THE NOVELS OF
edited by Anne Sr

The contributors to
essays approach H
widely different viev
book as a whole ta.
appreciation, and celebration, of the rich
variety of reading experience these novels
offer.

Contributors are: Barbara Hardy, who
argues for a more subtle appreciation of
Hardy's artistic maturity in *Under the
Greenwood Tree,* which she sees as 'a
novel about the imagination'; Robert
Heilman, with a hundredth anniversary
tribute to *The Return of the Native,* in a
re-examination of its themes and of the
successes and failures of Hardy's technique in this novel; Andrew Enstice, with an
overview of Hardy's fiction, which relates
it to the spiritual questing of the Book of
Job; Rosalind Miles, who studies the
female characters in the novels, and
Hardy's attraction to the women he himself created; Juliet Grindle, with an
analysis of the characterization of Michael
Henchard in 'Compulsion and Choice in
The Mayor of Casterbridge'; Rosemary
Eakins, who examines the ways in which
Hardy uses material from folk and
classical mythology in *Tess* to invest his
heroine with tragic stature; Patricia
Gallivan, who shows how Hardy was
influenced by his readings in contemporary psychology in the composition of
Jude; Philippa Tristram, with a discussion
of the importance of the physical am-
biance in the interiors of houses in
Hardy's novels; and finally Simon Gatrell,
who demonstrates how Hardy's compositors corrupted his own punctuation,
and argues for the restoration of Hardy's
own texts.

Front cover illustration: from a photograph of
Thomas Hardy, aged 19 years, by courtesy of the
Dorset County Museum, Dorchester.

Vision Critical Studies

General Editor: Anne Smith

The Novels of Thomas Hardy

THE NOVELS OF
THOMAS HARDY

edited by

Anne Smith

VISION

Vision Press Limited
11–14 Stanhope Mews West
London SW7 5RD

ISBN 0 85478 164 1

Printed in Great Britain
by Clarke, Doble & Brendon Ltd
Plymouth and London
MCMLXXIX

Contents

Introduction

This volume was not planned to give a thoroughgoing assessment of all Hardy's major novels, but rather to illustrate as many
approaches to them as were possible in the space available, and
to do this in a way which appreciates, and celebrates, the variety
of reading experience they offer. Appreciation of this kind is felt
to be all the more appropriate in view of the recent unsympathetic biography of Hardy's maturity, pounced upon gleefully by
Grub Street's equivalent of the inhabitants of Mixen Lane, to
whom nothing gives more satisfaction than to show that other
people's idols have feet of clay. Biographer's schizophrenia is a
pernicious disease in its dissociation of the man from the artist,
for its effect on the reader is to produce some sort of blurring
of the vision, and what he is made to see, in this instance, is a
mean ordinary little figure of a man, the disappointing kernel of
the luminous giant whom we imagine wrote the novels and poems.
But we owe it to Hardy to discriminate between the real and the
actual, to understand that the man of imagination can be moved
—and indeed, scarred—by other people's experiences. The artist
may have to choose between the bohemian, instinctual life and
some convenient degree of conformity; between destroying in his
own example what he perceives to be the 'false' order of the
society in which he lives, and conserving his energy by a superficial conformity to conventions which his work insistently seeks
to undermine: the choice depends on temperament rather than,
as the biographer implies, spiritual stature. Hardy, it seems, preferred to 'do his living in his head'; in his relationships he
preferred the ideal to the reality, so of course the hackneyed
observation can be made yet again, that art proceeds from sickness. If we might turn this piece of received wisdom on its head
and say that art proceeds from the sickness the artist perceives
in his fellow-men, we should probably be a lot nearer the truth—

if there is an appropriate image for the artist and his audience, it is surely that of the one-eyed man describing to the blind what he sees. The paradox of Hardy's work, in which a profound pessimism is given its biting edge by the relentless perception of what might have been, and the faithful celebration of eternal renewal in the natural world, is one that is universally true of human experience. Yet no other author has presented this paradox with such stoic honesty, or with such warmth of humanity: in showing us how sick we are, Hardy makes our sickness bearable. These essays, it is hoped, are a tribute to the real Hardy.

A.S.

Edinburgh, 1978

1

The Fruit of the Tree of Knowledge

by ANDREW ENSTICE

1

I frequently have the feeling that all possible philosophical abstractions of life have already been made. There is no truth to the idea of course, but in the study of literature it soon becomes apparent that certain themes are bound to recur. Life, death and love are the most obvious, but perhaps the most fundamental—expressed as early as the Book of Genesis—is simply Why? The search for a meaning in human existence, as Hardy knew, is the basis of much of our understanding of life.

The desire to eat of the tree of knowledge may not have been of the noblest motive, but in acquiring the understanding of death man found himself divided from the celestial beings only by his own mortality. It was to prevent him eating of the tree of life that he was driven from Eden; for gods, by any belief, guard jealously and well that immortality which relieves them of the need to justify their own existence.

Man has not been so fortunate. In discovering the dreadful secret of death he condemned himself to an eternity of torturing self-doubt. 'Wherefore is light given to him that is in misery?' asks Job, and all his wise friends can offer is the example of God's justice in the world. Yet it was as apparent to Job as to Hardy that there is no 'natural' justice in life. We need only consider the most basic facts of man's existence to realise as much ourselves. Where is the sense in creating so sophisticated a thing as the human mind when it ceases to function before it has even learnt its own possibilities?

It would appear at times as though we were the product of some particularly warped and sadistic cosmic sense of humour. Yet the understanding of Job lies eventually in realising that such a little thing as a man cannot hope to embrace the complexities of the universe. I know only one thing, that I know nothing. Only a god can compass all the illogic and injustice and see in it an order; or more realistically perhaps, in our use of the word 'god' we can express our realisation of all our inabilities. Like a Chinese symbol it means far more than can be said.

The choice of these two particular aspects of Old Testament teaching in a discussion of Hardy is not arbitrary. The 'wherefore is light' quotation will be familiar as the climax of Jude's suffering, and as a chapter heading in *The Return of the Native*. As in the tragedies of Shakespeare, with whose work some of Hardy's novels have been compared, there is a broad reliance on the Book of Job for imagery of despair and intellectual darkness:

> Sorrow and bitterness in the sky, and floods of agonised tears beating against the panes. I lay awake last night, and I could hear the scrape of snails creeping up the window glass.
>
> *(Woodlanders, ch. 27)*

But Genesis is less direct. Tess sees Clare as god-like, the being through whom she worships her undefined deity, and Grace Melbury imagines Fitzpiers her 'ruler' rather than her equal and friend. In this they follow closely the biblical precedent of Eve's view of Adam. It is in *Under the Greenwood Tree*, however, that paradise is formed:

> And the Lord God formed man of the dust of the ground, and breathed into his nostrils the breath of life; and man became a living soul. And the Lord God planted a garden eastward in Eden; and there he put the man whom he had formed.
>
> *(Genesis II. 7, 8)*

Hardy breathes life into his characters and sets them into a world where events are ordered, rules established, and no disturbance greater than the installation of an organ in the church ruffles the calm depths of placid souls.

In this 'rural painting' it is sound, practical commonsense that dictates the actions of the characters. 'The world's a very sensible feller on things in gineral, Dick' says Reuben (*Under the Greenwood Tree*, II, ch. 8), and indeed there is good cause for his opinion. The artisans' world of Mellstock is one of subtly-woven human relationships in which tradition and practice combine with personal experience, generation by generation, to create a pattern for living. Dick's unease in his courtship of Fancy is resolved by his father's advice, a combination of 'what all the common world says' (II, ch. 8) and Reuben's own experience in courting Ann. When at last the young couple marry they walk out in procession round the parish, following the established local tradition despite Fancy's 'respectable' qualms. 'Since poor mother did, I will' (V, ch. 1) is her capitulation after the briefest resistance, and the ancient demonstration of pride, the assurance that the wedding has actually taken place, binds her and Dick firmly to their rural paradise.

In the secondary theme of the story Mr. Grinham, the late vicar, is lauded for his policy of not interfering in village affairs. The new vicar's insistence upon taking Christianity into the cottage is an unsettling disruption of accepted practice. Mrs. Penny fears to go about her housework for ' 'tis such a confusing thing to meet a gentleman at the door when ye are in the mess o' washing' (II, ch. 2). Similarly it is the upset of established patterns that dismays the quire in the introduction of the organ, for life in *Under the Greenwood Tree* derives its strength and beauty from these patterns. Every character, from Enoch with his curiously profound musings upon the death of the bees, ' 'tis the money . . . without money man is a shadder' (IV, ch. 2), to Elizabeth Endorfield with her 'witchcraft' of commonsense, deals with life according to the accumulated wisdom of the society in which they live. Like the African tribal group it is the perfect organisation for the individual to whom life is a matter of practicality, day to day survival and simple pleasure in an existence that is relatively predictable from cradle to grave. In this situation the society itself is the justification for life, as well as its ordering. Marriage confers, through a predictable future for the unborn generations, a kind of immortality and a sense of purpose in life. In Eden there is no greater need to justify the ways of God to man.

The successful rural formula was carried over into *Far from the Madding Crowd* and Wessex was born as an image of Eden, a world of innocence to satisfy the cravings of a far from innocent Victorian world of commerce and Empire. Life in this concert of agricultural harmonies revolves around the everyday business of farming, and potentially sordid commerce is translated into something noble. The storm-threatened ricks become 'seven hundred and fifty pounds in the divinest form that money can wear—that of necessary food for man and beast' (ch. 36), while the small luxury of Oak's concern for his lambs' inevitable future helps to divert uncomfortable speculation. Oak is at heart a farmer before all else and his skill and dedication are, as his name implies, the solid foundation upon which the world of *Far from the Madding Crowd* is built. Worth and success are measured against his scale, with the emotional vagaries of Bathsheba and Boldwood evidence of their relative weakness.

Doubtless the success of *Far from the Madding Crowd* freed Hardy of some of the pressure to write to public taste. The Preface to *Under the Greenwood Tree* indicates his dissatisfaction with the enforced Eden when he says that 'circumstances would have rendered any aim at a deeper, more essential, more transcendent handling unadvisable at the date of writing', and the much later poem 'The Country Wedding', also based on the 'Mellstock quire', envisages a far from idyllic world, with the fiddlers playing the young couple to their wedding and their grave. From a vision of Genesis, however, to attempt to step to the profundity of Job is a daunting task for any writer, and *The Return of the Native* shows up the weakness of Hardy's argument only too clearly. 'Man is born unto trouble, as the sparks fly upward' says Eliphaz the Temanite (Job V. 7) and Hardy picks up the image with power and lyricism:

> In half a minute all that could be seen on Rainbarrow was a whirling of dark shapes amid a boiling confusion of sparks, which leapt around the dancers as high as their waists.
>
> (*Return of the Native*, I, ch. 3)

But it is still the imagery of Wessex which dominates the novel, and the ill-conceived themes of personal frustration and need are never fit partners for the biblical vision of darkness. 'Wherefore is light given to him that is in misery?' (Job III. 20) asks the first chapter of Book Five. Yet the 'light' given to Clym is the knowledge that Eustacia ignored his mother on the visit that caused her death. Such personal bitterness can hardly sustain the weight of human despair that moves Job.

The fact remains, however, that Hardy has attempted in this

novel to free himself of the cloying perfection of his rural Eden. There is a restless dissatisfaction apparent in Clym, Eustacia and Wildeve, and the Oak-like figure of Diggory Venn has lost the close involvement in the community which most distinguished Gabriel Oak. Eustacia derives from the heath a dignity which she might never have attained in the narrower confines of Budmouth, her more natural haunt, yet 'Egdon was her Hades', her place of darkness and torture; she draws from its spirit but is 'inwardly and eternally unreconciled thereto' (I, ch. 7). Clym for his part has a fascination with the ancient association of man and heath —a passion which he tries to communicate to Eustacia—but to the harsh realities of its environment he is blinded, literally and metaphorically, by his impractical vision of education. Wildeve, the feckless engineer who prefers the seclusion of Egdon to the realities of Victorian professional life, is so detached that outside the mechanics of the plot he makes virtually no impression on the novel.

Ill-formed, dissipated by the requirements of plot, and overwhelmed by the power of the Wessex setting, there is nevertheless a current of unrest flowing through *The Return of the Native*. Mere dedication to the immortality of society is no longer enough, and characters have begun to question the place of the individual in this rural world. Tentatively at first, men and women are groping their way towards a greater understanding of life than could be found in Mellstock or Weatherbury. The serpent has raised his head in the Wessex Eden.

2

> Cursed is the ground for thy sake; in sorrow shalt thou eat of it all the days of thy life . . . In the sweat of thy face shalt thou eat bread, till thou return unto the ground; for out of it wast thou taken: for dust thou art, and unto dust thou shalt return.
>
> (Genesis III. 17–19)

The first bite of the apple is taken, curiously enough, in a novel that adheres more closely to a vision of self-contained Wessex communities than did *The Return of the Native*. The power of that novel lay in its complete isolation. The heath brooded over everything without reference to other worlds. In

The Mayor of Casterbridge the town is aloof and independent, but by no means isolated. It is, however, an enclosed community in which the focus of the novel is the rivalry in commerce and love of the two mayors, Henchard and Farfrae, 'two-hundredth odd' (ch. 34) in line since the time of Charles I. The characters here are as completely a part of their society as any in Mellstock or Weatherbury; but in Henchard, stubborn and unreasoning as he is, Hardy creates the first truly dominant individual in his novels and the relentless pursuit of fulfilment that drives him up the ladder of success, then headlong to his own destruction, demonstrates him more concerned with the reality of personal human needs than the transient Farfrae. 'Part of his wish to wash his hands of life arose from his perception of its contrarious inconsistencies' (ch. 44); and in that one sentence is contained the first direct statement of an understanding that life is inconsistent, because it involves two such contrary features as the logic of nature's laws and the illogicality of human emotions. Elizabeth Jane, far more the daughter of Henchard than of Newsom, is the first to ask 'what that chaos called consciousness, which spun in her at this moment like a top, tended to, and began in' (ch. 18). But she, like Farfrae, is ready to bend with the vicissitudes of life and accept whatever benefits are allowed her. It is Henchard who shakes his fist at the universe, preferring to die alone rather than be submerged in the anonymity of life. There is an overwhelming feeling of despair in his understanding of life, untouched by any relieving hope. His last days are like the all-consuming anger of God after the first sin.

But the anger of God, the action which admits of no sense of logic or justice, does recognise that in his acquisition of knowledge 'man is become as one of us' (Genesis III. 22). 'And now, lest he put forth his hand, and take also of the tree of life, and eat, and live for ever: . . . the Lord God sent him forth from the garden of Eden, to till the ground from whence he was taken' (*ibid.* 22, 23). In *The Mayor of Casterbridge* Hardy retraces his steps to project that first moment of despair and leaden realisation which was passed by in the earlier philosophisings of *The Return of the Native*. However human and imperfect the world of Casterbridge, it nevertheless represents a self-contained ideal that, in return for unquestioning loyalty, offers comfort and modest security from the cradle to the grave. Mixen Lane is the

degenerate home of every form of human social failure or outcast, yet it offers protection and a kind of friendship to all in
trouble; and the bankrupt Henchard, even in his enmity for those
who have seen him fall, is offered money, premises and the hope
of a fresh start. It is only his own pride that prevents him taking
this second chance, for 'he had no wish to make an arena a second
time of a world that had become a mere painted scene to him'
(ch. 44). But the pride itself is, to Hardy, 'the ingenious machinery
contrived by the Gods for reducing human possibilities of amelior-
ation to a minimum' (ch. 44). This is the Catch 22 of the human
situation, reflected in the myth of Genesis, and repeated in the
struggle of every individual to apply logic to something too
great for logic. In the departure from Hardy's Eden there is less
a feeling of loss than a sense of betrayal. It outrages any concept
of natural justice that the two figures who have displayed some
greatness of soul, Henchard and Elizabeth Jane, should be condemned to the bitterness of understanding the world's injustice.
In the end Henchard loses everything, while Elizabeth apparently
gains all, but there is no order or meaning in either eventuality.
Failure and success owe little to personal worth.

It was this outrage of the justice to which most of us feel some
right that continued to preoccupy Hardy for some time after *The
Mayor of Casterbridge*. In *The Woodlanders* Grace picks up the
image of the fruit of the tree:

> The earth this year had been prodigally bountiful, and now
> was the supreme moment of her bounty. In the poorest spots
> the hedges were bowed with haws and blackberries; acorns
> cracked underfoot, and the burst husks of chestnuts lay exposing
> their auburn contents as if arranged by anxious sellers in a fruit
> market. In all this proud show some kernels were unsound as
> her own situation, and she wondered if there were one world in
> the universe where the fruit had no worm, and marriage no
> sorrow.
>
> (ch. 28)

The purity of the image of Eden is tainted now, like the first
purity of comprehension in *The Mayor of Casterbridge*, by more
present realities. 'My flesh is clothed with worms and clods of
dust; my skin is broken, and become loathsome. My days are
swifter than a weaver's shuttle, and are spent without hope' (Job
VII. 5, 6). It is Felice Charmond, detached from the troubles of

those around her, a woman who could be expressed in the one word 'Inconsequence' (ch. 27), who admits the reality of the biblical image in Hardy's world. 'Why,' she asks, 'were we given hungry hearts and wild desires if we have to live in a world like this? Why should death alone lend what Life is compelled to borrow—rest?' There is no answer. 'You must eat of a second tree of knowledge' says Fitzpiers (ch. 27), and quite suddenly we are aware that, in the subtle evolution of Wessex, Hardy has passed out of the gates of Eden and sits, with Job, in judgement upon the chaos of this world. The theme, 'Wherefore is light', that could not be sustained by *The Return of the Native*, emerges naturally from the natural logic of the woodland, 'for there is hope of a tree, if it be cut down, that it will sprout again . . . But man dieth, and wasteth away: yea, man giveth up the ghost, and where is he?' (Job XIV. 7, 10). Man, the individual, is doomed; and it is the cruellest paradox of all that man alone should feel the need to exist as an individual, not merely a link in the chain of survival.

In *Tess of the D'Urbervilles* Hardy turns from the apparently circular attempt to understand why we should exist at all, and concentrates on the concept of 'natural' justice—the theme that motivates the rather facile replies to Job's vitriolic assaults upon life. The recurring cry of Eliphaz the Temanite, Bildad the Shuhite and Zophar the Naamathite is that the wicked obtain their due punishment and the just their just reward. It is a ridiculous argument in human terms and, as the ending of the Book of Job indicates, equally ridiculous by any other standard. Tess's own life is an example of natural virtue brought low, and she displays very early on—before she can seriously be expected to realise the full import of what she says—that she understands the basic injustice of this world. To the Board school teaching, that the stars are worlds like our own, she adds the same vivid image that came naturally to Grace's mind: 'They sometimes seem to be like the apples on our stubbard-tree. Most of them splendid and sound— a few blighted' (*Woodlanders*, ch. 4). And our world, of course, is blighted. 'I shouldn't mind learning why—why the sun do shine on the just and the unjust alike . . . But that's what books will not tell me' (*Tess of the D'Urbervilles*, ch. 19). There is no visible logic to it all, and even to Tess, that most innocent of women, life seems a cruel gift to have bestowed:

The trees have inquisitive eyes . . . And the river says,—'Why do ye trouble me with your looks?' And you seem to see numbers of tomorrows just all in a line, the first of them the biggest and clearest, the others getting smaller and smaller as they stand farther away; but they all seem very fierce and cruel and as if they said 'I'm coming! Beware of me! Beware of me!'

(ch. 19)

Tess is the victim, not of any person or action, but of all the injustices and follies which, little or great, are the substance of life in our world. The understandings which illuminate her path through life are based on experience, unrefined by the subtleties of human thought, but they are the same as the understandings in the mouth of Angel Clare. The two kinds of perception attempted in *The Return of the Native*, the instinctive and the intellectual, are taken out of the crude shells of Eustacia and Clym, and transferred to the more human context of Tess and Clare. Ideals and god-like passions are muted to the frailties of a real situation, the man and the woman displaying all too clearly that they are capable of both sublime understanding and the most ridiculous short-sightedness. The coming-together of the raw country girl's experience and the sophisticated man's learning in an affair of head and heart allows Hardy the fullest scope to explore the weaknesses and strengths of life. 'The last grotesque phase of a creed which had served mankind well in its time' (ch. 12) is reduced to its real significance, as just one more aspect of the chaotic pressures of life. But the images of the Old Testament serve Hardy well. Once more we are delivered to the gates of Eden, but this time the features of man that were only hinted at in earlier novels are given plain statement, as innocence is translated into a knowledge too complex for comprehension, and death comes brutally upon the human victim. Clare and 'Liza-Lu walk hand in hand away from Wessex, as Adam and Eve walk away from paradise, full of the knowledge of good and evil, and the realisation of death. God answers Job, and says 'Where wast thou when I laid the foundations of the earth? declare if thou hast understanding' (Job XXXVIII. 4). For the truth, as the Book of Job declares, is that man cannot understand the vastness of the universe, or put reason to his own existence. 'God', or whatever one chooses to call the concept of power behind all things, can-

17

not be justified to man. We are too brief a span to comprehend even so small a thing as our own lives.

3

> Let the day perish wherein I was born, and the night in which it was said, There is a man child conceived. Let that day be darkness; let not God regard it from above, neither let the light shine upon it . . . Wherefore is light given to him that is in misery, and life unto the bitter in soul?
>
> (Job III. 3–20)

There is a cautious optimism in the ending of *Tess* that might in some senses seem the logical culmination of Hardy's Wessex novels. He has stepped outside the orderly regime of the early settled communities in search of some wider concept of justice and logic in life, and the image of the chastened, wiser Clare and still innocent 'Liza-Lu offers an unspoken hope of greater understanding through experience. But such an idea is still one step short of a complete exploration of the misery of individual human awareness. The very basis of human understanding, the cruellest cut of all, is the individual's need to come to terms with the paradox of life. No matter how many times the problem has been explored before, from Job to Tess, each new thinking man or woman must at some stage follow the same circular path of insoluble illogic. No man can answer for another.

In *Jude the Obscure* the need for personal understanding is finally removed from the aegis of the community and concentrated in the mind of one individual. Perhaps the most fascinating aspect of the novel is the impossibility of completely separating Jude's perception of life from Hardy's. The disparate elements of the search for human understanding which surfaced and vanished without great effect in previous novels are here drawn together in a determined effort to explore the possibilities of one man's life.

The start, for Jude, is not auspicious:

> Growing up brought responsibilities, he found. Events did not rhyme quite as he had thought. Nature's logic was too horrid for him to care for. That mercy towards one set of creatures was cruelty towards another sickened his sense of harmony. As you got older, and felt yourself to be at the centre of your time,

and not at a point in its circumference, as you had felt when you were little, you were seized with a sort of shuddering, he perceived. All around you there seemed to be something glaring, garish, rattling, and the noises and glares hit upon the little cell called your life, and shook it, and warped it.

(I, ch. 2)

The despondency and unembarrassed self-concern are characteristically youthful, as is his immediate change of mood, his positive decision to search for the great city of Christminster. The words, however, are the considered words of a man truly in the centre of his time—of Hardy, now in his fifties, as detached from his youth as Jude is from the place of his birth. The image is all of the mind, introverted and utterly different from the naturalistic portraits of the earlier novels. Where Tess's musings on the rottenness of this world are framed in the body of a blossoming country girl, a creature of passions and natural intellect, this eleven-year-old boy is 'a little cell' shaken by the inconsistencies and cruelties of life. Life has ceased to be a natural harmony and become an intellectual struggle for survival. This is the language of Job. Man is a body and a mind, the irreconcilable chained irrevocably together. There is no escape but death.

For Jude, however, such a conclusion lies only at the end of a lifetime of searching for purpose in this inconsistent world. The argument of Job begins with despair, 'let the day perish wherein I was born', but the whole argument, with all its false replies, must be put before God will answer—before the Socratic wisdom is vouchsafed. No man can understand the limits of his own knowledge until he has explored them, nor can he hope to find a meaning in his own life unless he searches.

Jude searches. In his vision of scholastic Christminster, the dream of imparted understanding; in the work of the mason's hands; in his hope of ordination; and in his love for Sue. But through the passages of his life, down all the twistings of the maze, there follows the image of his own mortality. Born of the lust for Arabella, a symbol of the flesh, Father Time's aged countenance presides over the death of every aspiration. Neutral in himself, he is the reminder that recurs through all the pettiness, hypocrisy, jealousy and bitterness that is now the vision of Hardy's Wessex. It has become irrelevant to consider whether Wessex is changing and innocence lost, for our own mortality

19

mocks us. Where is the purpose in searching, or the need for change, in a world that contains only the certainty of death?

Peace, the peace of the grave, is the final aspiration of *Jude*. The introversion has become total, and Sue is just a tortured cell which suffers life until the release of death. 'She's never found peace since she left his arms, and never will again till she's as he is now!' (VI, ch. 11). The irony of the peace that Sue and Jude found in each other, of course, is that it relied upon a total suspension of the knowledge of time and mortality:

> We gave up all ambition, and were never so happy in our lives until his illness came.

> (V, ch. 7)

It was the happiness of Eden once more, the paradise that Hardy rejected for his characters. Once more in the biblical image, man finds contentment only in the unconsidered joy before the fall. There is no understanding to be gained, to satisfy the dreadful craving of the mind. The curse upon the first Adam is within us all, and we must eat of dust though our souls aspire to God.

> Thy aerial part, and all the fiery parts which are mingled in thee, though by nature they have an upward tendency, still in obedience to the disposition of the universe they are over-powered here in the compound mass the body.

The quotation from Antoninus heads the fifth part of *Jude*, and is the prelude to inevitable death. Air, fire, earth and water are the elements, and man is compounded of them all. Eternally unreconciled, eternally changing and reforming, they are part of the inevitability of the universe. We know far more than Job, can comprehend the laws of Physics which seem to govern all things and realise that man too is so governed. Yet we are no closer to an understanding of ourselves. 'O! why were we given hungry hearts and wild desires if we have to live in a world like this?' (*Woodlanders*, ch. 27). After a quarter-century of writing, Hardy could go no farther than Job. 'Why died I not from the womb? Why did I not give up the ghost when I came out of the belly? . . . For now should I have lain still and been quiet. I should have slept: then had I been at rest!' (*Jude*, VI, ch. 11; quoting Job III. 11, 13).

We must go back to *The Return of the Native* to escape the introversion that is the legacy of *Jude* and see man once more as an integral part of the universe:

> There the form stood, motionless as the hill beneath. Above the plain rose the hill, above the hill rose the barrow, and above the barrow rose the figure. Above the figure was nothing that could be mapped elsewhere than on a celestial globe. Such a perfect, delicate, and necessary finish did the figure give to the dark pile of hills that it seemed to be the only obvious justification of their outline.
>
> (I, ch. 2)

Like Tess upon the scaffold at Wintoncester, the human shape brings order and logic to the scene. The logic may be cruel or seemingly pointless, but it cannot be denied. Each little cell that is a human being is part of the intricate structure of life, and life is part of the limitless web of the universe. As individuals we are frustrated by the paradoxes of life. As part of the web we have no need of point or justification. We are because we are. Like the universe itself, our search has no beginning and no end.

Hardy never wrote another novel to balance the introversion of *Jude*, but the ending of Job suggests very clearly the direction a further novel might have taken. 'Doth the hawk fly by thy wisdom, and stretch her wings toward the south? Doth the eagle mount up at thy command, and make her nest on high?' God asks of Job (XXXIX. 26, 27), and there is no answer. 'Behold, I am vile; what shall I answer thee? I will lay mine hand upon my mouth' (Job XL. 4). The wisdom of Job lies in his accepting that our lives are beyond our own understanding, but not worth the less for that. In his Introductory Note to *Winter Words*, his last volume of poetry, Hardy reiterates 'what I have often stated on such occasions, that no harmonious philosophy is attempted in these pages—or in any bygone pages of mine, for that matter.' Like Job, Hardy is aware that a consistent philosophy is an invention, something false even to man's limited understanding, and in 'A Philosophical Fantasy' he argues, like Job with God, to reiterate the impossibility of defining such a thing. Why, he asks God, did he let this world remain imperfect, 'its concept stand unfinished'? But before an answer is given he must apologise for not knowing whether God is man or woman:

21

Call me 'It' with a good conscience . . .
Call me 'but dream-projected',
I shall not be affected;
Call me 'blind force persisting',
I shall remain unlisting

What meaning do the definitions of a mere man have for this thing, whatever it may be called? What understanding, Hardy asks, does it have of grief, morals, ethics, justice, time or the very human frustration of 'unfulfilled intention'? 'Nor love I've given, but mindlessness' it says; why should man 'think my so-called scheming Not that of my first dreaming'?

Yet in the same mindless course of things which condemned Jude's every hope to frustration lies also the seed of man's essential nobility. By our own mortality we define all things, measure and find purpose. In grief we discover pleasure, passion in pain, justice in injustice, and meaning in our own frustration. We understand by opposites, finding humanity in all the things that 'god' is not. In the most essential way man is his own creation, and his own justification.

2

The Women of Wessex

by ROSALIND MILES

> Yonder a maid and her wight
> Come whispering by;
> War's annals will fade into night
> Ere their story die.
> ('In the Time of The Breaking of Nations')

He was always in love. First, with the lady of the Manor when he was nine or ten; then with a girl on horseback who chanced to smile at him as he came out of school, and whom he sought for, and got his friends to seek for, over a whole week before he got over 'this desperate attachment'. There was Louisa in the lane, though he never spoke to her—save to murmur once, 'Good evening', and there was Lizbie 'Browne' of the beautiful bay-red hair to whom he wrote a poem after she had lived in that 'encysting' memory for more than thirty years. In March 1888 we find him writing down his recollection of four village beauties, of whom Lizbie is one. These and many more lie behind the note he made when a young man in London: 'Walked about by moonlight in the evening. Wondered what woman, if any, I should be thinking about in five years' time'. Then there was the ubiquitous Tryphena, and Florence Henniker, and when he married Florence Dugdale at the age of seventy-three he made provision in his will for 'the first child of mine who shall attain the age of twenty-one' . . . The second Mrs. Hardy became seriously alarmed by her aged husband's infatuation with Gertrude Bugler who had delighted him with her playing of Tess in the dramatised version of the novel at Dorchester in 1924. Love is the overriding subject of his poetry, and the finest of these love poems was written when he was more than seventy. Time did indeed shake the fragile frame at eve with the throbbings of noontide, for it is true that they whom the gods love die young.

Hardy died young at seventy-eight. As the landlord of the Phoenix tavern said with a happy smile when asked if he could remember his fellow-townsman: 'Mr. Hardy was fond of the Ladies'.

(R. J. White, *Thomas Hardy and History*, 1974, pp. 5–6)

This is the conventional picture of Hardy as it has emerged over the years. Lord David Cecil observed that all Hardy's stories are love stories; and so they are; the story of Hardy's own endless love of women. Some part of Hardy never outgrew the susceptible schoolboy whose heart was wrung by the little girl who sat next to him in Sunday school; and few commentators have passed by without remark, whether of amusement or admiration, the vivid octogenarian flutterings of Hardy's romantic impulses.

But this is only the surface image, although one that Hardy himself was fond of cultivating. Certainly there were elements in Hardy's biography which contributed to his fictional presentation of women characters. But the interaction of fact and fiction is much subtler than this rather dated, stage-door-Johnny picture of the novelist as a connoisseur of women would suggest. Take, for instance, the theme of what Hardy himself called 'the lost prize'. Much has been made of Tryphena Spark's part in Hardy's life and work; overmuch perhaps. Hardy's heart may have been, like old china, crazed and crisscrossed with assorted cracks—but it never underwent a main fracture like that of Walter Scott or Dickens, both of whom recovered from one romantic disaster only to live and love thereafter at a permanently impaired level. And who can say which of Hardy's losses in love touched him more nearly? It is at least arguable that his most heart-struck injury was inflicted by Emma Lavinia, as she grew from his beloved girl into the emotionally deranged matron, bent on putting behind her with distressing firmness not only the bewitching young woman of Hardy's fancy, but also the young man, the ardent lover, that he had been, too.

Critics have brooded long over Hardy's own brooding sense of waste and futility, so strong as to amount to a sense of bereavement. Of what priceless and irreplaceable illusion had he been bereft, and at what stage? To a certain type of man, possession is loss, and one which may be harder to bear, with its daily reminder and ironic echo of the past, than a simpler grief. The theme of the lost prize, the unknown beloved, to which the commentators on Hardy so frequently revert, is perhaps to be connected less with Tryphena than with some insatiable desire to apprehend the romance of womanhood, womanliness, the female. This element is inevitably ephemeral, transient, since it is so firmly bound up in Hardy's imagination with physical attractiveness and intensity of feeling, the experience of which depends first upon the presence of youth and beauty, and then upon the moment of time which will throw them into sharp relief.

It is of course also possible that Hardy's elegiac feeling about women, the characteristically dark and tender presentation of his women characters, is not necessarily rooted in his biography at all. Many of his insights are clearly the product of constant, subtle, and sympathetic observation. He had, surely, a deeply intuitive understanding of female nature, as he well knew himself; he told Gosse that the only interesting thing about his first lost novel, *The Poor Man and the Lady*, was its 'wonderful insight into female character', adding with typical modesty (or disingenuity) 'I don't know how that came about' (*The Genius of Thomas Hardy*, ed. Margaret Drabble, 1970, p. 16). Hardy makes it the basis of Boldwood's personal disaster in *Far From the Madding Crowd* that 'he could not read a woman'. Hardy, from the onset of his career, always could. But this intuitive gift was combined with a felt awareness, and a highly conscious analytical interest; he watched, noted, picked up the trivial details, the very grain and texture of female existence; and upon this basis he built the characterisation of his women.

The novels do more, however, than simply parade Hardy's assortment of insights and observations; his women are never a collection of pinned butterflies in a glass case. Whatever the source of Hardy's haunting sense of loss, it certainly became his prevailing tone. As the early sweetness of fictional temper (in *Under the Greenwood Tree*, for example) refined into something approaching despair, Hardy learned as a lesson of life that 'delight is a delicate growth' ('In Tenebris'). More and more he sounded the mournful note of settled despondency, ranging from a still grieving bitterness to a dry bruised irony; this condition was summed up long ago in Gosse's pronouncement that 'the wells of human hope had been poisoned for him by some condition of which we know nothing' (Drabble, p. 35). Possibly so—but where the waters still rose true and sweet was in that area of his mind in which resided his feeling about women. Hardy's perceptions

sophisticated, but never cheapened; his did not become a coars-
ened or abraded mind. The more he succumbed to a pessimism of
the intellect, the more his tone darkened, then the more this
female element strengthened its primal hold upon his imagination, and indeed became its basic nourishment.

For what fires the eremitic novelist in the lonely wilderness of
the imagination? It takes more than a pretty face, or the memory
of a girl on horseback, to sustain the solitary act of creation.
Hardy's guileless and ecstatic response to women in life irradi-
ated his writing at every possible level. When he had what he
called in 'Lyonesse' 'magic in his eyes' (which for the reader trans-
lates as magic in his pen) it was invariably generated by his unusually acute awareness of the female force. It is not too much
to say that in Hardy the processes both of feeling and of thought
were centrally taken up with women, as human beings and as
fictional shadows of that reality. Certain untrodden regions of
his mind only spring to life at the passage of the female; while
his poignant concern for women enabled him to sustain, quite
amazingly, a lyrical intensity of treatment even in the harshest
ordeals which he imposed upon his characters. It seems as if, in
delineating the sufferings of Bathsheba, Tess, and Sue, Hardy
succeeded in tapping the vein of trembling wondering love which
had originated in him as a child, which had come to fulfilment
in his love of Emma Lavinia, and which, though it by-passed her,
never ceased to quiver and function.

It is surely this which brings his female characters so fully to
life as women before us. Many of Hardy's fictional assertions
about the nature of women can be summed up in Keats's well-
known phrase, 'the holiness of the heart's affections and the truth
of the imagination'. Hardy was and remained a true Romantic
in his insistence upon the supereminence of subjective feeling.
No writer was better at conveying the powerful effect of a
woman's emotional proximity, or the intensity of female passion.
With a continually resourceful imagination Hardy was able always
to discriminate the individual features of which such feminine
appeal is composed, to create heroines who are loving, wistful,
sweet, and hardly resistible. Is he sentimental? It is true that the
hollow blandishment of hearts, flowers, cherry lips, and kisses

sweeter than wine, are not totally absent from his work. But his heroines are never insipid or even irritating, as for example Dickens' so frequently are.

For in Hardy, the sense of women's charm is constantly linked to his awareness of their fatality. He saw women as dangerous simply in being, to themselves as well as to men. Consequently, no critic could ever fall into the trap of treating Hardy's fictional females as a repertory of ideal brides, as is so often the case with Dickens or Shakespeare. Despite the overspiritualisation of women which is undeniably a feature of Hardy's treatment it is through his female characters that Hardy mainly communicated his sense of that 'insupportable and touching loss', of the waste of human potential and the irrecoverable destruction of innocence. Heartsick at the world's cruèlty, or worse, indifference, Hardy solaced himself by creating feminine softness and constancy. He found a recurrent consolation in rendering with loving exactness, through the medium of these imaginary women, the sensations of the castaway.

For Hardy's loss of faith which we remarked earlier was not purely negative. It charged his vision with an acute immediacy. His imagination was galvanised rather than paralysed by images of irremediable suffering, and nowhere did he see suffering so precisely presented as in women. Female fragility, women's pain, the pain of living as a woman—Hardy was especially good at dealing with women's grief and experience of sorrow as *they* feel it, rather than as it looks from the outside to men (as D. H. Lawrence deals with it)—and in the general pointlessness of tragedy, the respectful attentiveness and the vitality of his indignation generated that point which it is in the nature of only the highest art to suggest. Mrs. Yeobright's last walk on Egdon Heath in *The Return of The Native* links with Fanny's Calvary in *Far From The Madding Crowd*; it is the human triumph in rising above fate, the triumph of will over matter; but all the more remarkable in being *female* will, *female* matter. So often Hardy, unlike other novelists, allows his women characters to carry associations, convey messages, which in the work of others are taken to appertain more properly to men. Fanny's workhouse death can be compared with Chapter I of *Oliver Twist* to illuminate the difference of method and purpose between the two writers. Dickens with his usual skill, displays his splendid facility for the excitement of the morbid voyeuristic strain in us, while Hardy goes for an identification of the reader's feelings with his subject. Hardy seeks to draw us as sufferers into his heroine's experience, where Dickens furiously compels us to view it as a spectacle and image of our social proceedings.

In this and in countless other examples it is evident that Hardy is master of the small female moment through which we glimpse the eternal. It is for these presentations of women's emotional exaltation or exhaustion, and all the range between, for the subtle fluid treatment of labile states of mind and feeling, that we turn again and again to Hardy's fiction. But Hardy is also interested in moral drama. Among his strengths are the ability to delineate moral confusion, and the uncertainty which accompanies the transition from one role or way of life to another. Again and again he works, in his characteristically painstaking way, through an examination of those growing points at which women find their dignity. Paradoxically Eustacia, preserving the secret of her lover's name at the expense of her marriage, or Fanny crawling on her knees to certain shame and death, have such an impact, such reverberation in the mind and soul of the reader, precisely because these are not, and never will be girls of an innate nobility and genuine moral sense like Dorothea in *Middlemarch*, who could never have known such a descent in the first place.

Hardy has always enjoyed a reputation for a keen penetration of the female mentality. Like that won by D. H. Lawrence, it is possibly more apparent than real. Hardy women *seem* different from one another—Bathsheba is mistress, Fanny is maid, Tess is rounded while Sue is slight—but on closer examination they all prove to originate from one prototype, with variations physical and social. What stimulated Hardy was the idea of a woman who was strongly individualised, who felt the pulse of 'her own precious life' beating irresistibly within her. This type is already formed in Bathsheba. Intelligent and 'an excellent scholar besides', she is in danger of cutting herself adrift from the life around her by being free-thinking and nonconformist—'She was going to be a governess once, you know, only she was too wild' (Chapter IV). Bathsheba is flirtatious, yet vacillating, and touchily repressive of the construction put upon her behaviour by Oak when he feels himself to be receiving a signal of some sort: 'I *hate* to be thought men's property in that way, though possibly I shall be had some day. Why, if I'd wanted you I shouldn't have run after you like this; 'twould have been the *forwardest* thing! But there was no harm in hurrying to correct a piece of false news that had been told you' (Chapter IV). Later, Sue's career and behaviour in *Jude the Obscure* constantly suggest what Bathsheba's might have been, with only a slight shift of focus and a turn of events against her. Like Bathsheba Sue seems more arresting and intelligent than any of the men around her: 'Her intellect sparkles like a diamonds while mine smoulders like brown paper,' observes Phillotson with justifiable gloom (Chapter IV, Part Fourth). And how evocatively does Sue's sad little self-justification echo Bathsheba's disastrous love career:

> Sometimes a woman's love of being loved gets the better of her conscience, and though she is agonised at the thought of treating a man cruelly, she encourages him to love her while she doesn't love him at all. Then, when she sees him suffering, her remorse sets in, and she does what she can to repair the wrong.
>
> (Chapter V, Part Fourth)

Yet despite their surface inconsistencies, often the product of a more deep-seated moral confusion, all Hardy's women have a sort of unshakeable integrity at bottom. Izz Huett identifies this quality in Tess with the vivid image-making of which the vernacular is capable: 'Her mind can no more be heaved from that one place where it do bide than a stooded waggon from the hole he's in' (Chapter XLVII). This capacity to be totally, even stubbornly themselves, and inability to shift and change even when it would be to their own advantage, is not only confined to Hardy's romantic heroines. Arabella is made to recognise in herself and Sue the same individualism: 'You are a oneyer too, like myself' (Part Fifth, Chapter II). And even Mrs. Yeobright the matriarch of Egdon, describes herself as 'a poor, weak, one-idea'd creature' (Chapter VI, Book Third).

How then does Hardy set about presenting and interpreting his unusual woman to an insufficiently understanding world? One of his standard techniques is to associate his heroines, in the words of Gabriel Oak, with 'nice flowers and birds'. Flowers in particular are used by Hardy with such insistent repetitiveness that the unsympathetic reader may feel that he is indulging in a favourite masculine pastime of the Victorian era in simply gathering a garland of gorgeous girls. Yet it is interesting to observe how his technique matures. At the bad news about Fanny, Bathsheba looks 'like a lily, so pale and fainty'. Here the flower is introduced simply for its colour value. But when we are told that at her re-marriage to Phillotson, Sue 'never in her life looked so much like the lily her name connoted as she did in that pallid morning light', the flower reference links Sue with her entire environment as pale and bloodless, while in addition the sacrificial and sacra-mental associations of this particular flower are marshalled to deepen our sense of the significance of Sue's self-immolation and to stimulate our awareness of her as a victim.

It is always such associations of tenderness and pathos that Hardy seeks to mobilise by these means. The appeal to the reader is made in a highly particularised way. Tess's appearance as 'a posy' of peonies, roses, fruit, Sue's panicky sense of herself as 'a little bird caught at last', Tamsin darting and skimming like a swallow, all call upon our emotions for an echo of the protective love and pitying empathy that Hardy himself so clearly felt for his creatures. Like Clym, Hardy 'could not help feeling that it would be a pitiful waste of sweet material if the tender-natured thing should be doomed from this early stage of her life onwards to dribble away her winsome qualities' (Chapter III, Book Sixth). Full many a flower may be born to blush unseen, but Hardy would give as many as he could room to blossom in the pages of his novels. But these associations are not merely decorative; they are progressively more functional as Hardy uses them with more pre-cision. The linking of his women with flowers conveys not only beauty, but delicacy and fragility. They are doomed to die, but in life their existence is rooted in the soil of reality, and they have an assertive natural vitality and place in the scheme of things— a short life, but a gallant show.

Important too in the overall effect are the physical associa-tions of flowers and fruit, their scent, texture, taste and colour. Hardy's deeply sensuous response to his female characters shows again in his fondness for bathing his admired women in shades of red and pink. He was fascinated with blushing; see the set-piece of 'the Maiden's blush' in *Far From The Madding Crowd* (Chapter II). And by extension, it is interesting to observe how very often his female characters appear in, or are associated with, shades of redness, as if the whole of nature signified its sense of

their presence with a flush of emotion. When we are first introduced to Bathsheba, we are told that 'the morning sun lighted
up to a scarlet glow the crimson jacket she wore'; she blushes
at herself, and seeing her reflection blush in her handmirror,
blushes the more. Eustacia Vye makes her first strange and fatal
appearance to Clym in *Return of the Native* at a window 'whose
panes blazed in a ruddy glare from the west', and when she speaks
to him, 'it was like garish noon rising to the dignity of sunset
in a couple of seconds' (here, of course, a faint but unmistakable sense of ill-omen accompanies the other strong symbolic
associations of redness). But Tess, as she epitomises the peak of
Hardy's use of the flower comparison device, is also the quintes-
sence of Hardyesque rosy glow. Her pinkness is unwearyingly
brought before us, not simply in the conventional 'rosy lips and
cheeks'; she is all pink, down to her pink milking gown and small
pink hands, 'a rosy warming apparition' of 'lush womanhood'.
Indeed, so keen is Hardy on the pinkness of Tess, with all its
blatant sexual connotations, that he even puts praise of her
'deep red lips' and an expression of approval of 'rosy-mouthed
girls', quite inappropriately into the elderly female mouth of the
vicar's wife, Angel's mother.

For Hardy really is a lover of women in the fullest physical
sense. E. M. Forster remarked that Hardy conceived his novels
from a great height, but his females are drawn from very close
up; there is an almost myopic insistence upon the grain of their
skin, and texture of hair. Sound, scent, mouth, cheeks, downy
plumpness—no detail of their physical presence is allowed to
escape our senses. Again, though, what these women have for
Hardy is not sensuous fulfilment so much as the promise of it;
the womanliness is tantalisingly there, but not enjoyed. Sue is
described as '*looking* warm as a new bun' (the verb is surely
highly significant here); Eustacia has a mouth 'formed less to
speak than to quiver, less to quiver than to kiss', so that Hardy
asks rhetorically, 'where was a mouth matching hers to be found?'
Yet he dodges the answer, so that what is implied here is never
followed up.

This indeed declares itself as Hardy's pattern in the treatment
of female sensuousness, and his own sensuous response to his
women characters. Tess is the apotheosis of Hardy's sensuous
realisation of womanhood, and he is lover-like in his attention to

her, in his tender dreamy delineation of her aura, the charm of her bodily existence:

> She was yawning, and he saw the red interior of her mouth as if it had been a snake's. She had stretched one arm so high above her coiled-up cable of hair that he could see its satin delicacy above the sunburn; her face was flushed with sleep, and her eyelids hung heavy above their pupils. The brimfulness of her nature breathed from her . . .
>
> Tess's excitable heart beat against his by way of reply; and there they stood upon the red-brick floor of the entry, the sun slanting in by the window upon his back, as he held her tightly to his breast; upon her inclining face, upon the blue veins of her temple, upon her naked arms and her neck, and into the depths of her hair. Having been lying down in her clothes she was as warm as a sunned cat . . .
>
> (Chapter XXVII)

All good stuff. But what, precisely, is intended to be the reader's relation or response to this sort of information? Hardy's main difficulty as a novelist lay in his inability to maintain a constant and rigorous self-monitoring. His surrender to the emotional experiences of his characters leads him too closely in upon them. As a lover he becomes too involved with his fictional creations; so that we feel that the blood that courses through the veins of his heroines is drawn straight from his own heart. Hardy tries hard to make the reader see these women in his way. By such phrases as 'our Eustacia', Hardy seems to commend them to our affection. But what he really means is '*my* Eustacia'. A true Pygmalion, Hardy seems to have undergone a series of verbal and imaginative love affairs with his creatures. In brooding over Tess's 'fluty' voice, or Eustacia's cloudy hair, Hardy solaced himself for the defeat of his love for Emma Lavinia, warmed himself on his dreary trek through the Arctic wastes of a long cold marriage. No wonder Emma Lavinia resented her husband's writing. As the sun shines deep into Eustacia's red mouth as into the inside of a tulip we can surely discern, within the exquisite sensuousness, the pain of longing. And is not Eustacia *in toto*, the 'woman who had advanced to the secret recesses of sensuousness', the dream of the repressed womaniser? Hardy's heroines are the fantasy projections, indeed the life work, of a man condemned to the yearning half-life of the solitary nympholeptic.

Not all Hardy's women, though, are condemned to be young, lovely and fateful. Somewhere in the more Gothic reaches of Hardy's sense of the macabre dwelt a whole tribe of women whom we may call his anti-females. Because he enjoyed so keenly feminine loveliness, he felt the more acutely the absence of it, or its replacement by coarseness and crudeness. Yet though each of his heroines may be 'a flower among vegetables', Hardy does not care to cultivate a patch without some examples of this humbler growth, and in his mature art he brings us to know and care about such swedes and turnips as Marion and Izzy in *Tess of the D'Urbervilles*. There is an affection implied even in the fun Hardy has at the expense of frizzy-haired brawny damsels, stout red-faced girls, or such as 'Bower o' Bliss' and 'Freckles' in *Jude the Obscure*. For older women Hardy has little use as women; indeed his old rustic women are not felt to be feminine at all; they are without gender, like tree roots. Late flowering blooms have no place in Hardy's garden. Where not comical or negligible they may be sinister and threatening, witch-like or evil (Eliza Endorfield in *Under the Greenwod Tree* and Susan Nunsuch in *Return of the Native* are examples here). With Mrs. Coggan in *Far From The Madding Crowd* Hardy demonstrates that he can draw with fond irony an ordinary, good-hearted, 'wholesome-looking' older woman going about her every day routine tasks; but even the friendliest treatment cannot lend to any other than young and beautiful women that special female magic.

But these crones and cards play an important part in the over-all scheme of Hardy's depiction of the female sex. Partially at least, they serve as devices enabling Hardy to work off some of his ambivalent, if not hostile, feelings about the sex 'bearing the legend "the Weaker" '. We have considered Hardy as a lover, and relished his relish of womanliness. But it is not 'roses, roses all the way'. The other side of the coin is Hardy's sexual pessimism, which can combine with his native distrust of life to sound like an abiding misogyny. Under this impulse, Hardy is fully capable of ironising even his beloved heroines. Bathsheba in particular is relentlessly made the vehicle of some of the worst of Hardy's resentful cynicism. The novel is full of lofty reflections upon such topics as 'woman's privileges in tergiversation', 'women's pre-scriptive infirmity', combined with nudging invitations to the reader: 'We know how women take a favour of that kind.' At times this heavy and intrusive irony spills over into a pedagogic scolding of this 'fair product of Nature in the feminine kind', as when Hardy informs us crossly, 'Such is the selfishness of some charming women.' On the inexperienced novelist the swaggering pose of the man who knows about women sits somewhat uneasily in this rather too effortful assumption of masculine superiority.

But this is rather a fault of tone than of content, and one which never occurred to the same extent again. Also, within the novel it is balanced not only by such warm touches as the picture of Liddy with her 'womanly dignity of a diminutive order', but also by Hardy's keen identification with Bathsheba's bitter sense of 'her spoliation by marriage with a less pure nature than her own'; 'Love is misery for women always, and I shall never forgive God for making me a woman.' Hardy always had the power to breathe into his women's speech the authentic accents of female despair; and in such moments the reader is brought to overlook a good deal. Further, Hardy genuinely expects us to accept his view that a beautiful and passionate woman is not guided by the same rules as lesser mortals. His comment upon Bathsheba's selfish dealings with Gabriel is 'such imperiousness would have damned a little less beauty; and on the other hand, such beauty would have redeemed a little less imperiousness' (Chapter XXI). Eustacia, too, ultimately defies criticism, in Hardy's design for her at least. She is not untouched with Hardy's reproving irony; consider what effect it produces in Chapter Six of Book First when she is made to use the child Johnny like 'a little slave' as part of her plan to call Wildeve to her. She is, further, idle, selfish and vain. But with what confident expectation of admiration does Hardy firmly inform us, 'The fantastic nature of her passion, which lowered her as an intellect, raised her as soul.'

These, then, are some of the key features of Hardy's response to, and presentation of, women in his fiction. An examination of *The Mayor of Casterbridge* will show them exemplified throughout. The title of the novel itself is in some degree a misnomer; for although it nominally centres upon Henchard, in fact it is built around the three women whose actions and reactions entirely direct and determine his course. The novel is a particularly

appropriate one for focussing our consideration of Hardy's treatment of women characters, for in it we see his techniques on the
verge of coming to fulfilment. Prentice work behind him, in this
book he rose to a level from which he could launch himself into
the novels which posterity has designated his masterpieces.

First, though, we have what amounts to a recapitulation of
Hardy's favourite trick of linking women with flowers, fruit, or
small appealing animals, God's lesser creation. Elizabeth-Jane
is at first a field-mouse, not a water-flower in bloom, and specifically displaying 'a field-mouse fear of the coulter of destiny'; in
this strong, literally cutting image, Hardy invites our sympathetic
identification with Elizabeth-Jane, wishes us to grasp her life as
she feels it, from the point of view of the minute powerless
creature about to go under the plough. Later the natural vitality
in Elizabeth-Jane begins to assert itself, and her face is seen as
a garden in which 'cheek-roses' bloom, and 'peachy cheeks' flou-
rish. At this point she becomes less of a mouse, and more of a
fawn, 'a dumb, deep-feeling, great-eyed creature'. More ephemeral
from the start, Lucetta makes her first appearance in Chapter XX
in association with a rainbow and a butterfly, both delicately
evocative of the frail loveliness of the evanescent; a fraility which
in this case is prophetic.

Familiar too is the way in which Hardy's romantic heroines are
set against other women whose absence of their special qualities
throw their charms into relief. Around Lucetta and Elizabeth-
Jane are set rough and ready coarse-tongued specimens like Nance
Mockridge: ' "Be cust if I'd marry any such as he, or thee either",
replied that lady.' Nance is of the same tribe as Mother Cuxom,
who, with her 'nods and becks and wreathed smiles' and her
impressive tonnage, is half Mother Earth and half a caricature
out of Jacobean citizen comedy (both she and Arabella in *Jude
the Obscure* have more than a whiff of Ursula, the great sow
turned pigwoman, from *Bartholomew Fair*). A more sinister part
is played by the furmity woman, roundly designated by Hardy
as an 'old hag'; this is not mere abuse, but an accurate description of the force of her contribution, when like avenging fate she
shuffles out of the long past to bring home to Henchard his
great offence against one of her sex, and to ensure that he pays
his debt. Rarely indeed does Hardy deploy his chorus of Wessex
women to such good effect elsewhere. We hear of Hardy's senti-

mentalising women, but Casterbridge is also a world in which the luckless Jack Griggs, forced to carry a vapourish Joan Dummett through the mud (her name indicates Hardy's view of her mental capacities), contrives to drop her in the cow-barton, a euphemism which every schoolboy will recognise. This action, with other recollections of 'such doggery as there was in them ancient days', is brought forward as a counterpoint to Henchard's mockery marriage with Susan in Chapter XIII. How wonderfully artful this is, how disingenuously simple-looking! One tale of a long-ago fall cannot but recall another, Henchard's original descent and original sin—as, in this and countless other small almost subliminal suggestions, we are prepared for the inevitably disastrous outcome.

As everywhere in Hardy, we have here displayed again the perennial tension of Hardy's ambivalence about women. On the one hand, there is the faithful rendition of the small feminine moments which another writer would fail either to observe or to consider worth recording; Elizabeth-Jane's 'latent sense of slight' when Farfrae omits to smile at her in Chapter IX; her ability to seize an idea 'at one feminine bound'; her efforts to protect her newly-sprung cheek-roses with a sunshade, 'deeming spotlessness part of womanliness'; the white parting of her hair arching from ear to ear. Lucetta, too, is written up in such a way as to make a similar appeal to our susceptibilities: 'Her heart longed for some ark, into which it could fly and be at rest. Rough or smooth she did not care, so long as it was warm' (Chapter XXIII).

Yet even within the framework of this tenderly sympathetic presentation, the reductive effect of the constant linking of women with dumb little creatures or inanimate phenomena of nature makes itself felt. Henchard is indeed made to articulate that masculine superiority which is the unattractive aspect of protectiveness when we are told that 'his old feeling of supercilious pity for womankind in general was intensified by this suppliant appearing here as the double of the first' (Chapter XXXVI). Again, Lucetta is a sweet creation, charming in her impulsiveness, and genuinely well-intentioned towards Elizabeth-Jane. But as with Eustacia Hardy is careful to insert, however lightly, the chip of granite which lies at the heart's core of the coquette: 'Lucetta had come to Casterbridge to quicken Henchard's feelings with regard to her. She had quickened them, and now she was indifferent to the achievement' (Chapter XXIII). She who once was the victim of Henchard, in so far as the combination of social *mores* with her own indiscretion put her in his power, at last makes him hers, even though she least wants to; and when in Chapter XXV she offers him an apple, we feel that refuse it as he may, Henchard will not in the event succeed in extricating himself from the toils of this daughter of our grandmother Eve. 'These cursed women—there's not an inch of straight grain in 'em!'—Henchard's bitter outburst would serve as an epigraph upon at least a subsection of Hardy's view of womankind.

In general, however, the women in *The Mayor of Casterbridge* do not serve merely on this trivial level to allow Hardy to luxuriate in ideas of womanliness or work off attacks of spleen. They have two functions of primary significance. First, they embody in living form the main theme of the book; that we are all prisoners of our past actions and bear along with us into the future the ghosts of our past selves. Second, the three central women are the main props of the novel's structure; they represent with almost diagrammatic simplicity the different stages of Henchard's passage through life, the progress of his tragedy. In addition, as mother, mistress, and child, Susan, Lucetta and Elizabeth-Jane come to incarnate, for the reader as well as for Henchard, the three forms of the eternal feminine, the three faces of the great goddess.

In Hardy's hands, of course, all this is much more subtly and allusively dealt with than such a summary makes it appear. Nothing is quite as simple as that. There are some inherent paradoxes; the mistress, for instance, is like a child, and the child Elizabeth-Jane, like Elinor Dashwood in *Sense and Sensibility*, has at times to be mother. Paradoxically too, for a man who loves and lives for and through three women, the Elizabeth-Jane who dies as an infant before she could know him is the only female whom Henchard ever really possessed or was entitled to. His tragedy is not so much that of the man who, as Chaucer expresses it in the Prologue of *The Monk's Tale*, 'is yfallen out of heigh degree / Into myserie, and endeth wrecchedly'; that, as we are shown, he can tolerate, albeit very grimly. Henchard's disaster is bound up very specifically with his wife, his child, and his lover; in women and in his loss of them, his three-fold loss; this is rather, as with Othello, the tragedy of one who, 'like the base Indian threw a pearl away / Richer than all his tribe'.

And of course, try as Henchard might, in Hardy's universe there is no reversing this. Inexorably time moves on. In his re-marriage to Susan and subsequent course of action, Henchard is chasing a ghost, a phantom of the family happiness he could have enjoyed (notice the significance, both prospectively and retro-spectively, of Susan's wraith-like pallor; it denotes her a ghost from the past, and conveys to us her approaching death in the not-too-distant future). The first Elizabeth-Jane, like Mamillius in *The Winter's Tale*, is the price paid, the victim, the sacrifice. The child was the symbol, living and visible, of the early married life of Henchard and Susan, its proof and product; and whatever there was between the two of them dies with her (link this with the symbolism of the voyage over the sea after the separation; the waters of forgetfulness as another poetic equivalent of death and oblivion). And as Henchard is created by Hardy to live a life dogged by woman trouble, so we cannot overlook the painful significance of the final paradox, that this of all men dies with-out any of the necessary female care which traditionally accom-panies a deathbed. No mother or wife, daughter or nurse, to soothe his passing and comfort his distress; and he is even denied the callous professional attention of the layer-out. There is an almost crushing finality in the presence of Whittle as his sole companion; for Henchard has, like Lear, been stripped down and cut away to nothing.

All this is a great distance away from the garden of gorgeous girls. This fully functional treatment of women is one of the elements which makes *The Mayor of Casterbridge* such a satisfy-ing experience, artistically as well as emotionally. Yet even from here, Hardy was preparing to go further, both in his presentation of, and through the means of, his fictional women. Hardy the lover and collector of women was evolving into Hardy the social critic and even prophet, interpreting women to men, to society, and to themselves. By a different though related process, Hardy the creative artist continued to find in women the appropriate vehicles for what he wanted to say about nature and life. In the female condition he discovered an objective correlative of his own emotional state, and his deep-rooted convictions about the entire system of things, the interlocking scheme of character, environ-ment, and incalculable providence. Hardy *used* women, fictionally, because in their combination of weakness with strength, fragility with capacity for suffering, endurance with so much to endure, he found an artistically appropriate image of the human condition at large. A woman in Hardy's hands could be made to bear a weight of suffering whose inflictions transcend the personal and move through human to sublime; he never found the same true of a male character. Consequently while Henchard's is the tragedy of an individual, Tess's becomes a tragedy of the human race.

Initially, though, if we look at Hardy as social critic it is both interesting and impressive to observe how his art moves him surely from ironic observation through to a more penetrating analysis of social processes. From his early work, Hardy was acutely aware of, and prepared to draw his reader's attention to, 'the certain degradation in renouncing the simplicity of a maiden existence to become the humbler half of an indifferent matrimonial whole' (*Far From the Madding Crowd*, Chapter XLI). Later he came to perceive how totally certain women are shaped by the needs and desires of the men who take them up; Tess for example being, to Angel, 'no longer the milk-maid, but a visionary essence of woman—a whole sex condensed in one typical form. He called her Artemis, Demeter . . .' Through Tess Hardy demonstrates, with that indignation which remains so touching a feature of his work, how utterly a woman's self-esteem, indeed her whole *raison d'être*, lives in the warm approval and support of the man who loves her; so that Tess, gazing dry-eyed into the ruins of her marriage, learning to live like Gwendolen in *Daniel Deronda* 'without pleasure or hope of pleasure', broods 'I shall always be ugly now, because Angel is gone, and there is no-one to take care of me' (Chapter XLII). Meanwhile the man who is the author of this emotional devastation plunges off into an ill-judged and hopeless enterprise in further pursuit of those half-baked intellectual convictions which too often seem but a rationalisation of his imperfectly understood emotional needs.

When he came to Jude, however, Hardy had moved on yet again. Now he has absorbed the truth of Meredith's pronouncement that 'in tragic life . . . no villain need be; passions spin-the plot'. He no longer needs to oppose against his heroine-victim an outside afflictive force in the shape of an oppressive husband or self-seeking lover. Hardy still sees the man as creating woman, or trying to, in the image of his own needs; on meeting Sue, Jude experiences a 'consciousness of at last having found an anchorage for his thoughts, which promised to supply both social and spiritual possibilities'; 'he thought what help such an Anglican would have been to him under happier circumstances'; and (perhaps most telling of all) 'he wanted something to love'. In this Jude is merely and more comprehensively repeating the fundamental error of his marriage with Arabella, when 'his idea of her was the thing of most consequence, not Arabella herself'. But through Jude's discoveries about himself, marriage, and society in his relationship with Sue, Hardy articulates a basic but profound piece of social analysis which today's feminists are still struggling to put across:

> . . . it is no worse for the woman than for the man. That's what some women fail to see, and instead of protesting against the conditions they protest against the man, the other victim; just as a woman in a crowd will abuse the man who crushes against her, when he is only the hopeless transmitter of the pressure put upon him.

> (Chapter IV, Part Fifth)

Ultimately, though, despite the success of Hardy's protest through Jude, we are concerned not with what Hardy says about women, but what he communicates *through* them. From their prime position in the centre of Hardy's mental landscape, women appear to have presented themselves as vessels capable of being filled with a far older set of associations and meanings than the contemporary struggle to be socially free. A hint of this comes from an unlikely source, the Hardys' parlour-maid:

> Mr. Hardy seemed to come out his shell when talking to younger women, as if a light was breaking through and he could see them in one of his books. Myself I do not think he thought of them as women, but just shadowy figures fitting into space like a jigsaw.

> (Drabble, p. 51)

Perhaps we can look a little more carefully at the ways in which Hardy's meticulous imagination shaped and worked these pieces.

From the beginning of his career, Hardy's fictional women are more than just ordinary females. We can see his desire to add significance at its crudest when he calls Bathsheba 'an Elizabeth in brain, and a Mary Stuart in spirit'. Elsewhere he was driven by the impulse to make women either the receptacles of the life force, 'the force that through the green fuse drives the flower', or else the victims, easily overcome, of a cruel fate whose blows are rendered heavier by the sensibility of their hearts. With his fertility and felicity of imaginative implication, coupled to his steadfast devotion to a small handful of views and convictions, Hardy was to find a variety of ways in which to use women to suggest opening vistas of allegorical possibility. Mrs. Yeobright, for instance, dying of the adder's bite on Egdon after her rejection, as she believes, by her son and his wife, fulfils various roles at one and the same time. She is, first, simply a country woman succumbing plausibly enough in naturalistic terms to a commonplace hazard of that life; but she is also a poetic symbolisation of motherhood receiving its emotional deathwound from callous or cruel offspring; and finally an allegory of Egdon itself, the eternal mother, perennially betrayed by the failure and incomprehension of her children, our denial of our own nature. Similarly Tess alternates in our concept of her between Eve and Ceres, Mary Magdalen and Persephone, through Hardy's consummately artistic mobilisation of the allegorical values implicit in folk, classical, and Christian mythology; while through Sue, at once a 'poor little quivering thing' and a noble representation of the crucifixion of her entire sex, we are made to share with Hardy his inescapable sense of all creation groaning.

For here at last we come near to confronting the tension, the contradiction that lay at the heart of Hardy's attitude to women and affected the use he made of them in fiction. Seen in one way, women for Hardy were an intrinsic part of what he called the 'timid animal world', small, weak, vulnerable, and not very bright. On their animal level they are subject to that law which makes the weaker the natural prey of the stronger; so that although they may call forth the kindly and protective impulse in one type of man, they will always be at the mercy of their own physical and emotional weakness. Instinctive predators like Troy or Alec can no more resist Bathsheba and Tess than the hawk may be expected to spare the field-mouse, or the fox the new-born lamb. In presenting these dumb, even dim specimens of females going like cattle uncomplainingly through the slaughter of human life, Hardy is alternately moved by the dynamic of agonised pity for which he has become famous, and a lingering irritable suspicion of women's worthlessness, their inherent deserving of such a

41

fate, which as we have seen tends to spill over into the scorn and contempt which is only relieved by continuous irony at their expense.

Yet from this very weakness women draw their greatest strength, in Hardy's interpretation of things. Our kinship with the natural world at a thousand points is an intrinsic part of the Hardy vision; and for women, more in touch with their own feelings and with the pulse of life about them than men are, this closeness is so much easier as to be almost instinctive. Hardy's women are by virtue of their womanhood more involved in the basic processes of human birth, growth, and death; they are the vital continuers of human evolution; they are more elementary in apprehension of good and evil. Because more elementary, ultimately they are elemental. In Hardy's apprehension they do not simply play a part as inhabitants, albeit dominant figures, on the landscape of the beloved 'Wessex' of his imagination. Women for Hardy embody or incarnate that aspect of doomed rural England whose passage he devoted his life to setting down before it was too late. Mourning the vanishing agrarian ways of life and the loss of pre-industrial tranquillity he found, in Tess for example, a living, breathing embodiment, a personification almost, of what was being destroyed and lost. She functions allegorically as the child of nature, polluted and destroyed, as the fair country undergoing the rape of capitalism, and worse, modernism. She is the human microcosm, the form taken by Hardy's requiem. Yet all this is achieved by Hardy without ever losing touch with Tess as a woman, and a woman living in that time and place, so that some of Hardy's very best moments are also his simplest:

> Thus Tess walks on; a figure which is part of the landscape; a fieldwoman pure and simple, in winter guise . . . Every thread of that old attire had become faded and thin under the stroke of the raindrops, the burn of the sunbeams, and the stress of the winds. There is no sign of young passion in her now . . .
>
> (Chapter LXII, Part fifth)

Through Tess and many others of his female characters Hardy makes his farewell to the past, voyages through and takes his leave of his country, his world, his Wessex. Yet even here women have not exhausted their contribution to Hardy's mind and imagination. In the last analysis, women for Hardy are linked, at a level too deep for conscious reason, with the very wellsprings of human existence; they are the primal and original force of nature. Womanhood for Hardy was an element in which his imagination throve and had its being, and from it he derived both his dark glimmerings of the shadows of suffering that lie almost too deep for tears, and the solace and strength which form the consolation for them. For Hardy, femininity was a value, an essence, an eternal and inescapable fact, a cyclical and essential function, at times palpably open, but in the final reckoning a secret mystery as old as time itself.

For Hardy as a man, and for us as his readers, the good fortune lay in his constant ability to rediscover and recreate this 'visionary essence of woman' throughout his life. From the 'subtle-souled girl' Elizabeth-Jane to the 'worn wet face' of Mrs. Yeobright, Hardy continually found, and offered to us, his awareness of its operation. One final example must suffice:

> Half an hour later they all lay in their cubicles, their tender feminine faces upturned to the flaring gas-jets which at intervals stretched down the long dormitories, every face bearing the legend 'The Weaker' upon it, as the penalty of the sex wherein they were moulded, which by no possible exertion of their willing hearts and abilities could be made strong while the inexorable laws of nature remain what they are. They formed a pretty, suggestive, pathetic sight, of whose pathos and beauty they were themselves unconscious, and would not discover till, amid the storms and strains of after-years, with their injustice, loneliness, child-bearing, and bereavement, their minds would revert to this experience as to something which had been allowed to slip past them insufficiently regarded.
>
> (*Jude the Obscure*, Chapter III, Part Third)

Hardy, one of a long line that stretched from Milton to Strindberg, felt at times that women's importance lay in the possession of a power and significance that they did not understand and did not try to control. Yet all around he perceived the workings of a society which made nothing of this, and seemed dedicated to treating its women in such a way as to form them into the least worthy vessels of masculine needs and desires. If Hardy's view of women can be reduced to a nutshell, it is in his own phrase about Tess, that 'she was no insignificant creature to toy with and dismiss, *but a woman living her precious life*'. It is because of this basic belief that Hardy's fictional women attain full humanity when others' are paper dolls, fluttering winsomely but flatly, agitated by the huffing and puffing of writers not empowered as Hardy was to breathe life into them. For Hardy the female was his starting point and the summit of his highest endeavour, his initial inspiration and his ultimate goal. In the long search of his lifetime Hardy kept alive a sense of essential elusive woman, the repository of something ineffably delicate and frail, the novelist's own soul dreaming upon impossible fulfilment. This dream of woman was a value that a sensitive man could know, but never be. This essential woman embodies a value that men can recognise, but can never, even the best of them, attain to. Privileged indeed, to Hardy's way of thinking, is he who may discover and cherish one such natural flame; and privileged are Hardy's readers that he made himself its guardian and devoted his efforts to sharing with us its warming glow.

3

Under the Greenwood Tree:
A Novel about the Imagination

by BARBARA HARDY

Although Thomas Hardy's novels show his interest in crafts and arts, religious, secular, and military music, verse, architecture, landscape painting, and story-telling on the public platform (in *The Hand of Ethelberta*), they do not directly reveal his interest in the art of fiction. He does not write artist-novels. Nevertheless, all his characters are active in the narrative forms of fantasy and memory, and in his most argumentative and ambitious novels, *The Mayor of Casterbridge*, *The Return of the Native*, *Tess of the d'Urbervilles* and *Jude the Obscure*, his interest in imagination is too wide to be confined to the nature and situation of the artist. Jude, Sue, Eustachia, and Tess, are examples of imaginative power. They all share a poor chance of survival, for their mental energy finds it impossible to conform to the restrictive and conventional demands of nature and society. To imagine is to imagine a better world, and in the Hardy world, to imagine a better world is to be subversive, and to be subversive is to be destroyed. Only one of his highly imaginative people, Elizabeth-Jane Farfrae in *The Mayor of Casterbridge*, comes to terms with life, and modestly but sensitively survives. However, she refuses to be 'demonstratively thankful', as Hardy says, for 'the doubtful honour of a brief transit through a sorry world'. She believes, and encourages others to believe, that life may be made endurable through 'those minute forms of satisfaction that offer themselves to everyone not in positive pain'. Even such mild anodynes are rare in Hardy.

Tess is more representative of his thinking characters. Her intelligence and imagination are articulated as finely as Elizabeth-Jane's, though she has less promising opportunity for intellectual self-improvement. Though at times inclined to speak with her author's voice, as when she compares our planet to a blighted apple, she speaks and meditates for the most part in a personal style. Her individual eloquence shows a profound, passionate, and properly generalised sense of her situation, as in her retort to Angel Clare's typically Victorian offer to help her take up some 'course of study—history for example?':

> '. . . what's the use of learning that I am one of a long row only—finding out that there is set down in some old book somebody just like me, and to know that I shall only act her part; making me sad, that's all. The best is not to remember that your nature and your past doings have been just like thousands' and thousands', and that your coming life and doings'll be like thousands' and thousands'.'
>
> (ch. xix)

I am less concerned with the content of what Elizabeth-Jane or Tess say, with their attitudes of pessimism or meliorism, than with their ability to ponder and perceive and their experience. They are endowed with an imaginative capacity sufficiently sophisticated and eloquent to act as a vehicle for Hardy to utter his ideas. But the vehicle is shaped, coloured, and fully characterised. He creates characters who meditate and formulate in terms that serve the dual purposes of the particularities of fiction and the larger lines of his own argument.

Like most writers, Hardy uses mouthpieces as well as examples. Of course, imaginative literature tends to be about imaginative people—Odysseus, Antigone, Lear, Hamlet, Henry Esmond, Dorothea Brooke, Marcel, Stephen Dedalus. But the imaginative artist's interest in imagination and creation of imaginative character may show itself less conspicuously and heroically. *Under the Greenwood Tree* takes its place with *The Woodlanders*, *Far from the Madding Crowd*, and *The Trumpet-Major*, all novels which speak of and through the superficially limited minds and styles of characters who are rarely permitted to generalise, but stay and speak from their allotted empirical experience. It seems inaccurate to call them naïve or even simple characters, because their apparent simplicity is not incompatible with intimations of imaginative grasp. The novels stand with other works of literature whose

46

authors have decided to exclude their own close kin, those characters who can act as examples of expressive, bold, far-seeing, and inventive imagination. Among writings which take such a self-denying ordinance are Wordsworth's *Lyrical Ballads*, George Eliot's *Scenes of Clerical Life*, and Joyce's *Dubliners*. These poems and stories exclude characters directly and broadly representative of their authors' powers, and attempt instead to work through less expressive and refined intelligences of people for whom the world of general ideas barely exists, or seems not to exist at all. Their concerns are with their day-to-day existence, with their immediate environment, with the place and society in which they find themselves, with their families, work, pastimes, pleasures, births, loves, marriages, and deaths. The last-named major events in the human cycle immediately signal the occasion for analysis, speculation, and debate, and the works I am concerned with often avail themselves of the enlarged experiences of social and religious ritual. But even on such occasions, the cyclical or major events of human experience are usually presented and discussed empirically, and the human actors are not strongly sceptical, subversive, or solemn in their attitudes to their own mortality, and are never unconcerned with immediate and particular action.

Under the Greenwood Tree can scarcely be said to have themes in the usual sense understood by literary critics. Its double plot joins the love-story of Dick Dewy and Fancy Day with a vital and fatal chapter in the history of the Mellstock Quire. It can be pressed into thematic conformity with Hardy's other novels through its concern with time and history, but although it certainly suggests or proposes views on change, conformity, continuity, tradition, and modernity, such suggestions do not amount to an informing and conspicuous theme. To insist on such generalisation as dominant would, I believe, reduce or abstract much of the book's vitality and particularity. But I am not so much concerned to examine all the concerns of this novel, as to suggest the way in which one of them emerges. The emergence is subtle, natural, and unusually implicit.

The novel presents the novelist's interest in imagination entirely through its accretion of particulars. In *Under the Greenwood Tree* the characters, actions, and environment, show the human mind sensitively, benignly, and creatively at work. Such work, however humble, is characteristic of what we commonly

47

call imagination. It synthesises and particularises, like Coleridge's favourite image of the shooting star which vividly condenses complex experience in Shakespeare's *Venus and Adonis*. The Imagination shows itself in *Under the Greenwood Tree* as founded on knowledge, sympathy, sensuous response and synthetic force.

Under the Greenwood Tree is a narrative unity which invites an orthodox analysis. It joins the obstacles and triumphs of the love-story with the dismissal of the Mellstock musicians, and its synthesis is made through parallels and contrasts. Fancy Day is the new organist who replaces the old choir, and her two un-successful lovers, the churchwarden and the parson, bring about the local change as a testimony to their feeling for her. The lovers are young and must hurry, the musicians middle-aged and old, and must give way. Attitudes to love, youth, ageing, and age are shown in fine blends and contrasts. The lovers are rapturous and blind, the middle-aged and elderly are calmly disenchanted. A sharply and fully realised natural environment creates Hardy's honest version of pastoral, neither wholly ideal nor wholly un-desirable, in which the bitter-sweet human experiences are all chronicled.

The pastoral exerts its binding-power. Each part of the novel is what Coleridge would call an organ to the whole, beginning with the resonant title's quotation from that earlier pastoral, *As You Like It*. Sentences are resonant, suggesting the motion of nature's rituals, 'And winter, which modifies the note of such trees as shed their leaves, does not destroy its individuality' (in Chapter I), or perfect harmony, 'a couple . . . so exactly in tune with one another as Dick and she' (in Chapter II) of the fruition and colour, in the description of grandfather William, 'an ardent vitality still preserved a warm and roughened bloom upon his face, which reminded gardeners of the sunny side of a ripe ribstone-pippin' (in Chapter III).

The image of William's face marks one of Hardy's favourite methods of describing his characters. He is closely attentive not only to appearances, but to the sensibility and sympathy which register them. He likes to show his characters through the vari-able responses of other people:

> William Dewy—otherwise grandfather William—was now about
> seventy; yet an ardent vitality still preserved a warm and
> roughened bloom upon his face, which reminded gardeners of

the sunny side of a ripe ribstone-pippin; though a narrow strip
of forehead, that was protected from the weather by lying
above the line of his hat-brim, seemed to belong to some town
man, so gentlemanly was its whiteness. His was a humorous
and kindly nature, not unmixed with a frequent melancholy; and
he had a firm religious faith. But to his neighbours he had no
character in particular. If they saw him pass by their windows
when they had been bottling off old mead, or when they had
just been called long-headed men who might do anything in the
world if they chose, they thought concerning him, 'Ah, there's
that good-hearted man—open as a child!' If they saw him just
after losing a shilling or half-a-crown, or accidentally letting
fall a piece of crockery, they thought, 'There's that poor weak-
minded man Dewy again! Ah, he's never done much in the world
either!' If he passed when fortune neither smiled nor frowned
on them, they merely thought him old William Dewy.

(pt. 1, ch. iii)

This joint attention to a man and to the shifting external view-
point which regards, interprets and judges him, is characteristic
of Hardy's medium of presentation in this novel. He is not altogether giving up the descriptive authority of the author, but in-
clines to share it provisionally with his characters, while reserving
his own total knowledge. He does not preserve this superior knowledge in order to create an ironical contrast between wisdom and
ignorance, as George Eliot or Henry James occasionally do, but
suggests and ultimately proves that good judgement and vision
are native to Mellstock. Hardy speaks about his people, through
them, and for them. To present a character is for him to present
a variable, not a constent, so as to recognise a local truth, and to
create a community of linked and separated people. He may be
omniscient, but masks the omniscience out of regard for the
minds and responses of his people, who have their own rights
and powers. If he is attentive to nature, so are they; and his
description of the natural world, like his description of people,
uses his people's eyes and ears.

The novelist's familiar knowledge, and his appreciation of individual human and natural life, is drawn from his characters
and is delegated to them. This is not a critical conceit. One might
truly suggest that Hardy learnt to see, hear, and know by observing the originals of his characters, the creation of art being a
circular process rather than an imitation of nature.

We learn then from Hardy's people how imagery and imagination function. The novel's first sentence reports that dwellers in a wood can tell trees apart by voice as well as feature; then Dick Dewy makes his entry, while his author observes that the plantation 'whispered thus distinctively to his intelligence'. The author's sensibility is interwoven with the character's. Hardy immediately proceeds to delineate Dick's nature, confining himself to Dick's confining darkness. Dick is first sensed and presented through the sounds he makes: 'All the evidences of his nature were those afforded by the spirit of his footsteps, which succeeded each other lightly and quickly, and by the liveliness of his voice as he sang in a rural cadence . . .' These evidences of his nature, which are allowed to speak for themselves, carry great weight through being unendorsed yet unmistakable. Many of the novel's people meditate, observe, and respond to the world outside through their 'intelligence', a word Hardy uses rather broadly to include mind, feeling, senses. Reuben Dewy, the tranter, for instance, is first seen as his friends and neighbours arrive at his house, knowing 'by their footsteps that they were the expected old comrades' and so not bothering to look up from the hogshead he is about to broach. His son Charley is contemplating his own face in a small looking-glass, 'to learn how the human countenance appeared when engaged in crying, which survey led him to pause at various points in each wail that were more than ordinarily striking, for a thorough appreciation of the general effect'. His daughter Bessy is comparing the faded and unfaded pattern of her plaid dress, his wife testing the temperature of flitches of bacon which seem to be in possible danger from the festive fire's great heat. Hardy likes to show people engaged in fervent, absorbed, and curious attention to the things around them, including themselves. The child Charley is worth all the children in the novels of George Eliot put together, for that look in the glass, as he cries, and for his marvellous question about the inside of the cider cask, 'Idd it cold inthide te hole?' Hardy's grown men and women, as well as his children, are engaged in this barefaced and unmonitored response to life. Old William loves two things best, splitting apple-wood and playing the bass-viol. At one time Hardy intended to call the novel, *The Mellstock Quire*, and the whole choir is ruled by a musical passion, delighting in performance, discussing the merits and history of their instruments, and forcing music upon Farmer Shines who can't stand their Christmas carols. This quality of fervour is a necessary aspect of imagination and sensibility, as Hardy conceives them. Fervour joins intellectual curiosity with physical and emotional response, to create the exhilarated and creative eating, drinking, singing, dancing and working of *Under the Greenwood Tree.*

The fullest instance of fervour is the music, a fervent labour and a fervent joy. But professional appreciation is also there in Fancy's expected 'sharp remark' which was expected of 'the village sharpener', in the villagers' disinterested praise of 'sellers' like old Sam Lawson, and in the tranter's history of his cider and its barrel. Reuben Dewy discourses on the subject of his cider, the apples of which it is made, their names (where known), and the places where they grew, the hoops and tap of the barrel, once used for port wine and dishonestly sold by Sam Lawson, in an articulate history. Professional fervour involves a way of organising and ordering experience, not exclusively or distortingly, like a humour, but affording an entry to experience and a means of organising it. It depends on knowledge of people, objects, and history. It is attentive to life, as Dick Dewy is when he attends to the swarm of bees even though it makes him slightly late for his wedding. It is presented through praise and delight. This knowledgeable fervour is more than a feeling for community and nature, for through its specialisation Hardy's people establish and order their lives and values. Mr. Penny not only knows about shoes and feet, but tells his shoemaker's anecdotes to reveal an implicit feeling for family, neighbourhood, and individual people. Ruling passions can blind or blinker vision, but Hardy makes his people benevolent and sympathetic in the exercise and defence of their jobs:

'Well,' said the shoemaker, seeming to perceive that the interest the object had excited was greater than he had anticipated, and warranted the last's being taken up again and exhibited; 'now, whose foot do ye suppose this last was made for? It was made for Geoffrey Day's father, over at Yalbury Wood. Ah, many's the pair o' boots he've had off the last! Well, when 'a died, I used the last for Geoffrey, and have ever since, though a little doctoring was wanted to make it do. Yes, a very queer natured last it is now, 'a b'lieve', he continued, turning it over caressingly. 'Now, you notice that there' (pointing to a lump of leather bradded to the toe), 'that's a very bad bunion that he've had ever since 'a was a boy. Now, this remarkable large piece' (pointing to a patch nailed to the side), 'shows a' accident he received by the tread of a horse, that squashed his foot a'most to a pomace. The horse-shoe came full-butt on this point, you see. And so I've just been over to Geoffrey's, to know if he wanted his bunion altered or made bigger in the new pair I'm making.'

(pt. 1, ch. iii)

and

'You used to know Johnson the dairyman, William?'

'Ay, sure; I did.'

'Well, 'twasn't opposite his house, but a little lower down— by his paddock, in front o' Parkmaze Pool. I was a-bearing across towards Bloom's End, and lo and behold, there was a man just brought out o' the Pool, dead; he had un'rayed for a dip, but not being able to pitch it just there had gone in flop over his head. Men looked at en; women looked at en; children looked at en; nobody knowed en. He was covered wi' a sheet; but I catched sight of his voot, just showing out as they carried en along. "I don't care what name that man went by," I said, in my way, "but he's John Woodward's brother; I can swear to the family voot." At that very moment up comes John Woodward, weeping and teaving, "I've lost my brother! I've lost my brother!" '

(pt. 1, ch. iii)

In such professional humours experience is incised, remembered, and narrated. The anecdotes have their guiding theme or *motif*, whether it is shoes, music, drink, or Mrs. Penny's harping on her marriage to her 'little small man'. As Penny talks to the group outside his shop window, he goes on stitching, and punctuates or emphasises remarks with the strong pulls of needle through leather. His special shoemaker's concern makes his responses sharply self-interested, and informed, and so keeps sympathy from spilling over into grandiose or sentimental effusions. Grandfather William's passion for strings allows him to remember warmly and acutely:

'Well, as to father in the corner there,' the tranter said, pointing to old William, who was in the act of filling his mouth; 'he'd starve to death for music's sake now, as much as when he was a boy-chap of fifteen.'

'Truly, now,' said Michael Mail, clearing the corner of his

throat in the manner of a man who meant to be convincing;
'there's a friendly tie of some sort between music and eating.'
He lifted the cup to his mouth, and drank himself gradually
backwards from a perpendicular position to a slanting one, during which time his looks performed a circuit from the wall
opposite him to the ceiling overhead. Then clearing the other
corner of his throat: 'Once I was a-setting in the little kitchen
of the Dree Mariners at Casterbridge, having a bit of dinner,
and a brass band struck up in the street. Such a beautiful band
as that were! I was setting eating fried liver and lights, I well
can mind—ah, I was! and to save my life, I couldn't help chaw-
ing to the tune. Band played six-eight time; six-eight chaws
I, willynilly. Band plays common; common time went my teeth
among the liver and lights as true as a hair. Beautiful 'twere!
Ah, I shall never forget that there band!'

'That's as tuneful a thing as ever I heard of,' said grandfather James, with the absent gaze which accompanies profound criticism.

(pt. 1, ch. viii)

These ruling passions are not despotic, and often divide their
rule. Penny plays the fiddle as well as making shoes, grandfather
William cleaves the apple-wood and knows how it will burn, Mr.
and Mrs. Dewy and Mr. and Mrs. Penny tell a chequered but not
cynical experience of married life. The passions chime in together.
Grandfather William's thought of singing to Fancy Day follows
Mr. Penny's story of the drowned man's foot, but takes place
with natural and easy enthusiasm, not jockeying for position.
There is room for stories about strings, cider, shoes, and marriage,
told by many story-tellers. Hardy's are not satirical humours.
No one 'peculiar quality' diverts and distorts the 'effects and
powers' of his people, making them 'in their confluction all to
flow one way'. The bias gives shape to imagination. These people
have a solid and special ground, from which to regard their own
and each other's lives.

Despite the great praise of strings, the choir can put aside their
special interest with tolerance and generosity. When their depu-
tation marches off to see the parson, it is not to give it to him
'hot and strong' as local intelligence expects, but to accept the
decision and ask modestly for a proper season for their going.
William's mild detachment refuses to be insulting or unjust to
their enemy the parson:

'Still, for my part,' said old William, 'though he's arrayed against us, I like the hearty borus-snorus ways of the new pa'son.'

'You, ready to die for the quire,' said Bowman reproachfully, 'to stick up for the quire's enemy, William!'

'Nobody will feel the loss of our church-work so much as I,' said the old man firmly: 'that you d'all know. I've a-been in the quire man and boy ever since I was a chiel of eleven. But for all that 'tisn't in me to call the man a bad man, because I truly and sincerely believe en to be a good young feller.'

Some of the youthful sparkle that used to reside there animated William's eye as he uttered the words, and a certain nobility of aspect was also imparted to him by the setting sun, which gave him a Titanic shadow at least thirty feet in length, stretching away to the east in outlines of imposing magnitude, his head finally terminating upon the trunk of a grand old oak-tree.

(pt. 2, ch. ii)

So Hardy evinces his approval of William's character and remarks. They are not sentimental, as their collective biography of the former parson makes clear:

'Ah, Mr. Grinham was the man!' said Bowman. 'Why, he never troubled us wi' a visit from year's end to year's end. You might go anywhere, do anything: you'd be sure never to see him.'

and

'And 'a was a very jinerous gentleman about choosing the psalms and hymns o' Sundays. "Confound ye," says he, "blare and scrape what ye will, but don't bother me!" '

(pt. 2, ch. ii)

The quality of the Mellstock imagination is well-wishing but not soft, self-respecting but not egotistical, specialist but not warped. These moral and intellectual qualities are invariably conveyed in those narratives that are the prevailing genre within the novel. Music may be a collective enterprise, but so is story-telling, ritualised in village feasts and gatherings, part of the ordinary social flow of reminiscence, gossip, praise, criticism, entertainment, hopes, fears, jokes and ruminations, and seemingly extended naturally to form Hardy's art.

A remarkable feature of his story-tellers is their co-operation in narrative. The community is brought to life in its daily activities and its properties. Every object and every event tells many stories, and the stories are generous, but the actual harmony and community of the telling testifies and ministers to the benevolence. The tellers quote and build on other stories. Hardy's storytellers are good men, and their sprightly and potent characters, with their ironic but tolerant acceptances, are expressed and implied in their stories. Perhaps the social psychology and morality of Hardy's narratives achieves its most complex response in the last sight we get of the community in *Under the Greenwood Tree*. In the last chapter, Hardy shows us the communal act of imagination, practised by the onlookers at the nuptial dance:

> Here the gaffers and gammers whose dancing days were over told stories of great impressiveness, and at intervals surveyed the advancing and retiring couples from the same retreat, as people on shore might be supposed to survey a naval engagement in the bay beyond; returning again to their tales when the pause was over. Those of the whirling throng who, during the rests between each figure, turned their eyes in the direction of these seated ones, were only able to discover, on account of the music and bustle, that a very striking circumstance was in course of narration—denoted by an emphatic sweep of the hand, snapping of the fingers, close of the lips, and fixed look into the centre of the listener's eye for the space of a quarter of a minute, which raised in that listener such a reciprocating working of face as to sometimes make the distant dancers half wish to know what such an interesting tale could refer to.
>
> (pt. 5, ch. ii)

Those whose dancing days are over remember festivities past, and loves and marriages are summoned up unromantically to testify to the binding-power of social ritual. The feeblest member of the Mellstock Quire is Thomas Leaf, who turns up, as so often, to take his place among his superiors. Like a good guest he makes his contribution to the ritual story-telling under the beech-tree. Thomas Leaf's story is scarcely an imaginative creation, but takes its place in the common ritual.

It is a feeble story, its rhetoric and form making it a model of how not to do it. His tale is one told by an idiot, flat, pointless, but generously offered for the occasion.[1]

'Once,' said the delighted Leaf, in an uncertain voice, 'there was a man who lived in a house! Well, this man went thinking

55

and thinking night and day. At last, he said to himself, as I might, "If I had only ten pound, I'd make a fortune." At last by hook or by crook, he got the ten pounds!'

'Only think of that!' said Nat Callcome satirically.

'Silence!' said the tranter.

'Well, now comes the interesting part of the story! In a little time he had made that ten pounds twenty. Then a little time after that he doubled it, and made it forty. Well, he went on, and a good while after that he made it eighty, and on to a hundred. Well, by-and-by he made it two hundred! Well, you'd never believe it, but—he went on and made it four hundred! He went on, and what did he do? Why, he made it eight hundred! Yes, he did,' continued Leaf in the highest pitch of excitement, bringing down his fist upon his knee with such force that he quivered with the pain; 'yes, and he went on and made it A THOUSAND!'

'Hear, hear!' said the tranter. 'Better than the history of England, my sonnies!'

'Thank you for your story, Thomas Leaf,' said grandfather William; and then Leaf gradually sank into nothingness again.

(pt. 5, ch. ii)

The tranter and his father, two of the best tellers, in this novel full of telling, move their generous vote of thanks. In *Under the Greenwood Tree* the chorus often ceases to be choric, to take its prominent place in the centre of our attention. It holds such a place through its imaginative appreciation of the past, well-preserved and alive, but naturally conservative and conserving. The middle-aged and the old men are constantly telling the comic story of courtship and marriage, wryly, drily, but not chillingly or cynically. The two lovers are naturally forward-looking. Hardy's appreciation of their amorous creations is beautifully balanced against the old stories. Dick's vision is a vision, delicately appreciated in its intensity and fervour, comedy insisting on its inventiveness and force. His exuberant ideality is contrasted with the acquired common-sense of the choir, whose unromantic and unvisionary look at love amazes the young lover. The choir's imagination dwells on the reliable pleasures of music, song, food, drink, and festivity, but they sigh over Dick tolerantly, their breath scarcely dimming the brilliant reflecting surface of creative love.

Dick Dewy sees visions. Fancy Day's imagination has been busy with a more complicated vision of future possibilities than Dick

Dewy's. She follows Thomas Leaf's unimaginative simple tale with her carefully kept secret and her white lie. She has made up her plain tale of love and marriage with Dick, but into this realistic construction has strayed the less palpable vision of higher things, thoughts of marriage with Parson Maybold. This is a vision entertained but not followed through. She chooses the plain tale, though Hardy makes it truthfully apparent that her imaginative endeavours, in their selective and creative efforts, are painfully struggling, as Coleridge says of poets, to idealise and unify. The choir's creativity takes an understated form, right for its stoicism and sense of proportion. Fancy's imaginative infidelity is also understated, remaining a straying of the mind which reminds us, like the novel's title, that idylls are fictions. The personal autobiography we are all engaged in constructing as we look before and after depends on visions and revisions.

NOTE

1   I have discussed Thomas Leaf's story more fully in *Tellers and Listeners* (Athlone Press, 1975).

4

The Return:
Centennial Observations

by ROBERT B. HEILMAN

1

To return to *The Return of the Native* after a long absence, and after some transactions with the later 'major' works, is to find much that is familiar and much that is, well, for lack of a better word, surprising. By 'the familiar' I do not mean matters remembered from a distant reading, but the recurrent practices that one thinks of as Hardyisms—sometimes excellent, sometimes mingling the more and the less effective, sometimes stirring the reader, willy-nilly, to the ho-hum response. Technical tours de force, sometimes brilliant, co-exist with methods that are careless or heavy-handed. What is 'surprising' is that the excellences make one think of the older novelist rather than the relatively young one that Hardy still was in 1878—thirty-eight. Although *The Return* is only the third of the seven 'Novels of Character and Environment', as Hardy called them, its ties are mainly with the final four[1] that begin with *The Mayor of Casterbridge* (1886) and end with *Jude the Obscure* (1895). To say that is to declare *The Return* worthy at least of the usual centennial rites. As ritualist I want to observe some aspects of Hardy's fictional art rather than focus on influences (Schopenhauer, Mill, Arnold, Greek drama, modern science, folklore, anthropology, etc.) and on ideas (Hellenism, Hebraism, paganism, Christianity, 'natural energy', harmony with nature, rural decline, fate, destiny, magic, Prometheanism)[2] that have received much attention.

2

The style[3] is like that of the later novels: it has the ups that gratify and the downs that disappoint. The talk of the rustics rarely lacks vitality. Grandfer Cantle describes his wife as a girl: 'a long-legged slittering maid, hardly husband-high' (I, 5);[4] Timothy Fairway says he is 'stiff as a ram's horn stooping so long' (III, 3). Hardy can approach this vein himself: the fifth of November fires 'dwindling weak' (I, 3); like Buonaparte, the reddleman belongs to 'the land of worn-out bogeys' (I, 9). Hardy draws good images from ordinary life: a road on the heath is like the 'parting line on a head of black hair' (I, 2); 'the oblique band of sunlight which followed her through the door became the young wife well' (III, 6); in 'upland hamlets . . . no dense partition of yawns and toilets divided humanity by night from humanity by day' (V, 2). Now and then there is that revision of the observed reality which almost excites the thrill of the surreal: the Vyes' pool 'lay on the outside of the bank like the white of an eye without its pupil' (III, 3). On the one hand Hardy can climax a physical description with an allusion to Keats—in the carboniferous period, 'nothing but a monotonous extent of leafage, amid which no bird sang' (III, 5); on the other he can remind us of Austen—as he often does, surprisingly—with a neat antithesis (Wildeve was a man 'in whom no man would have seen anything to admire, and in whom no woman would have seen anything to dislike' [I, 5]), or an almost epigrammatic generalisation: 'In the heath's barrenness to the farmer lay its fertility to the historian' (I, 3). He may use Austen balance, of course, to render a perception that goes beyond the limits of Austen comedy: 'He was not so young as to be absolutely without a sense that sympathy was demanded, he was not old enough to be free from the terror felt in childhood at beholding misery in adult quarters hitherto deemed impregnable . . .' (IV, 6). There is often the very apt phrase—the heath as an 'instalment of night . . . before its astronomical hour was come' (I, 1), or a tract of land that 'made itself felt as a vague stretch of remoteness' (I, 3); and at times the paradoxical phrase—Fairway's 'passionless severity of face' (I, 3); Eustacia's 'drowsy fervour of manner' (I, 6) and her '[growing] generous in the greediness of a new passion' (II, 7). Then there is the flashing near-paradoxical distinction between

59

states that one could readily think allied: 'Sometimes his condition had been one of utter remorse, unsoftened by a single tear of pure sorrow . . .' (V, 1). There is a poetic sureness in this opposition of remorse as hard inturning and sorrow as generous outgoing.

Hardy's range extends from the striking image to the disciplined syntax. Beside the compactness, precision, and imaginative freshness of which he is capable there is often the flaccid, the vague, the verbose, the bumbling, and even the opaque. If he can be brisk and tonic, he can also go soft, as in the sentimental diminutive ('a finch was trying to sing' but the wind 'twisted round his little tail, and made him give up his song' [III, 6]; Eustacia's 'little hands quivered' [V, 3], big girl though she has been said to be), and in the idea that the face of the heath, since it was 'lonely', suggested 'tragical possibilities' (I, 1). The tendency to pump up feeling artificially leads him into the pathetic fallacy. He all but makes an Iago out of an adder, which 'regarded the assembled group with a sinister look in its small black eyes, and the . . . pattern on its back seemed to intensify with indignation' (IV, 7), and a villain out of a storm which 'snapped at the windowpanes' (V, 8). But 'how ineffectively gnashed the storm!' is his triumphant note on another occasion, even though in the gale 'convulsive sounds came from the branches, as if pain were felt' (III, 6). The as-if clause contains the lame, awkward passive that Hardy often commits. Observers could locate each fifth of November fire 'by its angle and direction, though nothing of the scenery could be viewed' (I, 3). Another amateurism of Hardy's is the painful participle: Venn was 'singular in colour, this being a lurid red' (I, 2). Again, he could hardly find a more uncomfortable way of saying that a door opened directly on a room where people were dancing: 'It became evident at once that the dance was proceeding immediately within the surface of the door, no apartment intervening' (II, 5). One could make a longish catalogue of Hardy's dangling verbals, but I will stick to one example: 'On reaching the hill the sun had quite disappeared . . .' (IV, 3); one must work through the context to be sure that it was not the sun but Eustacia who reached the hill. Hardy's usual concreteness softens up at times, and he falls into a mushy 'type' or 'sort'. Mrs. Yeobright had 'features of the type usually found where perspicacity is the chief quality enthroned within' (I, 3).

What are those features, one wonders. A fire dies down because 'the fuel had not been of that substantial sort which can support a blaze long' (I, 3). Dry stream-beds 'had undergone a species of incineration since the drought had set in' (IV, 5); the dead Eustacia 'eclipsed all her living phases' (V, 9). These limp abstractions, often conjoined with a Latinate vocabulary, give the style a periodic taint of the academic or the bureaucratic. Hardy can be heavy, awkward, and vague all at once: the reddleman 'was an instance of the pleasing being wasted to form the groundwork of the singular, when an ugly foundation would have done just as well for that purpose' (I, 9). Finally, three brief quotations. In a tense confrontation between Clym and Eustacia, Eustacia says she thinks Clym will kill her, since 'No less degree of rage against me will match your previous grief for her' (V, 3). This non-colloquial antithesis, in the midst of passionate recriminations, approaches the laughable stiltedness of a ringing melodramatic statement on an outworn stage. There is a different effect when Hardy says, of the corpses pulled from the water at Shadwater Weir, that there was 'not a whiff of life left in either of the bodies' (V, 9). In 'whiff' the donnish in Hardy is replaced by an offhandedness that is trivialising. Finally 'the good shape of his figure' is singularly tautological (I, 2).

Such distracting ineptitudes remained with Hardy to the end. Still, they are like a scattering of potholes in an otherwise well-paved road: they cause discomfort but do not long impede the journey. They are far fewer than the stylistic adequacies and excellences. He can give a fine concreteness to his descriptions; his color sense is almost as active as George Eliot's. He often mixes colors, and he sees many hues, shades, and tints—whites (whitish, silver, burnished silver, pale, pallor of death, Parian marble), yellows and browns (amber, brass, copper-coloured, ensaffroned, bright yellow, gilt, gold, embrowned, neutral brown, russet, rusty, mud-coloured, tawny), reds (blood-coloured, crimson, ruby, scarlet, scarlet-red, metallic violet, lilac, purple), blues (pale blue, deep blue, brilliant blue, blue of the sea, sapphirine), greens (bottle-green, emerald green, olive-green, soft pale green), blacks (dark, frigid grey, crape, jet, sable, shade, shadowy, sooty). He sees light in different ways: 'sparkling starlight', 'shining facets of frost', 'lively luminousness', 'like a streak of phosphorus', 'eyes lit by a hot light'.

In describing Egdon Heath, perhaps the best known topographic personality in English fiction, Hardy perceives not only colors but shapes and textures and tones, the types and ways of flora and fauna, the changes that go with time of day and season, the interplay of person and scene (in heat and cold, fair weather and storm), the distortions of faces in flickering firelight. He records smells less often than sounds—the sounds made by insects and birds, by movements on the ground and against bushes, by different weathers, by winds blowing through different growths and foliages. With an air of ease, inevitability, and passion he gives the heath remarkable life. But for it he also feels a not quite controlled love and reverence, and he sometimes moves from audivisual virtuosity across the border to purple-passage excess;[5] he tends to overpictorialise the scene, especially with associational chromatics, and even more to give the picture an over-heavy frame of significance.[6] Still the heath survives, if less as a bearer of communicated meaning than as a provider of a not quite definable spaciousness—something like the spaciousness that wide grounds confer upon a dwelling even when essential life is centred within it.

Hardy sees the Heath as sombre, solemn, sublime, antique, durable; as 'untameable, Ishmaelitish', a home for a 'thoroughgoing ascetic'. It serves his mood when he is the doom-laden itinerant preacher. It is a 'Titanic form' that 'could only be imagined to await one last crisis—the final overthrow'; a little later the Titan is somewhat reduced, for the Heath is 'like man, slighted and enduring'; again, its 'sombreness' is 'absolutely in keeping with the moods of the more thinking among mankind' (I, 1). Here Hardy speaks as village pessimist, ready to blame reality for hostility to man (it is his good fortune, and ours, that he antedated the tedious vogue of the 'absurd'). Happily this is only a part of Hardy—less than half, one might say. Though Egdon is at times a savage place, and as such a symbol of cosmic unfriendliness to man, it is also the scene of ongoing life: virtually all the characters in *The Return* adapt well to it and are even devoted to it. Only Eustacia hates it (though Wildeve routinely agrees with her, 'I abhor it too' [I, 9], his emotions are not place-oriented), and the disasters that occur on it—far fewer than the working adjustments to it—are rooted in hearts, though the immediate instruments may be environmental. They always have to be: if one grows desperate in the Sahara, and plunges into some ultimate recklessness, drowning is not what happens to one.

When he makes Egdon symbolise an unfriendly reality, Hardy registers an almost sentimental conception of man as victim that also appears in sidemouth *obiter dicta* (though here less pervasive, I believe, than in the *Mayor* and less intrusive than in *Jude*). He comes up with the strange notion that handsome people are an-achronistic because faces are bound to reflect the 'view of life as a thing to be put up with, replacing that zest for existence which was so intense in early civilisations' (III, 1)—a view, he appears to think, made obligatory by 'modern perceptiveness'. Clym loses ambition, Hardy says, because he is at the 'stage in a young man's life when the grimness of the human situation first becomes clear', a stage in which, in France, 'it is not uncustom-ary to commit suicide' (III, 3). (That 'not uncustomary' charmingly reduces suicide to a vogue dictated by the makers of fashion.) Now and then Hardy borrows the voices of Clym and Eustacia for such plaints. Eustacia refers dourly to 'the cruel satires that Fate loves to indulge in' (III, 5), and Clym thinks at times that 'he had been ill-used by fortune, so far as to say that to be born is a palpable dilemma, and that instead of men aiming to advance in life with glory they should calculate how to retreat out of it without shame' (VI, 1). Hardy does save Clym for good sense by making that view temporary. But he immediately turns around and chastises Clym and mankind generally for hesitancy to 'de-grade a First Cause',[7] and to 'conceive a dominant power of lower moral quality than their own; and, even while they sit down and weep by the waters of Babylon, invent excuses for the oppression which prompts their tears'. Happily this sentimentalising of man as a victim of divine oppression[8] is a thing of the moment; at least it does not undermine the sense of reality which makes Hardy as artist present man's fate as congruent with his nature.[9]

3

In narrative technique Hardy wavers between an effortlessly progressive and formed narrative and, on the other hand, addi-tions, extemporisations, and manipulations that elicit minor rest-lessness and the involuntary retention, rather than the willing suspension, of disbelief. The rustics are lively, granted, but their talk-fests go on and on, as if Hardy could not arrest the flux of reportage.[10] On the other hand, he can neglect the dramatic documentation that could give a needed body or verisimilitude. Wildeve an engineer? Clym a 'manager to a diamond merchant'? Hardy seems to have hastily picked the roles out of a hat to serve a purpose: Wildeve's to define a comedown, and Clym's to make possible a rejection, which Clym elaborates at various times, even to an unlikely audience of rustics at a barbering (III, 1), with the somewhat windy rhetoric of scorn attractive to 'born-again' souls. The indefatigable study which nearly blinds Clym is a misty affair, for Hardy cannot identify a single work that Clym reads[11] (in contrast with the copious reading lists in *Jude*). The seven weeks' delay after the aborted Wildeve-Thomasin wedding is circumstantially vague; we know Wildeve's motives, but it is difficult to imagine, in this conventional community, a long social stasis when a crisis makes action seem inevitable. Then at the time of the marriage Hardy so amply reports the to-do which Clym and his mother make about it that it becomes important, and we expect to see more of the couple. Hardy, however, drops them cold until he can utilise them in the Clym-mother-Eustacia conflict. What he does is shift from documentation to design, from reportage to narrative form that has other necessities. It is a characteristic jump from one way of doing things to another.

Or Hardy may move into effective dramatic documentation from rhetorical generalisation. In the ultimately excellent portrayals of both Clym and Eustacia there is a marked departure from outsized intentions in the introductory accounts making claims that are not sustained. These set-piece descriptions are much noticed, but the key parts of them do not hold up under inspection. The famous notion that 'thought is a disease of flesh' (II, 6) is of such beguiling novelty that its inapplicability to Clym may escape detection. Though Hardy prophesies that Clym's 'beauty . . . would in no long time be overrun by its parasite thought' and asserts that he has 'a wearing habit of meditation', the character presented dramatically reveals neither a philosophic bent nor a suffering from 'a full recognition of the coil of things'.[12] Hardy goes from inapplicable theory (and surely erroneous theory: who has not seen deeply lined faces that go with conventional well-being, and recognised truly philosophic minds behind bland faces?) to half-truth when he declares that Clym's 'look . . . was a natural cheerfulness striving against depression from without, and not quite succeeding.' There is no sign of depression in newly arrived Clym, but much of 'natural cheerfulness'. Indeed the Comtian[13] positivism on which Clym was presumably nourished tends to beget optimism about the human scene, and the religion of humanity leads to such hopeful reformism as motivates Clym's educational fantasy.

Hardy's extended formal picture of Eustacia (I, 7), which used to be cited as an example of great description,[14] conforms a little better to the Eustacia developed in the later action. A beautiful woman, alluring in a limited environment where she seems exotic, she is intense, romantic, wilful, yearning, and resentful; Hardy says this, and he makes it good in the story (one wonders only why she is so unresisting to the hated heath-bound life imposed on her by her grandfather, who seems less a man of iron than a Smollett-Dickens nautical humour susceptible to management by an energetic woman whom Hardy calls an 'absolute queen' [I, 6] at home). What she cannot sustain—as who could?—are the implied comparisons with Clotho, Lachesis, and Atropos, with Artemis, Athena, and Hera, with Heloise and Cleopatra; the assertion that her style resembled 'the comprehensive strategy of a general' and that she 'could utter oracles of Delphic ambiguity'. All this is much too grand.[15] Partly Hardy has fallen in love with her, partly he uses her to express his annoyance at the heavenly mismanagement that accounts for the 'inequality of lot' and 'captious alternation of caresses and blows that we endure now'. Eustacia is not really 'the raw material of a divinity'; rather than a goddess manquée she is, as various readers have noticed, a full achiever in a human mode identified just two decades before *The Return* appeared—bovarysm. Eustacia is more intelligent and discriminating than Emma, but the basic kinship is there.[16]

Hardy's sense of the inner realities of advancing relationships and developing situations is generally very fine, but his external ways of bringing on change and crisis can stir resistance in even a submissive reader. When a character needs information that will determine what he does, Hardy may have recourse to the most fantastic overhearing since Richardson's Pamela picked up whole paragraphs of praise from anywhere nearby. I will cite just one example:[17] to plot his course as secret protector of Thomasin, Diggory must know what Wildeve and Eustacia are up to, so in the open heath he pulls off a remarkable feat of eavesdropping, creeping up unheard, and unseen under a couple of 'turves' (an Egdon Heath 'Birnam Wood'), to monitor a long conversation (I, 9). The coincidences which fill up so much space in Hardy's technical arsenal we must basically accept—few critics fail to reiterate this—as symbolisations of the untowardness of things that, in Hardy's *ex cathedra* pronouncements, afflicts humanity. But still his 'life's little ironies' and 'satires of circumstance' are of greatly varying artistic quality: they range from the heavy-handed and contrived to the convincing and the revealing.[18] Diggory's 'van' is the Grand Hotel of Egdon Heath: everybody happens in there when a hiding place or a shelter or a meeting with Diggory will be of use. A very effective irony results from Diggory's schemes to keep Wildeve at home with Thomasin: he so bedevils Wildeve, on his nocturnal expeditions to see Eustacia[19] that Wildeve resolves on a day-time trip, and at the same time Diggory encourages Mrs. Yeobright's growing desire for a reconciliation with Clym and Eustacia. Thus it is quite plausible that Wildeve and Mrs. Yeobright embark on visits at the same time and set up new troubles. But in working out the details Hardy starts manipulating: Wildeve and Mrs. Yeobright not only pick the same day for their visits but the same time of day (Mrs. Yeobright can even see Wildeve, whom she does not recognise, enter the cottage). After such a coincidence has set the stage, the crucial slip into disaster is entirely unforced: we understand Eustacia's not answering her mother-in-law's knock at the door, and her readiness to believe that Clym is waking up from a nap and will open the door (IV, 6). Then Hardy returns to coincidence: Clym does not wake up but has a dream which is a remarkable mirror-image of present events, and Mrs. Yeobright, on her return trip, runs into Johnny Nunsuch, who can hear and report her bitter statements and thus contribute to the remorse of her son. And on her walk, finally, comes an ultimate turn of the screw such as Hardy wilfully applies to guarantee disaster: as if fearful that Mrs. Yeobright may survive exhaustion and disillusion, he inflicts on her, of all things, the bite of a poisonous adder (IV, 7). The Lear allusion[20] includes several parallels: the thankless child, the closed door, the parent on the dangerous heath, and now an excessively literal serpent's tooth.

Mrs. Yeobright has picked an inordinately hot August 31 for

her six-mile walk. We are split between protesting that a woman
of such practical sense as she has been shown to have would
surely postpone the expedition, and acquiescing on the ground
that once she has resolved on the initiative, she is so eager to
get on with it that she is immune to the likely protests of good
sense. Be that as it may, this disastrous expedition must also
be seen in its quiet, unforced relationship to two others in which
good intentions lead to a bad end (though at times Hardy can
bark his wares very audibly, he can manage effective structural
repetitions so unobtrusively that we may be slow to notice them;[21]
critics say much about the over-all structure of The Return, but
little about these subtler contributions to structural cohesiveness).
One expedition takes place later, one earlier. The later depends
on one of the best ironies in the book: to please Eustacia, her
young admirer Charlie lights another evening fire and thus summons Wildeve and prepares for Eustacia's final journey, which
like Mrs. Yeobright's ends in a death assisted by the elements.
The earlier one, on the contrary, reveals Hardy in one of his most
mechanical devisings. On Clym's wedding day Mrs. Yeobright
despatches inheritances of fifty guineas each to Thomasin and
Clym. We can see, in retrospect, that Hardy wanted a major
break between Mrs. Yeobright and Eustacia, and a quicker action
than the slow heat of the inevitable friction between two women
different in nature and aspiration. So he suborned disaster by a
virtually preposterous series of events.

Whom does Mrs. Yeobright, a shrewed observer of the human
scene, pick to carry the hundred guineas (a large sum in the
1840s)? None other than Christian Cantle, who, if not quite
the village idiot, has been shown to be much too foolish, fearful,
and fragile for such a mission. Only such an incompetent bearer
could be deflected into gambling and, of all things, losing the
entire hundred to Wildeve (III, 7). But good news: ever-present
Diggory Venn spies on the whole thing, dashes out, forces Wildeve into an unwilling resumption of the game, and wins back the
whole hundred (the last twenty-one by the light of thirteen glow-
worms[22] drafted by Venn to replace a lantern extinguished by a
reckless moth). Surely never has chance reversed itself with such
insatiable consistency. Returning home, the miserable Wildeve
has to pass and see the happy newlyweds (a heavy irony reversed
when, at the lowest stage of her marital fortunes, Eustacia learns

that Wildeve has inherited £11,000 and has to be badgered about her choice of men by her grandfather [IV, 8]). But the deserving are by no means safe out of it, for Venn delivers the whole hundred guineas to Thomasin. Hardy is in there causing trouble again. For though Venn, spying on the Wildeve-Christian game of chance, has overheard so much that, when he is defeating Wildeve, he can crow over him by repeating to him the exact words that Wildeve had used to Christian, Hardy does not let him hear the key fact: [23] that half the guineas belonged to Clym (III, 8). Thomasin innocently keeps all the guineas. Mrs. Yeobright, dismayed that she receives no thanks from Clym, goes out to investigate, and Hardy forces her into two steps bound to work out badly. Does she first check out the matter with friendly Thomasin, as would be probable? No, she goes to Eustacia, and then sensible Mrs. Yeobright, of all people, puts her question in the one way bound to be irreparably offensive: 'Have you received a gift from Thomasin's husband?' (IV, 1).[24] What is more, she never explains what she means, even as Eustacia naturally falls into angry outbursts which it seems must elicit a clarification. Thus has Hardy made the breach immitigable. Next, Mrs. Yeobright tardily visits Thomasin and learns what happened; Thomasin conveys guineas and facts to Clym; but Clym does not pass the word on to Eustacia (IV, 2). Nor does Eustacia explain to Clym the grudge which she now nurtures. Rarely has disaster been led up to by such machinations, in which Hardy rather resembles the unkind divinities upon whom he likes to cast aspersions. When he is determined to prevent a human muddling through,[25] his darker sensibilities can produce an eminently resistible art.

Yet happily that is less than half the story, for the true artist in Hardy has the larger voice. For one thing, there is the unstrained continuity of events on the evening of 5 November; in an easy-flowing eight and a half chapters Hardy so traces the events of a few hours that he introduces all the main and supporting characters (even the absent Clym by talk of his expected visit) and all the principal situations (Diggory's rejection by Thomasin, the aborted Thomasin-Wildeve wedding, Mrs. Yeobright's hand in these relationships, the Thomasin-Wildeve-Eustacia triangle). Hardy manages a very fluent movement from hour to hour, from scene to scene.[26] In fact, long before films he hits upon a cinematic flow of episodes, and at times he uses a panning technique or a transition by contiguity:[27] we move effortlessly under the guidance, as it were, of a camera following people's steps and their eyes. It is a truism that Hardy likes to open a novel with out-of-doors movement: *The Return* employs a virtuosity of functional motion. Hiking a heath road, Captain Vye catches up with Diggory Venn and his pony-drawn van; inside is the woman who we later learn is Thomasin. Vye moves on, Venn stops for a rest, and we follow his eyes as he looks up and sees a woman's figure atop the highest elevation (Rainbarrow). She leaves, and many people replace her, carrying faggots for fires. We pan to such fires all over the heath, and then settle into a long close-up on the major community fire on Rainbarrow. While they talk, the rustics several times look down to a light which comes from the Quiet Woman Inn, Wildeve's place to which he is supposedly returning with his new bride. Later, when their fire and others are dying, the rustics see one fire which remarkably maintains a steady brightness: they locate it at Captain Vye's place and decide that it is his granddaughter's work. Diggory Venn comes up, looking for the road to Mrs. Yeobright's. She herself stops by to check on the festivities. We follow her when she leaves, walks down off the hill, comes to Diggory's van, meets Thomasin, gets the story of the failed wedding, and goes to the inn to accost Wildeve. We are there when the rustics come down from Rainbarrow for the shivaree which they have been planning. Among other activities they all look up at the Vye fire; Wildeve does too, and he starts to move in that direction. The camera now takes us back to deserted Rainbarrow: Eustacia, whom Venn had seen there earlier, returns, and we have a long close-up on her. As the others had done, she looks down at the Wildeve inn, and then she walks cross-heath to the bright fire we have seen several times—her own fire, of course. A wait, and then Wildeve, whom we have seen start, arrives. We get a sense of their relationship and then follow the homeward walk of Eustacia's fire-builder, the boy Johnny Nunsuch; he runs into Diggory, whom we have already seen twice, tells him about the Eustacia-Wildeve meeting, and thus inadvertently provides the information which determines Diggory's actions from now on. The sequence of actions which I have sketched should reveal Hardy's extraordinary skill in designing an easy flux of perspectives and scenes in which, without our ever having a sense of hiatus or of arbitrary placement of us by the author, or even of his steering presence, we glide among the many elements, animate and inanimate, that we must know.

This long night of 5 November, brilliant as an introduction, has structural importance: it is balanced by the long night of the next year's 6 November. The symmetry does not mean a too mechanical balance, for the account of the second long night is briefer and more intense; on one, hope sets in, on the other it dies out. The ties are elemental too: on the first, the actions revolve about fires, symbols of cheer and well-being; on the second, the same scenes are swept by wind and rain,[28] indeed a flood that destroys not a race but the self-chosen seeking escape (with a boat to France as ark). The compactness of the two long nights is matched by the compression of the over-all story; taking place in just a year,[29] it is tighter than *The Mayor* and *Jude*, which are life-histories. The year has its own cycle of seasons: a November day of community pleasures and lovers' problems, a new love ready to be born at Christmas (with its twentieth-century secularity), spring courting, June wedding, dog-days crises, November disaster. These seasons enfold a cycle of experience from old love to new, from new love to disillusion, from dreams to despair, from birth (Thomasin's baby, ironically named Eustacia) to death.[30]

4

Narrative skills and structural felicity[31] are the external manifestations of the fictional essence in which lies the strength of *The Return* to hold us and gain assent. The essence is the human reality that Hardy gets hold of in his major characters. In part he uses an unostentatious contrast; it is voiced by Eustacia when Diggory tells her that if he cannot have Thomasin he will do his 'duty in helping her to get [Wildeve], as a man ought'. Eustacia is incredulous. 'What a strange sort of love, to be entirely free from that quality of selfishness which is frequently the chief constituent of the passion, and sometimes its only one!' She hardly understands this, 'and she almost thought it absurd' (II, 7). Hardy can imagine the love that serves as well as the love that grasps; it is a skilful hedge against sentimentality to see the former through the latter. Eustacia's 'absurd' has another value too: in thus calling Diggory irrational, she establishes a subtle link with the loves of Wildeve, Clym, and herself. For the two men and she are, above all, irrational, and driven. And so is Mrs. Yeobright in her own way. Hardy sees in them a compulsiveness that would take all but very lucky people into disaster. (We need not fall back upon the psychological cliché 'self-destructive'; destructiveness is secondary to, rather than inherent in, compulsive action.)

In Mrs. Yeobright Hardy gets hold of interesting ambiguities.[32] As an influence on Thomasin she reveals conventionality of values, some perceptiveness, and some power of accommodation. She encourages Thomasin to think Diggory lacking in the status her suitors should have (I, 9): she is right in seeing that Wildeve is not good marital material; and then, having given in, she is as insistent on Wildeve's following through as she was once set against him (I, 5, 11), even though she feels an intelligent skepticism about his motives (II, 8). *Vis-à-vis* Clym and Eustacia, she is shrewd in perception but weak in accommodation. If it is snobbery or a superficial notion of 'success' that makes her want Clym to stay on in Paris (III, 2), she is accurate in treating his educational evangelism as one of his 'new crotchets', as 'wasting your life here', as 'the folly of such self-sacrifice', as 'a castle in the air' (III, 3). We are convinced in advance of what Hardy calls her 'singular insight into life' and of the limitations which he ascribes to her (III, 3). He sees clearly her mixed emotions. While she was jealous for Thomasin, she is jealous of Clym and Eustacia —the possessive mother. So she errs in making Eustacia the cause of Clym's conversion, and she condemns Eustacia too harshly. She is sound in insisting that Eustacia is not the right girl for Clym, but the shrill derogatory style that comes out of her defensive motherhood and sense of defeat contributes ironically to the outcome that her insight leads her to oppose—Clym's marriage (III, 5, 6). All this Hardy perceives brilliantly. He skilfully uses Mrs. Yeobright's point of view on the wedding day, and compresses the ambiguities of her feeling into a single sad comment: 'O, it is a mistake! . . . And he will rue it some day, and think of me!' (III, 7).

The heart of the matter is the Clym-Eustacia relationship, and here is Hardy's great strength. Though the grander things that Hardy claims for them—the divine and the Promethean—are not there, they are not essential to fictional magnitude. The big and impressive truth is the nature of the attraction between them and the compulsive inability of each to grasp the evidence that could modify the attraction. Hardy's extraordinarily late introduction of the title character as a physical presence (in the seventeenth of 48 chapters) is not only a rare technical *tour de force* in the Victorian novel but a device which helps define the amatory relationship. For first we see fully the toying, the fencing, the sparring of Eustacia and Wildeve—an excellently imagined affinity in which there is mutual erotic responsiveness but not the felt irresistibility that induces total commitment. They make use of each other, perhaps less as sex objects[33] than as ego-maintaining objects. Whether because he feels the incompleteness of Eustacia's devotion or because two girls are more gratifying than one, Wildeve gets engaged to Thomasin; then the power-love of which Hardy is deeply aware makes Eustacia pull him back to her (I, 6), though she is a little embarrassed to discover 'the dog in the manger' in herself (I, 11). Acknowledging the irrationality, she can tell him, 'and yet I love you', and still always feel that in some way Wildeve is not good enough for her; hence it is natural for her to feel no more need of him once she has met Clym, the hero from Paris, and begins to nourish other hopes. Dismissed and fearing 'to lose two women', Wildeve must salvage his ego by marrying Thomasin (and hoping thus to make Eustacia feel slighted). All this is very well done.

When Clym shows up, then, Eustacia is already known to the reader as a handsome woman who wants 'to be loved to madness' (I, 7), who has a strong sense of her own status and value, and who has some instinct for and experience in the politics of emotion. Hardy carefully shows both parties drawn in by forms of peripheral charm—the exotic, the unexpected, the preconceived—rather than by a center of congeniality. There is a touch of the Benedick-Beatrice psychology when Eustacia overhears rustics praising Clym and talking about a match between her and Clym; she adores the Paris which she assumes defines Clym— 'like a man coming from heaven'; she begins to have 'visions', a 'day-dream' (II, 1), a 'Great Dream', as Hardy puts it in the caption of a chapter in which he calls her 'half in love with a vision' (II, 3); later she thinks of Clym as a deliverer (II, 5). She creates him out of her needs and desires rather than observes the actual creature before her. When she takes a part in the mummers' play, Clym is struck by 'a cultivated young woman playing such a part as this' (II, 6). Taken for a witch and pricked by Susan Nunsuch wielding a needle, Eustacia becomes the victim bound to attract Clym's attention and sympathy; and each expresses concern for the other's risk of injury at the bucket-raising—a 'Timeworn Drama' as Hardy almost jestingly puts it in the caption (III, 3). From here on Hardy wonderfully records the way in which each one listens to himself and not to the other. Eustacia is quite explicit in her disavowal of interest in schoolteaching, but Clym doesn't hear it or doesn't believe it. Likewise with her hatred of the heath that he loves. The intensity of her romantic fascination with Paris does not dawn on him. And he pays not the slightest attention when she says, testingly or coquettishly but still truthfully, 'I shall ruin you . . . Kiss me, and go away forever' (III, 4). So they get engaged, she thinking that she can get him out of teaching and back to Paris, and he sure that they'll be happy in love and in improving heath-life. Despite their moments of doubt, the egotism of passion, which Hardy entirely understands, carries them ahead into marriage. The hubris of each is to think that the loved one can be subsumed under, or co-opted into, the social passion of the lover.

Once the initial excitement is over, their minds and feelings are more than ever back on their single tracks. One might wish that Hardy, evidently with the epic year in mind, had not chosen to speed disaster by making Clym go nearly blind[34] (mildly prepared for by brief references to eye-strain), by inventing the plot of the misdirected guineas, and by employing the adder to make sure that Mrs. Yeobright does not survive, but they are his way of reducing the inevitable to plot-form. What is unexceptionable is the tracing of the life within as it issues in visible conduct— Eustacia's seeking a little excitement with Wildeve, her concealment of his presence on the day Mrs. Yeobright calls, Clym's breakdown after her death, the self-righteousness of his fury against Eustacia when he learns the whole story, the mutual recriminations, Eustacia's mixture of almost unconscious footwork and desperation. What is especially good is Hardy's perception of the egotism that runs through the grief and despair on both sides, of the interplay in both characters, of tragic sense of guilt[35] and a strange *amour propre* which clings to intensity of blame, of others or obdurate circumstance or even of oneself. 'But I don't want to get strong,' complains Clym at one point

(V, 1)—a key-point in a continuing self-flagellation that borders on the self-indulgent. On the other hand, when he can say, after Eustacia's death, 'She is the second woman I have killed this year' (V, 9), his words lack the theatrical and hysterical note: here is the borne self-knowledge of tragic experience.

Likewise, on learning of Mrs. Yeobright's death, Eustacia can be toughly clear-headed for a moment: 'I am to blame for this. There is evil in store for me' (IV, 8). But she cannot tell Clym the truth; he ferrets it out and rages, and her awareness turns self-defensively from what she has done to what has been done to her, and to bitterness. At one moment Hardy can look at her with his tragic sense; at another he turns to his sympathy with the sense of defeat in a woman who finds it easy to believe herself an undeserving victim. As tragic observer he remarks that 'instead of blaming herself for the issue she laid the fault upon the shoulders of some indistinct, colossal Prince of the World, who had framed her situation and ruled her lot' (IV, 8). There he virtually spots in her a habit of his own mind: the flight from tragic awareness to the laying of blame on outer forces. She oscillates as he does. How well he imagines the anguish of the self that feels at once immaculate and preyed upon by an uninvited fate. Eustacia can perceive the difference between fact and hope (if not the illusion that feeds the hope): Wildeve is 'not *great* enough for me to give myself to—he does not suffice for my desire!' (V, 7). She goes on in a rage of unearned defeat: 'How have I tried and tried to be a splendid woman, and how destiny has been against me! . . . O, how hard it is of Heaven to devise such tortures for me, who have done no harm to Heaven at all!' Hardy catches beautifully the ecstasy of self-love and self-pity, a force as dangerous to the psyche as a suicidal guilt neurosis. It is the last of the governing irrationalities that he portrays with a vitalising mastery (and by which he makes us all but forget the artifices of the mediating actions).

5

The Return is somewhat of a border point between the earlier and later Hardy. The rustics remind us of an earlier world, and Thomasin has ties with Fancy Day. On the other hand, insofar as serious troubles precede the final happy love, she anticipates

Elizabeth Henchard. In the central triangles Hardy now crosses over from the soluble situations of comedy to the difficulties that issue in disaster: the Clym-Eustacia-Wildeve triangle anticipates the Alex-Tess-Angel and the Arabella-Jude-Sue affairs. In *The Return* he introduces materials or situations that he will repeat or use more fully later. There is his French connection. Here, Clym is a Comtian, and Wildeve is 'the Rousseau of Egdon'— 'the man of sentiment', whose nature it is 'To be yearning for the difficult, to be weary of that offered; to care for the remote, to dislike the near . . .' (III, 6). Later Sue Bridehead will appear as a 'Voltairean', albeit of a shallow variety.

Certain narrative devices appear here and will be used later. Clym's letter urging Eustacia to return fails of delivery, as does Tess's explaining her past to Angel; both might have changed the course of action. The heavy rains on 6 November appear again in *The Mayor* to compound Henchard's difficulties, and in *Jude* to amplify the troubles of the return to Oxford. Hardy begins to use preaching as an index of personality: Clym slowly finds it a way of life, Alex d'Urberville would find it a temporary satisfaction, and Angel Clare would renounce it. Eustacia's dislike of Clym's reading is interestingly duplicated in Arabella's attitude to Jude's learning and books. Eustacia's and Clym's opposite attitudes to Parisian life would be deepened in the opposition between Sue's rationalism and Jude's faith, the latter opposition to be ironically reversed. A subtler anticipation: when Eustacia handles searching questions of Clym by saying, 'Dearest, you must not question me unpleasantly, or it may make me not love you,' and by using several similar ploys (IV, 2), Hardy is discovering a kind of female strategy that he would explore more fully in Sue Bridehead. Eustacia is a forerunner of Sue in that both are wilful and crave power without defining power as a conscious end. Eustacia, however, has read the travel books and comes up with a conventional desire for self-gratification in a glamorous city, whereas Sue wants to be the ruling divinity only in the life of one unglamorous man. In Clym, Hardy is getting into two aspects of human nature that later he would carry into further implications. After his mother's death Clym clings to a sense of guilt that borders on the pathological, but he does come around; after the death of her children, on the other hand, Sue falls into a sense of guilt that, as Hardy well sees, has such deep roots in her personality that it must intensify into an illness beyond therapy. When Clym finally learns the death-day facts that Eustacia has not told him, his verbal chastising of her contains a good deal of self-righteousness. Likewise Angel Clare when he learns facts about his wife's past: wounded ego, censoriousness, self-righteousness. But just as Sue's guilt is deeper than Clym's, so is Angel's punitiveness.

If such partial duplications tell us something about continuities and developments in Hardy's imagination, some comparisons outside the Hardy *oeuvre*[36] may help place the range and depth of his perceptiveness. *The Mayor* conquers time by looking backward; it is reminiscent of *Oedipus the King*, and to say that is to say that it transcends a local history in a specific time and place. *Jude* transcends its own times by looking ahead: it makes formulations of character perhaps more familiar now than in 1895. Jude prefigures what we now know as the 'narcissistic student', the type whose self-concern inhibits an adequate openness to realities that need to be understood. But still more significant is Sue, in whom Hardy has caught, more than half a century before it surfaces in often disturbing social phenomena that are widely visible, an excessive dependence on rational structurings of life and hence a violent rebound into sub-rational or apparently supra-rational experiences that represent a neglected human need.

Like the later novels, *The Return* looks beyond its own time. Mrs. Yeobright is the possessive mother who is a fixture on the twentieth-century stage, though she is a larger character than many of her successors because of her intelligent grasp of the world in which she lives. Eustacia looks backward in time and forward in time. As a sister of Emma Bovary she so yearns for an overpowering romance that any available life is not going to satisfy, though she is complicated by a precocious sense of the transitoriness of things that makes her doubt the relationship with Clym before its insufficiency has become evident. In the next century Eustacia's longing to be whirled away by some more than life-size force might lead to the beds of presidents or prime ministers, to drugs, or to political adventurism of a millennial coloring. Yet in all these courses there is an infusion of the vulgarity that Eustacia, whose taste is insecure, would avoid if she could, witness her final judgment of Wildeve (whose ironic fate it is to achieve, despite himself, a certain largeness, as of a Diggory rendered reckless: the self-gratification of plucking forbidden fruit turned into the self-abnegation of risking death in the weir). If Eustacia had talent one might think of her as the poet desperately weighed down by a sense of injuriousness and duplicity in the *natura rerum*.

Though Clym is never the thinker that Hardy asserts him to be, he is a very successful character: in him Hardy catches the archetypal lineaments of what we now call the do-good-er,[37] and he anticipates the ironic treatment of the type that would be the life of Dorothy Sayers' *The Devil to Pay* (1939) and Duerrenmatt's *An Angel Comes to Babylon* (1953). Clym is sure that 'with my system of education, which is as new as it is true, I shall do a great deal of good to my fellow-creatures' (III, 5). By a do-good-er we mean a theorist in benevolence who pays very little attention to human actuality and who hence may be a fantast, a busybody, or an enforcer (the man of good will whose will is to impose his good on man). It is not that good does not get done in the world, but that the professional benefactor is not the most effective agent of good. There is a nice structural interplay between Clym and Diggory Venn, who does good as it may be done: he consults the will of a specific person who has a specific desire and does his best to see that it is satisfied (in striving to bring and keep Thomasin and Wildeve together, Diggory is not striving to impose on others some theoretical good of his own). But Clym has an abstract idea of what is good for local humanity generally—'instilling high knowledge into empty minds without first cramming them with what has to be uncrammed again before true study begins' (III, 5). It sounds noble, but it is hard to tell what it means. If as observer of education Hardy approves of Clym's idea, as artist he is unable to come up with a single concrete formulation that would give life and meaning to the theoretical program. Clym does seem to think that Susan Nunsuch's anti-witch operation—sticking Eustacia with a needle—proves the need of a new education, but Hardy gives no sign of sharing the belief. In fact, Hardy rather enjoys setting it off against furze-cutter Humphrey's view that some such 'rum job or other is sure to be doing' whenever anyone from Egdon goes to church (III, 2).

Hardy portrays, not a period freak, but the *a priori*, dogmatic improver who belongs to every age. This type pays no attention to conditions and possibilities. These are implicitly recorded by local observers when Clym announces his desire for a 'rational occupation among the people I [know] best': Timothy Fairway is sure that 'In a few weeks he'll learn to see things otherwise,' and 'another' that 'he had better mind his business' (III, 1). The type pays no attention to historical appropriateness; Hardy himself notes that the 'rural world was not ripe for him' and that his 'mind' was not 'well-proportioned'. This type pays no attention to lack of appropriate experience; Clym does not listen when his mother says, 'The place is overrun with schoolmasters. You have no special qualifications' (III, 5) and when she prophesies accurately, 'Your fancies will be your ruin' (III, 2). In a particularly shrewd perception Hardy sees that the type absolutises personal philosophic ideas and regards them as a sound center for reform: 'teach them [i.e. 'half the world'] how to breast the misery that they are born to'. The type is ascetic, immune to the pleasures made available by maturing culture: 'I cannot enjoy delicacies; good things are wasted upon me.' The type instinctively subsumes persons and relationships to the mission; Hardy does very well to have Clym ask the turf-cutter whether Eustacia 'would like to teach children' (III, 2) and pay no attention to the answer. He hardly takes it in when she wants to talk about Paris; he categorically refuses a return because 'It would interfere with my scheme' and feels he can command her, 'Don't press that, Eustacia'; he doesn't really listen when she accepts his proposal on the ground that 'You will never adhere to your education plan' (III, 4); and when, after their marriage, she makes an effort to get Paris into their plans, he is shocked and responds by working harder than ever at his books (IV, 2). Eustacia learns the approximate truth of what Mrs. Yeobright has told her, that Clym 'can be as hard as steel' (IV, 1). Clym may look less like the rigid ideologue when, nearly blind, he takes to the rough life of the furze-cutter and thus seems to make peace with actuality instead of seeking a way to compel it. But in finding his way out of difficulty, he pays no attention to his wife; he arbitrarily rejects the financial help that could come from Captain Vye, and in his relative contentment he is insensitive to Eustacia's grave discontent (IV, 2); he is almost resentful that she can 'cling to gaiety so eagerly as to walk all the way to a village festival in search of it', although he does finally tell her to go (IV, 3); the egoist inside the benevolent idealist bursts out fully when Clym, sure of grave misdeeds by Eustacia, attacks her with the crude fervor of a prosecuting attorney[38] (V, 3).

To show that Clym, despite basic decency and good intentions, is not a very good matrimonial risk (a social scientist informs me that the domestic-success rate for cause-addicts is low; the excitement of battling conspicuous evil reduces the capacity for doing humble good, *vide* Dickens' Mrs. Jellyby, the archetype) is to round out the portrait of the strong-willed do-good-er that transcends historical boundaries. In the final stroke in that portrait Clym appears as itinerant preacher—exactly the right outcome for the character as created. It would be less so if Clym had a strong sense of actuality (human habits and needs) and a talent for collaboration and what we now call organisation. But his bent is toward the prophetic voice, the unclear saving vision, and solitary summons to better things that have become present to him after he has read a book and looked outward through the interstices of daily routines. A gentle egotist with a flair for moral theatre, he needs only a little ladder and a Hyde Park, and Clym finds his on Rainbarrow and elsewhere in Wessex.[39]

6

Thomasin escapes from her aunt's sense of marriage as a preservation or improvement of status and settles down into the sensible problem-solver, even playful and humorous as she finds and sticks to the right road, a fixture in English fiction. Diggory looks backward in the history of the novel and, with a quite fascinating unexpectedness, forward too. On the one hand he is the faithful lover who derives from Thackeray's Dobbin.[40] On the other hand he is the ancestor of a character who appears with vast frequency in popular fiction of the twentieth century—the 'private eye', the fixer, the amateur detective who manages to find things out and to be at the right place at the right time, the 'good guy' who is at least of peripheral help to the deserving, the jesting troubler of misbehavers. There is no artistic softening-up in the story of his and Thomasin's marrying. Hardy is simply wrong in thinking that the original ending in which Venn disappeared and Thomasin remained a widow represents an 'austere artistic code' and a 'more consistent conclusion' and the 'true one'.[41] One side of Hardy likes to hector happiness and point bitter fingers at the gods who do not work harder for human felicity. But another side of Hardy sees that humanity does include people who have their feet on the ground, who do effect an accommodation with reality, who do manage to like suitable members of the opposite sex and find adequate lives with them. Thomasin and Diggory earn each other; it is not a case of Hardy's interfering and giving each one to the other to gratify a public not up to his darker view of things. The final evidence of the truth of this relationship is the naturalness, spontaneity, and vivacity of the chapters in Book VI.[42] They work; they are not forced, casual, or flatly dutiful. Hardy's art contradicts his official opinion of the cosmos, but it does not betray his insight. His imagination embraced a fuller reality than he supposed.

One could hardly pay a better centennial tribute than that.

NOTES

1 Cf. Robert Gittings, *Young Thomas Hardy* (London, 1975), p. 214. Irving Howe, *Thomas Hardy* (London and New York, 1967), p. 58, is in a minority of critics who do not place *The Return* in the top rank of Hardy's novels.

2 Various anthropological issues are canvassed by Eliott B. Gose, Jr., in *Imagination Indulged: The Irrational in the Nineteenth Century Novel* (Montreal and London, 1972), pp. 99–125, and by Louis Crompton, 'The Sunburnt God: Ritual and Tragic Myth in *The Return of the Native*', *Boston University Studies in English*, 4 (1960), 229–40. John Paterson indicates his conviction in his title, '*The Return of the Native* as Antichristian Document', *Nineteenth Century Fiction*, 14 (1959), 111–27. While Paterson piles up all the evidence that tends to convert the novel into a polemic, he is at his soundest in a brief self-protective observation that runs counter to the general direction of his thought: both sides are subject to 'irreverent ironies' (126), and in the end *The Return* is 'as much a dramatic exploration and exposition of the pagan-Christian polarity as an unqualified denunciation of the Christian outlook' (127). Eleanor McCann, in 'Blind Will or Blind Hero: Philosophy and Myth in Hardy's *Return of the Native*', *Criticism*, 3 (1961), 140–57, applies Schopenhauer and Freud in an explication of Clym's thought and psyche. Approving of this reliance on Schopenhauer, Lennart A. Björk, in 'Visible Essences as Thematic Structure in Hardy's *Return of the Native*', *English Studies*, 52 (1972),

52–63, treats the novel as a fictionalised 'ideological' conflict between
Eustacia's 'Hellenism' and Clym's Christianity. Many critics discuss
what Hardy thought.

3   The only other full discussion of the style of The Return that I know
of is in John Paterson's The Making of 'The Return of the Native',
University of California Publications: Studies in English, 19 (Berkeley
and Los Angeles, 1960), pp. 135–46. Paterson is concerned mainly
with Hardy's stylistic revisions in the various steps from MS. to final
authorised edition. He finds that Hardy regularly tried to 'naturalise
his idiom' and reduce the 'predominantly Latinistic character of his
vocabulary' (136). However, it 'remained fundamentally Latinate'
(137), a quality that contributed to the desired 'effect of Sophoclean
grandeur' (138). In revising, Hardy tends to move from statement to
a connotative and imagistic language, which collaborates with other
elements and with the 'larger context of the novel' in amplifying meaning (140). Henceforth I refer to this work as The Making. In 'The
"Poetics" of The Return of the Native', Modern Fiction Studies, 6
(1960), 214–22, Paterson traces patterns of image and allusion—e.g.
those of divinity (Eustacia), of 'exotic antiquity', of Promethean fire
(a central theme), of 'antique nobility and grandeur' in the heath—
which he contends do more to structure the novel than does the
architectonic influence of Hardy's well-known efforts to assimilate The
Return to classical drama. There are a few good observations on style
in Evelyn Hardy's Thomas Hardy: The Life and Work (London, 1954),
pp. 166ff., and in F. M. Halliday, Thomas Hardy: His Life and Work
(Bath, 1972), pp. 83–4. Irving Howe finds Hardy's style marked by
'pretentiousness' as well as 'sublimity' (Thomas Hardy, p. 59) and the
description of the heath 'overpraised' (p. 61).

4   Since The Return is available in various English and American editions,
it seems most useful to locate quoted passages by book and chapter
rather than by page. The text that I have used is that in Signet
Classics (New York, 1959).

5   This has probably never been put more emphatically and uncon-
ditionally than by Morton Dauwen Zabel in 'Hardy in Defense of his
Art: the Aesthetics of Incongruity', The Hardy Centennial Issue of
The Southern Review, 6 (Summer, 1940): 'Even the famous overture
of The Return of the Native shows so exaggerated an air of por-
tentous solemnity and so much overwriting, dragging erudition, repe-
tition of motives, and rhythmic orotundity that it takes all the
subsequent weight of the novel, all its passion, rustic naïveté, and
counterbalancing melodrama, to overcome the ponderous effect of the
first chapter' (pp. 142–43).

6   Nearly all critics discuss the symbolism of the heath, which is interpreted in different ways, and often rather solemnly. In Thomas
Hardy: The Forms of Tragedy (Detroit, 1975), Dale Kramer explores
the complexity of meanings of the heath (pp. 54ff.).

7   Hardy has a higher opinion of some First Causes than of others. The
fifth of November bonfires are admirable: creating a 'radiant upper

81

story of the world,' they are related to 'Festival fires to Thor and Woden'. At the same time the fires are a renewal of 'Promethean rebelliousness'; here we are on the side of revolt. Then Hardy recalls 'Let there be light', a fiat which now comes, however, not from a divine creator but from 'the fettered gods of the earth' (I, 3). Then the 'black phenomenon' below the level of the fires is equated with Dante's Limbo, so that a medieval Christian ordering of the universe comes into play (later the lower parts are called 'Tartarean'—I, 4). Hardy's allusiveness is imperfectly syncretistic.

The numerous Biblical analogies are more pictorial than helpfully communicative. To say that Wildeve 'started like Satan' (II, 7) is to imply a moral dimension quite lacking in this troubled and finally reckless romantic. Clym Yeobright seems to Hardy a John the Baptist (III, 2) and to himself and Eustacia an Apostle Paul (III, 2; IV, 6)— two roles rather beyond his range. When the angry adder reminds Christian Cantle of the snake in Eden (IV, 7), we are probably meant to laugh once again at Christian, but we are not sure that Hardy himself does not fancy the unlikely analogy; after all, he has said that on 'fine days' on Egdon 'any man could imagine himself to be Adam' (II, 1). In the treatment of Venn, there is no problem when his redness suggests 'the devil' to the rustics (I, 3), but Hardy himself cannot resist calling reddlemen 'Mephistophelian visitants', comparing their redness to 'the mark of Cain' (I, 9), and even using 'sinister redness' to describe Venn (II, 7). In 'Hardy's Mephistophelian Visitants', *PMLA*, 61 (1946), 1146–84, J. O. Bailey works rather hard in pushing the 'Satanic symbolism' (1154). But, as F. B. Pinion observes in *A Hardy Companion: A Guide to the Works of Thomas Hardy and Their Background* (London and New York, 1968), pp. 156–57, Venn is not Mephistophelian at all; all that can be said is that reddlemen were 'at one time terrifying "bogey's" to young children'.

8 Related to this desire to indict some spiritual Primum Mobile of defective quality is Hardy's occasional tendency to pump up a difficult physical situation into a destructive monster. The rainstorm on the night of 6 November, Hardy says, made one think of 'all that is terrible and dark in history and legend—the last plague of Egypt, the destruction of Sennacherib's host, the agony in Gethsemane' (V, 7). Yet only two people perish.

9 That Hardy's characters who go down are not victims of Fate but 'largely victims of themselves, that is, of behavior that springs from their temperaments' is well argued by J. O. Bailey in 'Temperament as Motive in *The Return of the Native*', *English Fiction in Transition*, 5, No. 2 (1962), 21–9. The quoted passage is on p. 21. Cf. Bruce Mc-Cullough: 'Happily in his best productions, his sensibility acted as a leavening influence upon his ideas . . .' (*Representative English Novelists: Defoe to Conrad* [New York and London, 1946], p. 242). Equally relevant is Paterson's observation that despite all the critical focusing on Hardy's 'philosophy' his 'mind was not basically a conceptualising one. It followed the lead of a powerful, groping imagin-

ation, only half conscious of its profoundest tendencies and ends' (*The Making*, p. 131). A defense of character as the cause of events, and an attack on the idea that difficulties are caused by a 'cruel Fate', 'blind or malign Fate', or 'indifferent or incompetent God' are made by Charles Child Walcutt in 'Character and Coincidence in *The Return of the Native*', in *Twelve Original Essays on Great English Novels*, ed. Charles Shapiro (Detroit, 1960), pp. 153–73, especially pp. 160–2. Roy Morrell's *Thomas Hardy: The Will and the Way* (Kuala Lumpur, 1965) vigorously attacks the view that in Hardy man is a victim of anything but his own weakness and lack of will. Morrell's later 'Thomas Hardy and Probability', in *On the Novel: A Present for Walter Allen on His Sixtieth Birthday, etc.,* ed. B. S. Benedikz (London, 1971), pp. 75–91, argues that in *The Return* people drift into disaster because they postpone action rather than try to deal with misunderstandings, etc.; thus they illustrate the Second Law of Thermodynamics. Albert Guerard remarks wittily that in most of his books 'Hardy's dramatic energy generally dominated his ideas about his characters, though it failed to dominate his ideas about his ideas' (*Thomas Hardy*, Norfolk, Conn., 1964, p. 68).

10 Irving Howe calls the rustics 'charming puppets' and thinks them over-used (*Thomas Hardy*, p. 61).

11 J. I. M. Stewart is one of the few critics to point out how 'nebulous' is Hardy's presentation of Clym's background, plans, and intellectual life (*Thomas Hardy: A Critical Biography* [New York, 1971], pp. 99ff.).

12 Several critics regard Clym as a potential Hamlet. But in arguing rightly that Hardy fails to endow Clym with the heroic-classical-tragical qualities of a Prometheus or Oedipus, Paterson also identifies Clym's shortcomings for the role of Hamlet (*The Making*, pp. 60ff.). David De Laura attributes Hardy's ideas about Clym's face to Pater. See ' "The Ache of Modernism" in Hardy's Later Novels', *ELH*, 34 (1967), 380–81.

13 Various critics (De Laura, p. 383; Kramer, p. 52) say that the reference may be to Comte, Fourier, or St. Simon. Of these, only Comte is mentioned in Florence Emily Hardy's *The Life of Thomas Hardy 1840–1928* (rpt., New York, 1962), pp. 98, 146, 179.

14 Ian Gregor notes that this passage, once a touchstone for good writing, is now likely to be taken as an unfortunate example of 'fine writing' (*The Great Web: The Form of Hardy's Major Fiction* [Totowa, N.J., 1974], pp. 85–86). Gregor is at some pains to deny the latter charge (pp. 86–90). He relates the style to the duality of Eustacia, and he approves the approach of David Eggenschwiler in 'Eustacia Vye, Queen of the Night and Courtly Pretender', *Nineteenth Century Fiction*, 25 (1971), 444–54. Eggenschwiler believes that Hardy is ambivalent about the 'Queen of the Night' portrait, seeing Eustacia as grand and Promethean, on the one hand, and, on the other, as 'slightly ridiculous' (448) and as 'comically pretentious' (450); hence Eggenschwiler can refer to 'this satire' and can assume that Eustacia is 'variously a heroine and the parody of a heroine . . . ridiculed by

mock-heroic techniques' (451–52). This does not seem quite Hardy's dish of tea. Somewhat more to Gregor's purposes would be Robert Schweik's earlier 'Theme, Character, and Perspective in Hardy's *The Return of the Native*', *Philological Quarterly*, 41 (1962), 757–67, which discusses the duality of Eustacia as 'goddess' and 'schoolgirl' and argues for a similar doubleness in both Clym and Mrs. Yeobright, as Gregor also does (pp. 86, 108).

15 David Jarrett's 'Eustacia Vye and Eula Varner, Olympians: The Worlds of Thomas Hardy and William Faulkner', *Novel*, 6 (1973), 163–74, assumes that both writers have succeeded in endowing their characters with 'heroic grandeur' (165). Jarrett mentions an article by Robert Evans—'The Other Eustacia', *Novel*, 1 (1968), 251–59—but pays no attention to its contents: an inclusive catalogue of the moral deficiencies which render Eustacia completely untragic. Hardy's efforts to picture a tragic Eustacia, Evans declares, are 'little more than a sustained blast of rhetoric' (257). Pinion says more mildly that the 'Queen of Night' portrait is 'overdone' (*A Hardy Companion*, p. 33). Cf. Douglas Brown, *Thomas Hardy* (London, 1961), p. 63, and David De Laura, ' "The Ache of Modernism" in Hardy's Later Novels', p. 382. In 'Heroism and Pathos in Hardy's *Return of the Native*', *Nineteenth Century Fiction*, 15 (1960), 207–20, Leonard W. Deen argues that the images and allusions in the description of Eustacia are too numerous; hence they 'so complicate our impressions of her that it is almost impossible to form a consistent image of her'; she does not 'demonstrate or justify the dazzling array of qualities Hardy ascribes to her' (208). Paterson, however, believes that Eustacia does become a 'splendid creature' and a 'tragic protagonist' (*The Making*, pp. 17, 133). See also his 'The "Poetics" of *The Return of the Native*', pp. 216ff. J. I. M. Stewart speaks of the 'absurdity' of the 'notorious' Queen of the Night description and remarks that Eustacia does not gain from its 'inflationary pressure' (*Thomas Hardy*, pp. 101, 103). Cf. Michael Millgate, *Thomas Hardy: His Career as Novelist* (New York, 1971), pp. 131ff.

16 The resemblance was first noticed in a review in *Athenaeum*, 23 November 1878, reprinted in *Thomas Hardy: The Critical Heritage*, ed. R. G. Cox (New York, 1970), pp. 46–7. The reviewer regrets Hardy's spending time on an 'imperfect' portrait of 'a type which English opinion will not allow a novelist to depict in its completeness' (p. 47). The first twentieth-century critic to mention the Bovary likeness was Pierre d'Exideuil, who also equates Eustacia with 'other unhappy women' such as Jocasta, Hecuba, and Polyxena (*The Human Pair in the Works of Thomas Hardy*, tr. Felix W. Crosse [London, 1930], pp. 21–2). The next critic to remark on the 'affinities' of Eustacia with Emma was Walter Allen in *The English Novel: A Short Critical History* (London, 1954), p. 236. Allen contrasts the two treatments of the type. F. B. Pinion hazards the suggestion that Flaubert's character 'may have had its influence on the creation of Eustacia Vye; if not directly, then through the medium of Miss Braddon's *The*

Doctor's Wife' (*A Hardy Companion*, pp. 31–2). The possible influence of Braddon on Hardy is discussed by C. Heywood, 'The Return of the Native and Miss Braddon's *The Doctor's Wife*: A Probable Source', *Nineteenth Century Fiction*, 18 (June, 1963), 91–4. Slightly earlier Louis Crompton made the interesting proposal that Clym and Eustacia are related to 'the great fictional studies of the pathology of the romantic imagination . . . *Don Quixote* and *Madam Bovary*' ('The Sunburnt God', p. 234). Clym, we need hardly say, is not quite a Quixote. Robert Evans argues that Hardy is not nearly so perceptive about Eustacia as Flaubert is about Emma ('The Other Eustacia', pp. 257–259). He also compares Eustacia with Hedda Gabler (p. 257). Eustacia is likened to Caroline Lamb by Desmond Hawkins in *Hardy: Novelist and Poet* (London and New York, 1976), p. 76.

17 There are various others. Eustacia's imagination must be focused on Clym before he arrives, so, *inside* the Vye house, she manages to hear a couple of *outside* furze-workers—their voices come down the chimney, for the furze-stack is 'not far' away—talk at length about what a fine pair she and Clym would make (II, 1). When the Christmas mummers are *outside* the Yeobright house, unable to enter until the dance within is over, one of the mummers thinks that their time has about come because of something he overhears one dancer say to another *inside* the house! (II, 5). In reconnoitering the 'turf shed' where Mrs. Yeobright is dying, Wildeve does not come close enough to be observed; still from somewhere *outside* picks up the story of the snakebite, and so on, as it is implied in the conversation going on *inside*. During the violent storm on the night of 6 November, Diggory Venn, sleeping in his van with the door closed, is awakened by 'the brushing of a woman's clothes over the heath-bushes just outside' (V, 8)—amazing auditory acuteness.

18 The best record of the major ironic reversals in *The Return* is in Robert W. Stallman's 'Hardy's Hour-Glass Novel', *Sewanee Review*, 55 (1947), 283–96, especially 288–91. Stallman believes, however, that all the ironies are equally good; that chance is the narrative mode of 'an inexorable determinism'; and that 'Coincidences . . . have become integral to the mechanics' (286). Walter Allen is more accurate, for he accepts the principle but sees that it is used in ways that have to make us rebel: 'It is silly to blame Hardy for the emphasis he places on coincidence; simply, he believed in coincidence . . . But Hardy, as though not wholly convinced himself, does not know where to stop. He spoils his case by overstatement: . . . we begin to protest. *We begin to feel that the author has aligned himself with the nature of things against his characters, that he is manipulating fate against them*' (*The English Novel*, pp. 239–40). I add italics to call attention to an admirable statement.

19 It is an amusing coincidence that Hardy, when describing the success of Diggory's rather melodramatic actions to deter Wildeve from his evening rambles, falls into a cliché of melodrama, 'nipped in the bud' (IV, 4).

20 Mentioned briefly by Crompton, 'The Sunburnt God', p. 237.
21 There is an occasional interesting interplay between folk-action and major action: e.g., Christian Cantle, as the man no woman will marry, is a sort of comic version of Wildeve and Clym, whom we might say no woman should marry. There is, of course, a much more overt relationship between Susan Nunsuch and Eustacia: the literal witch-craft used against the supposed witch whose emotional witchcraft is well dramatised. In Hardy's original conception, Eustacia was to be a demonic character (Paterson, *The Making*, pp. 17ff.).
22 This scene, which I find labored, is vastly admired. One representa-tive example: Douglas Brown calls it 'one of the most personal and memorable in all Hardy' (*Thomas Hardy*, p. 111).
23 Otis Wheeler not only notices this difficulty but believes that Hardy was aware of it and in the course of revisions tried to minimise it. See 'Four Versions of *The Return of the Native*', *Nineteenth Century Fiction*, 14 (1959), 30, 34.
24 Pinion notes the implausibility of this as well as of Clym's dream (*A Hardy Companion*, p. 33).
25 Leonard Deen notes Hardy's tendency to pile up an excess of external difficulties, as if to make sure that the characters will not escape. 'This supererogation of tragic effects blurs the psychological and dramatic structure . . . an effort to indict the universe' ('Heroism and Pathos', p. 216). It is a pity that Deen here loosely uses the word *tragic*, for he goes on to note, rightly, that the effect is one of pathos, in which characters are victimised rather than responsible. His main argument is that in the later novels Hardy 'slips more and more into the diminishing ironic and pathetic mode' (p. 207).
26 Cf. Brown, *Thomas Hardy*, pp. 56–7.
27 George Eliot used the technique very skilfully just a half a dozen years earlier in *Middlemarch* (1871–72). I do not know of earlier instances.
28 Cf. Gose, *Imagination Indulged*, pp. 119ff.
29 Several critics deal with the chronological aspects of the overall structure.
30 The cycle has some interesting echoes in Book VI. 'No more Novem-bers' might be the principle of this section. The key occasion for Thomasin and Diggory is May Day, also a day of ritual festivities, and they are married in August—a blotting out, as it were, of that long August two years before in which everything went downhill for all the Yeobrights. Even in what we may call the outlying parts of the story Hardy uses regularities of dating. On the first fifth of Novem-ber we learn that Diggory had received a letter of refusal from Thomasin just two years before (I, 9) and that just one year ago Eustacia summoned Wildeve by a fifth of November fire (I, 6). It is just a year, too, since Mrs. Yeobright rejected Wildeve as a husband for Thomasin (I, 4). For four years running, then, November is a time of significant events. (In *Tess* Hardy would use the months of May [hopeful starts] and October [subsequent troubles] similarly, several

times with two-year intervals.) Hardy gives us one dating clue which, if we can assume that he was using an actual day of week and month, makes it possible to work out a complete calendar of events. In IV, 5, he identifies 31 August as a Thursday: this would put the main action in either 1843 or 1848, since in the Preface dated July, 1895, Hardy says that the date of the actions 'may be set down as between 1840 and 1850'.

31 J. I. M. Stewart emphasises 'the skill of the story-teller' and says that 'the organisation of the novel as a dramatic spectacle is very notable indeed. This holds both of its larger dimensions and of the detailed fabrication of its crucial episodes' (*Thomas Hardy*, p. 106). Criticism gets into weighty exegesis more often than into accounts of fictional art.

32 The duality of Mrs. Yeobright—the strength and the limits of her understanding—is well analysed by Robert Schweik in 'Theme, Character, and Perspective', pp. 762–65. Walcutt believes she has an 'ungovernable temper and animus' and is 'self-destructive' ('Character and Coincidence', p. 168).

33 Virtually all critics assume that Eustacia was Wildeve's mistress, and they note certain key passages. Eustacia blames Wildeve for acting 'as if I had never been yours life and soul so irretrievably', and she insists, 'you may tempt me, but I won't give myself to you any more' (I, 6). After her marriage she tells him, 'We have been hot lovers in our time, but it won't do now' (IV, 6). That the sexual terminology for the relationship became more explicit in the 1895 edition and then was toned down in the 1912 edition is noted by both Wheeler ('Four Versions', pp. 36, 39) and Paterson (*The Making*, pp. 113, 163–64). The terms that are left (principally the ones quoted above) seem plain enough to a modern reader. But since they occur in a story in which the references to Thomasin's pregnancy are so vastly delicate that a reader might not guess what they mean, one may perhaps risk wondering whether the Eustacia-Wildeve expressions do not seem more outspoken than they are and imply only activities short of intercourse. After all, 'Wildeve was never asked into the house by his proud though condescending mistress' (I, 11). It is difficult to imagine Eustacia's visiting Wildeve at his inn. That leaves only the out-of-doors, the 'heathy, furzy, briery wilderness' (I, 1), where there are bushes but no trees, where there are brambles that are regularly mentioned, where the 'heath-croppers' (wild ponies) seem always likely to gallop up disturbingly, where poisonous adders apparently abound, and where the weather seems to alternate between blazing heat and furious storms. Granted, Wildeve says, 'Eustacia, how we roved among these bushes last year, . . . and the shade of the hills kept us almost invisible in the hollows' (I, 9). This may be a tip that concealment is possible out there; still he only says 'almost'. But quite aside from the discomforts and dangers, Eustacia, though Hardy says she 'had advanced to the secret recesses of sensuousness' (I, 10), still seems a little too fastidious to join the 'girls' who 'Under the hedge . . .

had given themselves to lovers,' as Hardy puts it in *Jude the Obscure* (I, 2). Besides, just when he is talking about their hikes among the bushes, Wildeve accuses Eustacia of having 'served me cruelly enough' (I, 9). Would 'cruelly' be used of a woman who had been cooperative sexually but also had been—what, condescending? Wildeve seems hardly sensitive enough to take as 'cruelty' some incomplete emotional acceptance of him by a girl who was erotically unreserved. Besides, if her virginity was long gone, might we not expect Clym to make an inquiry or two? Constantly Eustacia strikes us as less hungry for sex than for power; we might expect of her the Sue Bridehead style of implicit invitation and explicit rejection. But these are speculations rather than argument. Other side of the fence: C. C. Walcutt takes Eustacia to be a 'sophisticated, promiscuous sensualist who is willing to take almost any risk to attain new intensities of passion' ('Character and Coincidence', p. 158).

34 This leads Hardy to liken Clym to Oedipus (V, 2). Even Paterson, who in general believes that the mythic and other classical allusions do create magnitude, regards this as a mistake ('The "Poetics" of *The Return of the Native*', p. 221). Likewise Crompton, 'The Sunburnt God', p. 238, and Deen, 'Heroism and Pathos', p. 214. Perhaps even without the Oedipus reference someone would have used the narrative materials to turn the Clym story into a textbook case of oedipality, as Eleanor McCann does in 'Blind Will or Blind Hero', pp. 140–57; she thinks that Clym's problems reflect some problem of Hardy's own. Clym is a 'sick man' (p. 157). Walcutt preceded McCann in moving in this direction. He says that Clym's insistent reading 'is the act of a man who is subconsciously bent on self-destruction' and calls Clym's withdrawal of his objection to Eustacia's going to a party 'a model of sick martyrdom and self-pity' ('Character and Coincidence', pp. 165, 170). On the other side of the fence: Richard Benvenuto regards Clym, up through Book V, as a true hero, 'a fiercely independent and conscientious man,' who 'loved to excess people who were not worthy of his love' and of 'the sacrifices he made for them'; hence his 'essential nobility'. See '*The Return of the Native* as a Tragedy in Six Books', *Nineteenth Century Fiction*, 26 (1971), 92. And Hardy: 'I got to like the character of Clym before I had done with him. I think he is quite the nicest of my heroes, . . .' (Florence Emily Hardy, *The Life of Thomas Hardy*, pp. 357–58).

35 Most critics accept *The Return* as tragic and as a major tragic work. Few define *tragic*, which often seems to have only its popular meaning of death, unhappiness, etc. It is a relief when Robert Evans says that Eustacia fails entirely of the self-knowledge essential to tragic experience ('The Other Eustacia', p. 259). Actually she does approach the knowledge at times, as Clym does, but they both tend either to flee it or to revel masochistically in its harsher contents. Various critics believe Hardy too much involved with both Clym and Eustacia to reach greatness through them. This is, I think, a part truth; Hardy oscillates between involvement and judgment. One critic who does

have a firm conception of the tragic is Dale Kramer, who regards *The Return* as Hardy's 'least successful effort at high tragedy' in that Eustacia's 'perspective is so myopic' and Clym's 'allegiances are so varied' (*Thomas Hardy*, pp. 58–64). Ian Gregor sees Hardy as achieving, at least in certain episodes, the 'status of genuine tragedy' (*The Great Web*, p. 94).

36 Resemblances between episodes in Hardy and other novelists may be matters of chance—e.g. the double drowning in *The Return* and in George Eliot's *Mill on the Floss* (1860). Still, it is a rather interesting coincidence when Clym and Dickens' Pip (*Great Expectations*, 1860), have identical ironic experiences: all passion spent, Pip decides to propose to Biddy, only to find her heart committed to Joe; Clym decides to propose to Thomasin, only to find her heart committed to Diggory—two somewhat complacent heroes in the same anticlimax. Eustacia's infatuation with Paris anticipates the longing for Moscow that appears repeatedly in Chekhov's women, especially in *The Three Sisters*.

37 Desmond Hawkins makes an analogous identification of Clym: 'what we should now recognise as a drop-out, a recruit to the "alternative" society' (*Hardy: Novelist and Poet*, p. 71).

38 Cf. Millgate, *Thomas Hardy*, pp. 138–40.

39 Most critics who comment on the sermon-on-the-mount scene regard Hardy's attitude to Clym as ambiguous or ironic. See De Laura, ' "The Ache of Modernism" in Hardy's Later Novels', p. 384; Kramer, *Thomas Hardy*, p. 54. Richard Benvenuto thinks Clym by now a wretchedly shrunken figure, a 'harrowing picture of high aspirations corrupting themselves' ('*The Return of the Native* as a Tragedy in Six Books', pp. 92–4). On the other hand, Merryn Williams, *A Preface to Hardy* (London and New York, 1976), p. 101, is sure that 'in this last paragraph' Hardy shows 'affectionate feelings toward his hero'.

40 Jarrett surprisingly sees, in Venn's efforts to assist the marriage of Wildeve and Thomasin, 'a weak perversity like that of Thackeray's Dobbin' ('Eustacia Vye and Eula Varner', p. 171).

41 Hardy's note at the end of VI, 3. One justification for the Thomasin-Diggory story at the end is the amount of space accorded to them earlier in the novel; they are not aesthetic second-class citizens in this community. Interestingly, most critics of the novel either ignore Book VI or assent routinely to Hardy's adverse judgment of it. Benvenuto, however, is much more emphatic than Hardy in condemning it. In his view, Hardy's 'original conception' was of 'a systemless, morally chaotic world', whereas in Book VI he apostasises and 'delivers an ordered world of regulated expectancies' ('*The Return of the Native* as a Tragedy in Six Books', p. 90). Benvenuto would deny to Hardy the duality of vision which saves him from the simplistic dogma to which, in his lower moods, he is somewhat prone. The fullest and most careful discussion of Book VI is that of Ian Gregor in *The Great Web*, pp. 104–6; he does not easily dismiss it. He points out, as does J. I. M. Stewart (*Thomas Hardy*, p. 93), that Hardy, in the course of

revisions extending over many years, never saw fit to remove Book VI or rewrite it or present it as one of two alternatives. Millgate says outright that the present ending has a ' "rightness" of its own which only Hardy's intrusive footnote disturbs' (*Thomas Hardy*, p. 142).

42 In contrast, for instance, with the casual and even flaccid tone of Dickens' alternative ending to *Great Expectations* and, to shift to drama, of Tennessee Williams' alternative ending to *Cat on a Hot Tin Roof*.

5

Compulsion and Choice in
The Mayor of Casterbridge

by JULIET M. GRINDLE

There are hints in the first chapter of *The Mayor of Casterbridge* that a sense of crisis has been brewing in Henchard for some time. A hay-trusser, he enters Weydon Priors with a wife and child at a time when, as anyone would know, there is no hay-trussing work to be had. Descending to the fair where the only remaining business is 'getting away the money o' children and fools' (10)[1], he gets drunk and at last succeeds in making Susan and his audience take seriously an idea which he has apparently voiced a number of times in the immediate past—the idea that he could sell off his wife and start again.

It is evident when we first see Henchard that he is in many ordinary respects a powerful man, full of unused and unapplied energy, who, however, experiences himself as absolutely powerless. One senses that a life comprising only endless responses to the endless demands of survival has built up in Henchard an overwhelming need to initiate. As he grows less and less able to tolerate his present limitations, his mind turns to ridding himself of them—the most obvious to him being his obligation to support a wife and daughter. If only he weren't tied in this particular way, he reasons to himself, if only he were a free man again, he would be able to accomplish anything he wanted: he would 'challenge England' in the fodder business, he would know nothing but success, he would be worth a thousand pounds. It is a dream of total mastery over the situation which currently defeats him; instead of sweating and scraping to obtain enough food for three mouths, he will become a corn merchant, an emperor of food.

At the moment that Henchard conjures up the image of this triumphant change of life, he hears the voice of the auctioneer outside inviting bids on the last of the horses. One might expect of the man who has been complaining so bitterly of his helplessness, his ties, his inability to control his own destiny, that he would identify with the creature being sold, but his mind has at some stage made a sudden imaginative leap, and he identifies with the seller who can not only escape the restrictions of destiny by virtue of his 'freedom', but can bring about those restrictions on others. Henchard can escape his disposal at the hands of fate and simultaneously play at being himself the disposer. Susan is his problem and his restriction, and instead of suffering her he can get rid of her. Thus he goes from victim to master in one daring stroke.

One of the reasons that Henchard stands out from among the other characters in *The Mayor*, and indeed from among all Hardy's characters, is that he approaches the acquisition of power not only with a singleminded energy but also with an extraordinary degree of faith that power solves all problems. His selling of Susan, and Susan's acquiescence in being sold, seems to expose their relationship itself as one in which power is the central issue. At the moment of the sale, Henchard believes he has power over Susan in the same sense that he has power over five guineas: both are, sequentially, his to exchange, and he can only realise the power by effecting the transaction.

If one of the purposes of Henchard's act is to exercise the only power remaining to him, it also leaves him with no-one over whom to exercise such power except himself. This he accordingly does in making his vow of sobriety, which he binds with— for him—the ultimate penalty-clause: '. . . may I be strook dumb, blind, and helpless if I break this my oath!' (22)

Henchard's commitment to controlling himself gives us some idea of the strength of the man whose story we are about to learn. Although it is apparently made for the sake of being able to master himself and thus prevent a recurrence of such a terrible act of mastery as he has just exercised over Susan, it will also have the effect of tempering and hardening the instrument (himself) by which he is able to exercise such mastery over others. His vow is going to enable Henchard to carry out his boast of the previous evening, that if he were a free man, he would be a rich, powerful and successful man.

The narrative leap over the nineteen years in which Henchard achieves all his ambitions and more, has something of the effect of a magic wand waved in response to his wish. Suddenly, there is Henchard transformed into the mayor of Casterbridge, with all the wealth and power he could reasonably want. But by the time the story begins its main business with Susan's return, Henchard has only two years of his vow to go. His great symbolic act of self-mastery is nearing its term, and we may be sure that the rearrival of his wife will hasten it on its way. On the morning after the sale, Henchard had said bitterly of Susan: 'Meek—that meekness has done me more harm than the bitterest temper!' (21) —and he is to repeat the sentiment when he eventually realises that his unassuming wife came to Casterbridge largely in order to gain his material support, without his knowledge, for her and Newson's daughter.

With the simultaneous arrival in Casterbridge of Susan, Elizabeth-Jane, and Farfrae, Henchard comes once more into close contact with people who have quite different kinds of strength from his own, and it becomes apparent in the course of the novel that those kinds of strength are superior to, or at least more effective than, Henchard's. In the trials of strength which take place between Henchard and each of them, it is never Henchard who wins, although it is only ever Henchard who sees winning as necessary.

Henchard is full of remorse for his sale of Susan, though in many respects the sale goes ridiculously wrong—he finds himself laughed at as an abandoned husband and spends the price of his wife in looking for her—but there is ample evidence that nineteen years later he still perceives the connections between people as ones of debt and obligation. He pays a double debt to Susan in symbolically buying her back with the five guineas and in remarrying her when his feelings amount to little more than a distant pity. We learn of a rather similar attitude towards Lucetta: 'she suffered much on my account,' Henchard tells Farfrae, 'and didn't forget to tell me so in letters one after another; till, latterly, I felt I owed her something . . .' (82). When Henchard concludes that his debt to Susan is the greater of the two and must be paid by remarriage, he makes plans to pay Lucetta off with money; she, like Susan, has a cash value.

Perhaps one of the reasons why Henchard finds Farfrae at once so attractive and so disturbing, is that he is uninvolved in the whole undercurrent rigmarole of debt and obligation. His free gift of his corn-curing secret contrasts strangely with the tense and untrusting bartering which has been going on between Henchard and his audience during the King's Arms dinner. Henchard is astonished by Farfrae's gift—'from a stranger!' (52)—and is uneasy until he can even the score. Thereafter he attempts to dominate and obligate Farfrae—his arm on Farfrae's shoulder 'bearing so heavily that his slight figure bent under the weight.' (93) His failure to do so is signified by the Abe Whittle episode, where the very thing they clash over is the degree of obligation enforceable in a relationship between employer and employee, which is essentially a power relationship. When Farfrae behaves like an equal in the matter of the public celebration, and especially when he sets up in business like an equal, Henchard feels that he has, variously, rebelled against him and betrayed him, and their relationship is at an end.

Between Henchard and Elizabeth-Jane, the question of ownership is a crucial one. He says of the child that Susan took with her to Newson, 'She'd no business to take the maid—'tis my maid.' (19) Years later, he cannot bear the Elizabeth-Jane he supposes to be his daughter not to acknowledge his ownership. For this reason he breaks his resolve to keep Elizabeth-Jane in ignorance of her real father and, in case her affection should not be entirely automatic as a result, he barters for it thus: 'I'll be kinder to you than *he* was! I'll do anything, if you will only look upon me as your father!' (125) So kindness itself becomes a pawn in an exchange, the terms of which are: *if* you'll look on me as your father I'll be kind to you; if you acknowledge your *obligation*, I will *repay* you.

Henchard's ownership of Elizabeth-Jane is to be symbolised by her adoption of his name—'You shall take it as if by choice' he says, and he is later to describe the proposed contract of marriage between himself and Lucetta as 'my name in return for your devotion' (125). It is perhaps not entirely unfair to mention in the same breath that Henchard's name is over the gateway to the business part of his premises and on the sometime ubiquitous waggons which carry his corn. In some respects all of these name-bearers for Henchard are extensions of himself in his own eyes, and the people are accordingly to be commanded much like the objects.

It is one of the most striking features of *The Mayor of Caster-bridge* that the central relationship is not only *not* a sexual one, it is one which defies acceptable labelling altogether. Over it hovers the possibility that these two are parent and child, or if not, that they are tied to each other as parent and child are tied, with what Hardy refers to in the novel as the 'tenderest human tie' (176). The novel plays repeatedly on this question of whether or no the possibility will be realised. Is she or isn't she his daughter? And, intertwined with that, does he or doesn't he care about her? The answer to the first question moves through four stages whereby initially Henchard thinks that Elizabeth-Jane is his daughter, while she thinks that she is Newson's daughter; then Henchard and Elizabeth-Jane both think they are father and daughter; then Henchard knows she's not his daughter but Eliza-beth-Jane thinks she is; and lastly they both know that she is not. In the early stages, the question of whether Henchard cares for her or not corresponds closely with the question of their blood relatedness: Henchard cares for her when he thinks she's his daughter and doesn't when he thinks she isn't. But by the middle of the third stage Henchard's love or need for her have taken hold of him, and operate independently of the blood con-nection which originally seemed to him so crucial.

On one level, then, the novel deals with a simple uncertainty, or series of uncertainties, about Elizabeth-Jane's identity. Because we see the child Elizabeth-Jane at the beginning of the novel, we are liable to sympathise with Henchard's notion of a 'real' Elizabeth-Jane. The 'real' Elizabeth-Jane is Susan and Henchard's child, who dies soon after her parents' separation, and what Henchard has to contend with on Susan's return is an *un*real Elizabeth-Jane. One of the most important tests of his last years is the test of whether he can, symbolically reversing his estrange-ment of Susan, accept a stranger as a daughter and knowingly love the 'wrong' Elizabeth-Jane, the one who does not in any ordinary sense belong to him. It may be worth remarking, in this context, that the problem of Elizabeth-Jane's concealed paternity gives her a 'past' comparable to the conventional 'past' of an imperfect wife (Lucetta and Susan both have such pasts), for it turns out that someone else has a prior claim on her, and Henchard moves through the conventional husband-like reactions of repulsion and jealousy.

The series of reversals and denials which mark the relationship between Henchard and Elizabeth-Jane, however, are by no means exclusive to it. Susan finds that she is not, or is no longer, Henchard's wife. Just as suddenly she discovers that she is not legally or morally Newson's wife. Elizabeth-Jane learns one day that Newson was not her father, another day that Henchard is not after all her father. Henchard, quite separately, discovers that Elizabeth-Jane is not his daughter. One could perhaps add to these Farfrae's discovery that Henchard is not a friend, and Elizabeth-Jane's discovery that Lucetta is not a friend. There is a widespread theme in literature whereby the protagonist discovers that the person he has most regarded as a stranger or an enemy is actually his brother (or mother, or father, or daughter, or friend). In *The Mayor* this theme is turned on its head, for where there were thought to be indissoluble legal, moral and social bonds, there turn out to be none. It transpires that the brother is a stranger.

The effect of these ironic reversals is partly to expose the futility of clutching and claiming such as Henchard's. We are invited to ask, what constitutes belonging? what causes or fails to cause people to behave to each other as if they were kindred? Can we in fact behave in such a manner without an essentially superstitious network of beliefs about who belongs to us and who doesn't?

The complexity of the web of relationships between the six major characters in *The Mayor of Casterbridge* is partly brought about and greatly augmented by the truly remarkable amount of lying which is done. Henchard pretends to have a sufficiently respectable past for him to be Mayor of Casterbridge, which involves him in the particular pretences of being a widower and of courting Susan on her return. He pretends not to have known Lucetta before she came to Casterbridge, which involves another pretended courtship (or attempt at it). He pretends to Elizabeth-Jane that she is his daughter, which involves him in the further pretences to her that Newson is dead and to Newson that Elizabeth-Jane is dead. Susan pretends to Elizabeth-Jane that Henchard is barely more than an acquaintance and to Henchard that Elizabeth-Jane is his daughter. Newson pretends to Susan that their 'marriage' is valid, and when that pretence fails he pretends to be dead. Lucetta, over whose door in Casterbridge is the image of a mask which has now been almost chipped away, pretends not to have known Henchard before she came to Casterbridge and, for a time, pretends not to know Farfrae. All speak 'mad lies like a child, in pure mockery of consequences' (293), as is said of Henchard when he sends Newson away from Casterbridge grieving.

Every single one of these lies is a lie about a relationship and represents in part an attempt to conform to orthodox rules about relationships. The necessity for each lie arises because the rules have been transgressed (only Farfrae and Elizabeth-Jane, the two thoroughly successful innocents, transgress but fail to see the need for lying). The relationships lied about are all affected by the preordained obligations of marriage and parenthood, of which ground rules common to both are that the relationships should be exclusive and irreversible. Husband and wife may not part, let alone in the rather too telling manner of Susan's auction, so Henchard lies to conform with what people may do. Sexual relationships must be both exclusive and legally sanctioned, hence Henchard's lie about Lucetta. People only love those to whom they belong or who belong to them in a socially recognised way, so Henchard must maintain the lie about Elizabeth-Jane's paternity if he is to retain her love. Elizabeth-Jane and Newson are each led to believe that the other is dead because there cannot be two fathers.

The collapse of each of these lies compels change. When the selling of Susan is told in court, Henchard's relationship with the whole world changes. When his connection with Lucetta is known, Lucetta dies (thus escaping the impossibility, according to the rules, of living in the same town with two 'husbands'). In anticipation of Elizabeth-Jane's learning, at one stroke, that Henchard is not her father and that Newson her real father is alive, Henchard leaves the town and solves the problem of Elizabeth-Jane's two fathers. Henchard's discovery of Elizabeth-Jane's real origins makes him look on her as an intrusive stranger, not as a daughter. Susan's discovery about the real nature of her marriage with Newson compels the abandonment of that relationship, so that Susan can go in search of her 'real' husband, Henchard.

Henchard, before he is finally driven to learn that relationships don't reside in law or blood, complains thus:

> The mockery was, that he should have no sooner taught a girl to claim the shelter of his paternity than he discovered her to have no kinship with him.
>   This ironical sequence of things angered him like an impish trick from a fellow-creature. Like Prester John's, his table had been spread, and infernal harpies had snatched up the food. (128)

What the events of the novel suggest, is that the mockery is largely self-mockery: Henchard is the impish fellow-creature and the person he tricks is himself. The infernal harpies are perhaps those conventions, seized on so trustingly by Henchard, which distinguish between 'real' (formal, named, involuntary) and 'not-real' relationships. Again, after Henchard has told Newson that Elizabeth-Jane is dead, he says to himself: 'at this moment her heart is as warm towards me as mine is towards her . . . Yet before the evening probably he will have come; and then she will scorn me!' (295) We are specifically told that Henchard is wrong. Elizabeth-Jane 'could not urge what she did not know—that when she should learn that he was not related to her other than as a stepparent she would refrain from despising him, and that when she knew what he had done to keep her in ignorance she would refrain from hating him' (311); but Henchard describes what is a common experience in *The Mayor of Casterbridge*: now you see it, now you don't—or rather, now you have it now you don't. The feast is whipped away by harpies. Just as, however, it is Henchard himself in the previous passage who removes the feast by his refusal to love the 'wrong' Elizabeth-Jane, so here it is Henchard who brings about the destiny he fears by his false assumption that Elizabeth-Jane will refuse to love the 'wrong' father.

At several points in *The Mayor of Casterbridge*, there occurs something akin to a strange and terrible vision which makes a vivid, forcible connection between one moment in time and another, between a man and himself at different times, between different places and between different people. Such is the effect made by the furmity woman's apparently demented testimony: —
'Twenty years ago or thereabouts I was selling of furmity in a tent

at Weydon Fair—' (202). Words equally as bizarre and disturbing because equally displaced are heard by Lucetta when Henchard reads aloud to Farfrae from her love letters. When Mixen Lane comes to Corn Street at the climax of the skimmity-ride, with the object of saying (like the furmity woman) 'you're no better than we', there is a confusion of time and place alike; Lucetta, Farfrae's wife, looks down from her window and sees herself, Henchard's lover, parading the streets, before the whole show vanishes 'like the crew of *Comus*' (282). The skimmity-ride offers a vision of the future as well as of the past, for when Henchard looks down into the water in which he is about to drown himself, he sees—himself drowned. The event, which is a major turning point in his life, makes him a seer in the double sense of both perceiver and visionary, like Conjuror Fall and the 'discerning silent witch' Elizabeth-Jane.

The cycle of ambition in Henchard's life ends with his unhesitating acknowledgement of the truth of what the furmity woman says in court. There is something profoundly mysterious about Henchard's refusal to let her be silenced, for he abandons in an instant his consistent and successful pretence of burgher-like respectability. It is perhaps for him a moment of true illumination about his own identity, for he says to the furmity woman, in effect, yes I am that man, and yes that does mean that I've no business sitting here and judging you.

All the manifestations of Henchard's supremacy vanish in the wake of his stepping down from the magistrate's chair. He loses Lucetta (now a considerable prize), goes bankrupt, becomes an employee of Farfrae's, and abandons the temperance occasioned by his twenty-one-year-long vow. One way to interpret his actions in the period that follows is to see them as explorations of his new-found powerlessness. Not as in the past before the selling of Susan, Henchard now has the experience of being a powerful man by which to measure his limits. It is perhaps this knowledge of power which enables Henchard to make the new exploration without capitalising on what power remains to him, for he does no more than attitudinise.

In what is surely one of Hardy's most cunning satirical moments, Henchard first engineers the delivery of God's own curse, in the form of Psalm the Hundred-and-Ninth. If he could only control Farfrae, as God can, by dictating his absolute destruction in a series of well-thought-out stages . . . Yet it is within Henchard's power to destroy Farfrae's happiness and his life itself, and Henchard feels and measures that power but disdains to use it. He plays lengthily with the idea of revealing the authorship of Lucetta's love-letters to Farfrae, but when the moment comes he cannot do it 'in cold blood' (242). When Lucetta pleads with him the following day, Henchard perceives the full extent of the power that he has to fulfil his own wish and see her harmed, but the very perception shames him—'Such a woman was very small deer to hunt' (251). After Henchard's exclusion from the Council's plans to welcome the Royal Personage, he meets Farfrae head on beneath the royal gaze, where Henchard's power to embarrass Farfrae in all his mayoral dignity is considerable, but again Henchard 'by an unaccountable impulse gave way and retired.' (266) Henchard then ties one hand behind his back so that he cannot blame himself for hunting too easy a quarry, fights Farfrae, masters him and has his life in his hands. Once more he withdraws: 'though I came here to kill 'ee, I cannot hurt thee! Go and give me in charge—do what you will—I care nothing for what comes of me!' (274)

The very same night, Henchard sees his own desire to harm Lucetta and Farfrae carried out, not by himself but by Jopp and the people from Mixen Lane. This frightening and irreversible triumph of spite gives birth to a new desire for affection in Henchard. Suddenly, he finds that he wants Elizabeth-Jane, not because she in any way 'belongs' to him, but because he at last perceives her own affection and its value: 'above all things what he desired now was affection from anything that was good and pure.' (287)

Henchard is still caught in his own toils, however. He assumes that it is only a matter of time before Elizabeth-Jane's affection for him is killed by Newson's return. Judging his last desire to be a hopeless one, and perceiving himself as a man without a single wish capable of fulfilment, he decides to end the desiring self and commit suicide. Just as he saw a previous wish retrospectively fulfilled and Lucetta and Farfrae harmed when he no longer wished them to be so, he now sees his wish anticipated and himself already dead in the water. He withdraws from harming himself as he withdrew from harming Farfrae, and in making that decision he relinquishes a desire beyond the desire for Elizabeth-

Jane's affection, namely the desire to exercise control over his own fate.

From this moment Henchard is a 'changed man', 'as far that is as change of emotional basis can justify such a radical phrase' (329). He stops fighting and edges towards a state of acceptance. He accepts all that Elizabeth-Jane is and does, he accepts his own agonised fear of losing her, he accepts Farfrae's and then Newson's claims to her, and he accepts the prospect of a life apart from her.

Henchard leaving Casterbridge inevitably recalls Henchard entering Casterbridge twenty-one years earlier. Just as, following the sale of Susan, Henchard loses the only people close to him and changes his life utterly in consequence, so here 'There would remain nobody for him to be proud of, nobody to fortify him . . . Susan, Farfrae, Lucetta, Elizabeth—all had gone from him, one after one, either by his fault or by his misfortune.' (295) The similarity of the two moments is underlined by the glaringly fraudulent complaint of the narrator (who may, however, merely be voicing Henchard's thoughts):

> Externally there was nothing to hinder his making another start on the upward slope, and by his new lights achieving higher things than his soul in its half-formed state had been able to accomplish. But the ingenious machinery contrived by the Gods for reducing human possibilities of amelioration to a minimum —which arranges that wisdom to do shall come *pari passu* with the departure of zest for doing—stood in the way of all that. He had no wish to make an arena a second time of a world that had become a mere painted scene to him. (319)

If we look back to the Henchard of twenty-one years before, young and ignorant enough to be full of zest for doing, we find him saying much the same thing: 'a fellow never knows these little things [the terrible consequences for a man of marrying at eighteen, for instance] till all chance of acting upon 'em is past.' (13) In the context of the belief that the Gods devise clever machines to thwart human progress, it should be noted that Henchard believed the Gods and not the skimmity-riders were responsible for the vision which saved his life, the image of himself drowned.

All that the passage implies, moreover, is brought into question by Elizabeth-Jane. Her role in the novel suggests rather that wisdom to do comes *pari passu* with the absence of opportunity

101

for doing, and that this state of affairs is not the product of divine malice but of the simple connection between passivity and perceptivity—between the absence of opportunity for 'doing' and the presence of opportunity for observing. It is said of Elizabeth-Jane, for instance, at tea with Lucetta, Henchard and Farfrae, that she 'being out of the game, and out of the group, could observe all from afar, like the evangelist who had to write it down' (182). Of Henchard on the same occasion, failing to notice Lucetta's loving glances at Farfrae, it is said that he 'was constructed on too large a scale to discern such minutiae as these by an evening light, which to him were as the notes of an insect that lie above the compass of the human ear.' (183) And Jopp in the same period has learned Henchard 'by virtue of the power which the still man has in his stillness of knowing the busy one better than he knows himself.' (183) Learning is the reward for such inaction, but disengagement is the cost; Henchard looking through the window from the street at Elizabeth-Jane's wedding party, sees what the participants cannot see, as did Elizabeth-Jane and Susan looking through the window of the King's Arms at Henchard's mayoral banquet; the price is his non-participation.

The idea of the arena has a central importance in *The Mayor of Casterbridge*. Within it, creatures may be exposed for a spectacle, traded, or killed, but always beneath the thoroughly unsympathetic gaze of onlookers. In Casterbridge's ancient amphitheatre, Romans have cheered the death of gladiators and thousands have flocked to watch executions. The malice hasn't changed, as witness the delight occasioned by the planning of Lucetta's downfall, nor has the indifference. Casterbridge has a modern arena, too—the market place where human as well as animal lives are exchanged and disposed of, the agricultural labourers in search of work having a market value outside their control which leaves them forever at the mercy of unpredictable change.

A series of highly informative images of animals can be linked with the image of the arena. The first occurs immediately after the sale of Susan, when we are told:

> In contrast with the harshness of the act just ended within the tent was the sight of several horses crossing their necks and rubbing each other lovingly as they waited in patience to be harnessed for the homeward journey. (18)

There are many occasions in Hardy's writings when he compares humans with animals in respect of both their predicaments (usually similar) and their response to it (usually different). Here the pathos of the horses' situation is matched not only by their inclination to comfort each other because of it but by their tolerance of it. Henchard, restricted as they are, performs an act which is not only unloving, but which represents an extreme rejection of the notion of waiting in patience to be harnessed. An extended metaphor is provided by the treatment of bulls in Casterbridge, towards whom everything is done—quite unnecessarily, we are told—that is most likely to 'infuriate the viciously disposed and terrify the mild' (206). Of the bull which temporarily traps Lucetta and Elizabeth-Jane, the point is made that it had 'perhaps rather intended a practical joke than a murder' (208). The same is true of those who organise the skimmity-ride, yet—though Lucetta does actually die in consequence—nobody looks on them as brutish and dangerous, or attempts violently to subdue them as Henchard subdues the bull.

Images of the bulls have, of course, a particular bearing on Henchard, who is bull-like in respect of his largeness, slowness, clumsiness, strength, unpredictability, and—in the end—the manner in which he is susceptible to being tamed. Hardy speaks of the *breaking-in* of Henchard when he goes to work for Farfrae.[2] During the royal visit he is like a bull breaking *out* of its pen.[3] Towards the end of Henchard's life, when he is thoroughly 'mastered' by 'his once despised daughter', Hardy suggests both a more fearsome and a nobler creature by calling him a 'netted lion' (302). Henchard too, imagining living with Farfrae and Elizabeth-Jane, projects an image of himself as 'a fangless lion' (309). Henchard may have lost his teeth at this point, but there is a further and apparently extraordinary diminution to come, for the last of such images is that of a caged *bird*. To this transition I will return in a moment.

In the skimmity-ride the fate of the animals is linked overtly with that of the humans: man, woman and donkey are all tethered together. And yet, consistently, the animals are held up as exemplars not only in respect of their greater innocence and freedom from malice, but also in respect of the vastly superior dignity with which they encounter the limits on their freedom. If each of these captive animals is presented to us as at once admirable and moving, then we must question whether the long slow 'breaking in' of Henchard is to represent a gain as well as a loss.

Henchard in his state of acquiescence after returning to life from Ten Hatches weir, comes closer to achieving the state of the horses outside the tent at Weydon than would have seemed possible at the novel's opening. In the perfectly-shaped circle of Henchard's life, the essential difference between the last point and the first is that he no longer wants anything. It is not that he has conquered desire and holds his own desires in subjection, but that he has parted company with desire, and thus parted company with the only thing that could lift him back up into a new life-cycle.

The fact that Henchard accepts his coming death absolutely while refraining from hastening it in any way, is perhaps an important aspect of his Will. The proscriptions of his Will are those of a man who chooses not to cling to life in any of the commonplace symbolic ways whereby the dead are enabled, in a sense, to exist. There are to be no acts of remembrance, mourning, honour or ceremony; the only person who might care about his death is not to be told of it; and, in what might be seen as an extreme statement of non-belonging, Henchard asks not to be buried in consecrated ground.

There is something of a literary-critical problem regarding Henchard's Will, some readers finding it as hard to swallow as, say, Little Father Time's farewell note to his parents. But it is doubtful that we should regard Henchard's Will as the words or intentions of a man who—like the attempted suicide of popular myth—wants sympathy rather than death. The man who writes the Will is not the same as the man who felt aggrieved when his wife took him at his word and stood up to be sold. Elizabeth-Jane, in fact, has 'independent knowledge that the man who wrote them meant what he said' and that they were 'a piece of the same stuff that his whole life was made of'(333). And naïve as Henchard may in some respects be in comparison with Elizabeth-Jane, it is perhaps her own naïvety which makes her remark 'what bitterness lies there!' (333) Elizabeth-Jane has after all been protected from experiences as overwhelming as Henchard's by the continually successful maintenance of her own poise. Henchard's solution to his life problems, which are no different from hers, is not the solution of an artificial man, but is perhaps the solution of a man who treats problems in as radical a manner as he knows how. If we were to imagine each as posing the question of their own identity in the face of the limitations by which they are restricted, we might characterise Henchard's answers as, sequentially, 'I am the possessor of this much freedom', 'I am the possessor of these many people—the man to whom Susan, Elizabeth-Jane, Farfrae and Lucetta all belong', and 'I am nobody.' Elizabeth-Jane's unchanging answer is, 'I am a person who uses her available measure of freedom in the following ways.'

One of Hardy's most persistent offences in the eyes of his contemporaries was that he wrote as if the 'problem of pain' referred to a commonplace personal problem rather than a theological one. Henchard and Elizabeth-Jane typify two approaches to that problem as Hardy saw it. Elizabeth-Jane's approach, as it is described on the last page of the novel, consists in 'the cunning enlargement, by a species of microscopic treatment, of . . . minute forms of satisfaction' (334). Henchard's, which unlike hers will answer to 'positive' pain, is to devalue, minimise and deny the self which experiences pain. When Elizabeth-Jane rejects him on her wedding-day, the chief reason that he does not attempt to change her mind is that 'he did not sufficiently value himself to lessen his sufferings' (326). There is no doubt that Elizabeth-Jane is the stronger of the two in the sense that she is far and away the better candidate for survival, but—as with Henchard—her energy is commensurate with her appetite, which is small. Part of Henchard's greatness, then, comes from his willingness to take risks, his lack of hesitation, his readiness to accept the consequences of his own actions, and his indifference to considerations which would keep his appetite or his energy within common bounds.

One of the several complex ideas about 'fate' to be found in Hardy's novels is that fate is a limitation, or series of limitations, which it may be more sensible to embrace than to struggle against, the reason being that 'fate' provides a discipline within which survival can be transformed from an unspeakable brawl into a highly sophisticated art. The art may be that of the gladiator in the arena, whose life is indisputably violent, short, and unjust, but it has the incalculable merit that the practitioner provides a creative response to what is outside his control. In

Hardy's famous poem, the bird which sings even though it has had its eyes put out and is forever trapped in a small wire cage, is pulling fate by the tail, and Hardy, immensely moved by the idea of its response, calls it *divine*, suggesting that it has attained the highest state that could possibly be aspired to.

It would be hard to make out a case that the slow-witted and leaden-hearted Henchard sings in response to his eventual fate, and yet it is impossible to interpret Abe Whittle's presence as other than a sign of grace. Henchard leaves Casterbridge referring to himself as Cain ('I—Cain—go alone as I deserve' [313]), but dies cared for by Abel. The man who has spent his life worrying about how to secure his claims to other people and test their claims to him, in the end finds a relationship which is based on the voluntary return of a kindness. He does, after all, find the long lost (or rather, long undreamed-of) 'brother' of the myth.

The exploration in *The Mayor of Casterbridge* of different kinds of power and different kinds of mastery leads the reader to question in what precisely mastery resides. For Henchard, initially, it seems to reside in having the greatest possible influence over the lives of people other than himself, and Henchard's fall from a position of influence in Casterbridge can be seen in the light of traditional kinds of moral fables which stress the uncertain and unreliable nature of such power as this, and its especial vulnerability to envious destruction. Another kind of mastery is Elizabeth-Jane's—and in the end, by a different route, Henchard's too—and that is the mastery over states of fear, pain, and astonishment which Hardy seems to present as those states in which we are obliged to live unless by some deliberate exercise of spirit we learn a means of subduing them.

NOTES

1 All page references are to Thomas Hardy's *The Mayor of Casterbridge*, Macmillan, 1965.
2 'When . . . Henchard had become in a measure broken in, he came to work daily on the home premises like the rest' (229).
3 Henchard says to Farfrae, 'He drove me back as if I were a bull breaking a fence' (270).

6

Tess: The Pagan and Christian Traditions

by ROSEMARY L. EAKINS

Dorset folk legends and customs figure prominently, together with classical allusions, in all the Wessex novels of Thomas Hardy. Some of the traditional material derives from the history of local families of Norman descent, and some relates to relics from Anglo-Saxon and Roman times (barrows and other burial grounds, old roads and fortifications). Hardy's country people have their own proverbs, superstitions and songs. Some of their seasonal festivals and rites have descended from primitive religions whose origins and original significance are, by Hardy's time, all but forgotten, but traces of witchcraft linger.

In the early novels, Hardy used this traditional material simply as local colour, to establish a setting and perhaps the frame of mind of some of his characters; it was not integral to his conception of the novel. In *Tess of the D'Urbervilles*, however, traditional material becomes the very fabric of the book, woven into almost every aspect of the tragic story. Furthermore, the folk materials selected by Hardy for inclusion in *Tess* are peculiarly suited to the story of a woman victimised by the dual standards of nineteenth-century morality.

Hardy associates Tess not only with the lore of Wessex, but with many old traditions pertaining to goddesses both Christian and pagan. At Marlott, in her unspoiled innocence, she had participated each year in a local Cerealia. At Talbothays, Hardy describes Tess as Eve and the Magdalen, and Angel Clare calls her Artemis and Demeter. When Tess travels to Flintcombe Ash seeking employment, she passes through an irregular chalk table-land, 'bosomed with semi-globular tumuli—as if Cybele the Many-breasted were supinely extended there'. These associations universalise Tess. Essentially she is a simple country girl cruelly wronged; but as Eve she is all women, as the Magdalen she is betrayed, as the chaste Artemis she remains eternally pure, and as Ceres or Demeter she is the earth goddess and mother of all.

The Wessex folk material used in *Tess* and Hardy's other work is all genuine:

> I may say, once for all, that every superstition, custom, etc., described in my novels may be depended on as true records of the same, whatever merit they may have in folklorists' eyes, and are not inventions of mine.[1]

Hardy recorded Dorset superstitions, customs, and anecdotes about the supernatural in a series of journals, which he kept for many years because he thought that these and other notes might be useful for his novels and stories. He gathered many of these tales from local people, and was himself familiar with local customs from boyhood. The subject matter of the journal entries is varied. Hardy records several ghost stories; he describes Midsummer Eve, Midsummer Day, and All Hallows' Eve customs; he gives an account of a conjuror; he tells the legend of the Cerne Giant. For example, in July 1876 he made the following entry:

> Mr. Warry says that a farmer who was a tenant of a friend of his, used to take the heart of every calf that died, and sticking it full of black thorns, hang it on the cotterel, or cross-bar, of his chimney: this was done to prevent the spread of the disease that had killed the calf. When the next tenant came the chimney smoked very much, and examining it, they found it choked with hearts treated in the manner described—by that time dry and parched.[2]

Hardy knew of the antiquity of such survivals as the Maypole dance, for instance, and of their descent from primitive religious rituals. It is possible that he may have read—with a poet's interest, rather than that of an anthropologist—some of the early studies in cultural and social anthropology published in England in the second half of the nineteenth century (beginning with the pioneering work of Sir Edward Tylor, whose *Researches into the Early History of Mankind* was published in 1865, and continuing up to the publication in 1890 of *The Golden Bough* by Sir James

Frazer). Evelyn Hardy, editor of some portions of his journals, assumes that Hardy did have some knowledge of, for example, fertility rites. Hardy's knowledge of folklore was not, however, systematically acquired. He himself testified that he learned what he knew through informal observation. In a letter to J. S. Udal he wrote:

> I have never systematically studied Folk Lore, nor collected dialect words. If I had done either I might have gained some valuable material in both kinds. I used in [my] fiction such folklore as came into my mind casually, & the same with local words.[3]

Hardy's interest in the traditions of his native Dorset was personal and pragmatic, not that of the antiquary. The complex of legends and superstitions surviving from the distant past and the tangible relics he saw around him formed part of the background of his whole life. Certainly he did not believe in most of of the superstitions held by his neighbours; but he was nevertheless affected by them. He always retained two personal superstitions: he did not like anyone to touch him, and he never allowed himself to be weighed, as he considered both to be unlucky.[4] He would have liked to believe in the supernatural, and he admitted, half jokingly, that he partly did. In a letter to Dr. Caleb Saleeby, he wrote:

> You must not think me a hard-hearted rationalist for all this [Hardy's comment that Bergson's philosophy amounts to Dualism]. Half my time (particularly when I write verse) I believe—in the modern sense of the word—not only in things that Bergson does, but in spectres, mysterious voices, intuitions, omens, dreams, haunted places, etc. etc.[5]

In conversation with William Archer, Hardy touched on the same theme:

> I am most anxious to believe in what, roughly speaking, we may call the supernatural—but I find no evidence for it! People accuse me of scepticism, materialism, and so forth; but, if the accusation is just at all, it is quite against my will. For instance, I seriously assure you that I would give ten years of my life— well, perhaps that offer is rather beyond my means—but when I was a younger man, I would cheerfully have given ten years of my life to see a ghost—an authentic, indubitable spectre.[6]

Hardy lived in an age of change. Although he knew that many of the social changes in his native Dorset were for the better, he nevertheless regretted the passing of some of the old ways of life and the end of the traditions and beliefs of his own youth. In a letter to Rider Haggard, he lamented this loss:

> But changes at which we must all rejoice have brought other changes which are not so attractive. The labourers have become more and more migratory . . . The consequences are curious and unexpected. For one thing, village tradition—a vast mass of unwritten folk-lore, local chronicle, local topography, and nomenclature—is absolutely sinking, has nearly sunk, into eternal oblivion . . . there being no continuity of environment in their lives, there is no continuity of information, the names, stories, and relics of one place being speedily forgotten under the incoming facts of the next. For example, if you ask one of the work-folk . . . the names of surrounding hills, streams; the character and circumstances of people buried in particular graves; at which spots parish personages lie interred; questions on local fairies, ghosts, herbs, etc., they can give no answer: yet I can recollect the time when the places of burial of even the poor and tombless were all remembered, and the history of the parish and squire's family for 150 years back known. Such and such ballads appertained to such and such a locality, ghost tales were attached to particular sites, and nooks wherein wild herbs grew for the cure of divers maladies were pointed out readily.[7]

Reflecting perhaps on the changes taking place around him, in his journal for 16 June 1875, Hardy made the following entry:

> Reading the *Life of Goethe*. Schlegel says that 'the deepest want and deficiency of modern art lies in the fact that the artists have no mythology.'[8]

Hardy took Schlegel's dictum seriously, and he provided the world of his novels with both Christian and pagan mythologies. They exist in Hardy's Wessex, as they did in Dorset, in continued tension and often in open conflict. (Note that Tess's ancestor, the knight d'Urberville who came from Normandy with William the Conqueror, is given the Christian name of Pagan.)

The richness of the traditional material in *Tess of the D'Urbervilles* might encourage readers to think, romantically, that Hardy intended Tess to be a personification of old Wessex, and that her tragic end suggests the passing of a way of life which (despite its hardships) offered country people a sense of dignity and identity. But although Tess's beliefs and her response to life are inseparable from her Wessex upbringing, her tragedy is an individual tragedy.

Tess of the D'Urbervilles tells the story of an individual victimised by the unfair standards of morality which condemn in a woman behaviour condoned in a man.

Hardy universalises Tess by means of a complex plot: in it she works out her destiny and, at the same time, moves through a series of events representing the failure of hopes for the future, the failure of present happiness, the failure of both recent and ancient traditions. She experiences profound distress and temporary happiness; as each misfortune overcomes her, she hopes for consolation first in the future, and then in the present. Later she she seeks comfort in the past, and finally in the remote past.

With each of Tess's attempts to find peace and fulfilment Hardy associates Wessex pursuits, the traditions of old families, or surviving remnants from pagan times. He prefaces her first appearance in the novel with an old legend and with an account of the annual May Day club-walking in Marlott. (The village of Marlott lies in Blackmoor Vale, once the home of a legendary white hart which was hunted and killed in the reign of Henry III.) Hardy describes the club-walking, in which the women and girls of the parish walk around the village, each dressed in white and carrying a peeled willow-wand in her right hand and a bunch of white flowers in her left:

> It was an interesting event to the younger inhabitants of Marlott, though its real interest was not observed by the participators in the ceremony. Its singularity lay less in the retention of a custom of walking in procession and dancing on each anniversary than in the members being solely women. In men's clubs such celebrations were, though expiring, less uncommon; but either the natural shyness of the softer sex, or a sarcastic attitude on the part of male relatives, had denuded such women's clubs as remained (if any other did) of this their glory and consummation. The club of Marlott alone lived to uphold the local Cerealia. It had walked for hundreds of years, if not as benefit-club, as votive sisterhood of some sort; and it walked still.[9]

Hardy calls the club-walking a Cerealia, indicating that he knows the rite celebrates the coming of Spring, and the return of

Ceres' daughter Prosperine. Tess first appears, therefore, clad all in white like the legendary White Hart of Blackmoor Vale, participating in an old ritual celebrating the return of life to the earth. As she walks with her companions, her father rides by in a carriage, drunkenly muttering to himself, 'I've-got-a-gr't-family-vault-at-Kingsbere —and knighted-forefathers-in-lead-coffins-there!' (p. 12). He has heard from the parson that he is ' "the lineal representative of the ancient and knightly family of the d'Urbervilles, who derive their descent from Sir Pagan d'Urberville, that renowned knight who came from Normandy with William the Conqueror, as appears by Battle Abbey Roll" ' (p. 4). Hardy has begun to introduce the theme of the d'Urberville coach and he has hinted, by John Durbeyfield's drunkenness, at the disaster that association with the d'Urbervilles will bring to his family.

As Tess dances on the green after the club-walking, Angel Clare and his brothers pass by on a walking tour. Hardy contrasts their tour with the club-walking: the young men read a chapter of *A Counterblast to Agnosticism* every day on their trip, while the young women welcome spring with an old pagan rite. Angel Clare joins the dancing for a while, but, although he notices Tess, he does not dance with her (pp. 16–17).

The Durbeyfields' troubles begin in earnest shortly after this episode, when Tess's momentary inattention causes the death of the horse on which their livelihood depends. This incident suggests, again, the legend of the d'Urberville coach, even though Hardy does not tell the whole story until much later. He introduces the theme gradually, so that when it is fully stated it recalls and illuminates earlier passages.

As a result of the horse's death, Tess is persuaded by her mother to ask for help and employment from the d'Urbervilles at Trantridge. These d'Urbervilles, however, are not really related to Tess's family: they have arbitrarily adopted the old local name. When Alec seduces Tess it is in The Chase, one of the oldest woods in England, a place that links Tess again to ancient rites of fertility:

> Far behind the corner of the house—which rose like a geranium bloom against the subdued colours around—stretched the soft azure landscape of The Chase—a truly venerable tract of forest land, one of the few remaining woodlands in England of undoubted primaeval date, wherein Druidical mistletoe was still

found on aged oaks, and where enormous yew-trees, not planted by the hand of man, grew as they had grown when they were pollarded for bows.

(pp. 42–43)

Long after, Angel Clare hangs a bough of mistletoe over the bridal bed which he later refuses to share with Tess. The mistletoe links the first violation with a second, Angel's refusal to consummate the marriage. The mistletoe bough, emblem of fertility, is bitterly ironic (p. 299).

In describing the sun over the fields where Tess works after the birth of her child, Hardy suggests the traditional associations of the harvest and evokes the past when the sun was worshipped as a god:

> The sun, on account of the mist, had a curious sentient, personal look, demanding the masculine pronoun for its adequate expression. His present aspect . . . explained the old-time heliolatries in a moment. One could feel that a saner religion had never prevailed under the sky. The luminary was a golden-haired, beaming, mild-eyed, God-like creature, gazing down in the vigour and intentness of youth upon an earth that was brimming with interest for him.
>
> (p. 109)

Tess's relationship with her supposed family has brought her nothing but disaster, culminating in the illness of her child. When Tess realises that her child is dying, a further grief is added to her distress, for her father forbids her to have the baby baptised. In despair, she baptises him herself, giving him the name Sorrow (p. 119), before he dies and is buried in unconsecrated ground among the parish suicides and murderers. With him are buried Tess's hopes for the future.

With the coming of another spring, Tess's spirits rise enough to enable her to seek work again. As she enters the Froom Valley on her way to Talbothays dairy, she sings the words from the Book of Common Prayer she knows well:

> 'O ye Sun and Moon . . . O ye stars . . . ye Green Things upon the Earth . . . Ye Fowls of the Air . . . Beasts and Cattle . . . Children of Men . . . bless ye the Lord, praise Him and magnify Him for ever!'
>
> (p. 134)

Hardy comments here on Tess's religious beliefs; although Christian by training, she has something of the pagan in her as well, he writes:

> And probably the half-unconscious rhapsody was a Fetichistic utterance in a Monotheistic setting; women whose chief companions are the forms and forces of outdoor Nature retain in their souls far more of the Pagan fantasy of their remote forefathers than the systematized religion taught their race at later date.

> (pp. 134–5)

In the Vale of Great Dairies, Tess's dairy work brings her spiritual regeneration, and there she meets and falls in love with Angel Clare. As she and the other dairymaids go about their daily chores, with Angel watching them, Hardy gives the women dignity and stature by using a series of metaphors evoking a classical rather than a pastoral tradition (perhaps harking back to the club-walking in honour of Ceres). He describes the evening milking:

> The sun, lowering itself behind this patient row, threw their shadows accurately inwards upon the wall. Thus it threw shadows of these obscure and homely figures every evening with as much care over each contour as if it had been the profile of a Court beauty on a palace wall; copied them as diligently as it had copied Olympian shapes on marble *façades* long ago, or the outline of Alexander, Caesar, and the Pharaohs.

> (pp. 136–7)

As the milking proceeds, Dairyman Crick tells of the bull that knelt to pray at the sound of the Nativity Hymn. An intruding voice (Angel Clare's) interrupts with a comment which destroys the atmosphere created by Crick's tale. ' "It's a curious story; it carries us back to mediaeval times, when faith was a living thing!" ' (p. 143). Clare violates the peace of Talbothays more than once, for he cruelly disappoints Tess and also disrupts the lives of three other dairymaids, Izz, Retty, and Marian.

When Clare hears the d'Urberville name from his father, he exclaims at it. He is interested in the old family although he knows nothing of Tess Durbeyfield's connection with them. In Angel's exclamation, Hardy introduces his first explicit reference to the legend of the d'Urberville coach. ' "Not one of the ancient d'Urbervilles of Kingsbere and other places? . . . That curiously historic worn-out family with its ghostly legend of the coach-and-four?" ' (p. 213).

Tess is disturbed by the ancient coach which Clare arranges as transport on their wedding day: ' "I seem to have seen this carriage before, to be very well acquainted with it. It is very odd —I must have seen it in a dream" ' (p. 272). She denies Clare's suggestion that she must have heard the legend of the d'Urberville coach. He begins to tell her the story: ' "A certain d'Urberville of the sixteenth or seventeenth century committed a dreadful crime in his family coach; and since that time members of the family see or hear the old coach whenever—" ' (p. 272). He breaks off and refuses to say more, but Tess seems to have an instinctive knowledge of the legend (and, of course, she remembers how she rode with a spurious d'Urberville in his smart gig). She asks Clare whether the d'Urbervilles hear the coach when they are about to die or when they have committed a crime. He does not answer her. Legend is memory.

Clare takes his bride to an old farmhouse at Wellbridge, whose exterior features are so well known to all travellers through the Froom Valley; 'once a portion of a fine manorial residence, and the property and seat of a d'Urberville, but since its partial demolition a farm-house' (p. 276). On the walls are painted the portraits of two long-dead d'Urberville women. Clare sees in their harsh features a disquieting resemblance to Tess; she is frightened by them.

On their last night at the house, after Tess has told Clare of her relations with Alec d'Urberville and he has decided that they must part without consummating the marriage, Clare walks in his sleep. He picks up Tess and carries her across the river into the grounds of a ruined church. 'Against the north wall was the empty stone coffin of an abbot, in which every tourist with a turn for grim humour was accustomed to stretch himself. In this Clare carefully laid Tess. Having kissed her lips a second time he breathed deeply, as if a greatly desired end were attained' (p. 318). Tess's husband has betrayed her in the home of her ancestors and in the presence of their portraits. Her lineage cannot help her; the Christian church can offer only a place of burial. Clare's burial of Tess in the abbot's coffin means the death of her hopes for present happiness, and the fact that he rejects her even in his sleep suggests that for him Tess has indeed died.

After they separate, Alec d'Urberville enters Tess's life again. One day when she has been daydreaming and thought she heard a carriage, Alec tells her the whole story of the d'Urberville coach:

> 'If you are a genuine d'Urberville I ought not to tell you either, I suppose. As for me, I'm a sham one, so it doesn't matter. It is rather dismal. It is that this sound of a non-existent coach can only be heard by one of the d'Urberville blood, and it is held to be of ill-omen to the one who hears it. It has to do with a murder, committed by one of the family, centuries ago . . . One of the family is said to have abducted some beautiful woman, who tried to escape from the coach in which he was carrying her off, and in the struggle he killed her—or she killed him—I forget which. Such is one version of the tale . . .'
> (p. 452)

Hardy does not dwell upon the legend of the coach; he mentions it explicitly only four times. Yet there is an implicit connection between the death of the Durbeyfields' horse and the legend of the d'Urbervilles' coach. Tess was guilty of inattention: she should not have slept and allowed the cart to travel on unwatched. Small chances may have great consequences; the 'coach' of Tess Durbeyfield—be it the horse-cart, her wedding carriage or Alec d'Urberville's gig—carries her to eventual disaster, and Alec d'Urberville re-enacts the role of the doomed abductor.

Tess's mother, Joan Durbeyfield, insists on moving to Kingsbere, ancient seat of the d'Urbervilles, for she fondly hopes that good luck will come if she is close to the old lands of the family. The Durbeyfields arrive there to find that the rooms promised to them have been let to someone else, and so Tess finds refuge for her mother and the children under the walls of the d'Urberville Aisle of the church.

> The door of the church was unfastened, and she entered it for the first time in her life.
>
> Within the window under which the bedstead stood were the tombs of the family, covering in their dates several centuries. They were canopied, altar-shaped, and plain; their carvings being defaced and broken; their brasses torn from the matrices, the rivet-holes remaining like martin-holes in a sand-cliff. Of all the reminders that she had ever received that her people were socially extinct there was none so forcible as this spoliation.

> She drew near to a dark stone on which was inscribed:
> Ostium sepulchri antiquae familiae d'Urberville.
>
> (p. 464)

Alec d'Urberville intrudes even here, terrifying Tess when she discovers him reclining like an effigy on the oldest tomb in the Aisle. When she refuses to accept his renewed offer of help he delivers a veiled threat. After he leaves, Tess bends down over the entrance to the vault and murmurs (surely with the memory of the abbot's tomb still vivid in her mind), ' "Why am I on the wrong side of this door!" ' (p. 465) She has sought refuge in the burial place of her ancestors and found that even there she is not safe. Her ancestral past has failed her, and she wishes only to be buried with the d'Urberville dead.

When Tess, distraught beyond endurance, has found the courage to stab and kill Alec, and has run after the returned Clare, they travel together through the Great Forest and come to Stonehenge. Tess asks whether it is the heathen temple, and Clare replies, ' " Yes. Older than the centuries; older than the d'Urbervilles! . . ." ' (p. 502) Tess does not want to leave the place, although Clare fears they are being pursued. She tells him that she feels at home among the great monoliths, and then she lies down on the Stone of Sacrifice.

> 'One of my mother's people was a shepherd hereabouts, now I think of it. And you used to say at Talbothays that I was a heathen. So now I am at home.'
>
> . . . . .
>
> 'I like very much to be here,' she murmured. 'It is so solemn and lonely—after my great happiness—with nothing but the sky above my face. It seems as if there were no folk in the world but we two . . .'
>
> (p. 502)

Tess asks Angel whether sacrifices to God were made at Stonehenge, and he replies, ' "I believe to the sun. That lofty stone set away by itself is in the direction of the sun, which will presently rise behind it" ' (p. 503). The mention of sun-worship recalls the passage describing the harvest at Marlott, where the autumn sun shone on Tess and her child. She begs Angel for some reassurance that they will be reunited after death, but he cannot give her the answer she wants. His silent renunciation of the Christian faith and her silent acceptance of his unspoken response is their

last private communication, for she falls asleep, and in the morning they are awakened by the officers who have come to arrest her.

The ruins of Stonehenge are monuments of the pagan culture
in which Tess is an unwitting participant, and her night on the
stone altar represents her death in the pagan past, the fourth and
last in the series that began with the burial of her child. The
Christian church has failed Tess throughout the story: her child
was denied a Christian burial: her marriage according to its sacra-
ments was a travesty; her seducer returned to torment her in the
guise of an itinerant lay preacher; her husband has denied that
there is life after death. The pagan world has long since passed
away, and although a few muted echoes and relics of it (such as
the monoliths at Stonehenge) still linger in Wessex, the customs
and beliefs they once represented are powerless to give Tess anything more than belated consolation. Tess feels at peace among
the great stone slabs; she feels that in some way she belongs
among these relics of the past. Whatever happiness she has
sought in her life has been denied her, even twisted around to
destroy her. She has participated in the traditional pastimes and
pursuits of Wessex, but the modern world is gradually affecting
the countryside and destroying the old customs. Stonehenge is
the most notable monument to pagan British tradition; Hardy
clearly makes the point that tradition can offer a measure of
comfort when all else fails.

Omens were a special part of the local folklore that so interested Hardy. Each of the misfortunes in Tess's life is heralded
by an omen which she herself recognises and comments upon.
Alec d'Urberville showers roses and strawberries upon her when
she first visits Trantridge, seeking employment from her supposed kinfolk: a thorn from one of the roses stabs her chin.
'Like all the cottagers in Blackmoor Vale, Tess was steeped in
fancies and prefigurative superstitions; she thought this an ill
omen—the first she had noticed that day' (p. 50). When a letter
arrives from the d'Urbervilles, offering her work, her mother urges
her to accept it, but Tess has a premonition that she ought
not to go. When her mother asks her why she wants to stay
at home, she replies, ' "I'd rather not tell you why, mother; indeed, I don't quite know why" ' (p. 52).

At Talbothays, when she has consented to marry Angel Clare,
she admits that they have seen each other before:

'Ah, then I *have* seen you before this summer—'
'Yes; at that dance on the green; but you would not dance with me. O, I hope that is of no ill-omen for us now!'

(p. 244)

As Tess tries on her wedding gown, she remembers the lines of a ballad her mother used to sing about Queen Guénever's robe:

That never would become that wife
That had once done amiss.

Although she has tried to tell Angel of her relations with Alec and of the child, she has not been able to do so. Now she wonders if her wedding dress could betray her guilt. 'Suppose this robe should betray her by changing colour, as her robe had betrayed Queen Guénever. Since she had been at the dairy she had not once thought of the lines till now' (p. 263).

The worst omen of all occurs when she and Angel leave Talbothays on their wedding trip. A white cock flies up on to a fence and crows three times in the middle of the afternoon. Tess is upset, and Dairyman Crick shoos the bird away. Mrs. Crick knows immediately what Tess and Crick are thinking. ' "It only means a change in the weather," said she; "not what you think: 'tis impossible!" ' (p. 275) Tess has interpreted the omen correctly, however.

The powers of conjurors and witches are another particular aspect of Wessex folklore firmly believed in by Joan Durbeyfield and the folk at Talbothays. Joan lives in such dread of her witch's book, *The Compleat Fortune Teller*, that she will not allow it to remain in the house over night; she stores it in the outhouse when she is not consulting it. When she persuades Tess to visit the d'Urbervilles at Trantridge, she tells Tess's fortune with this book and she convinces herself (correctly) that her daughter will marry a fine gentleman.

Dairyman Crick thinks of consulting a conjuror when the butter will not come in the churn at Talbothays. A discussion of several local conjurors ensues.

' 'Tis years since I went to Conjuror Trendle's son in Egdon—years!' said the dairyman bitterly. 'And he was nothing to what his father had been. I have said fifty times, if I have said once, that I don't believe in en; though he do cast folks' waters very

119

true. But I shall have to go to 'n if he's alive. O yes, I shall have to go to 'n, if this sort of thing continnys!'

. . . . .

'Conjuror Fall, t'other side of Casterbridge, that they used to call "Wide-O," was a very good man when I was a boy,' said Jonathan Kail. 'But he's rotten as touchwood by now.' 'My grandfather used to go to Conjuror Mynterne, out at Owlscombe, and a clever man a' were, so I've heard grandf'er say,' continued Mr. Crick. 'But there's no such genuine folk about nowadays!'

(pp. 170–1)

The conversation takes a more cheerful turn, however, when Mrs. Crick suggests that the butter will not come because some-one in the house is in love.

All of these legends and traditions and the environment itself provide a haunting counterpoint to the action of *Tess* and rise at last in a major key to parallel and transcend the personal themes and to express Hardy's sorrow over the loss of generations of tradition. The story of Tess, however, is fiction, and what Hardy expresses about the Wessex of his imagination in the 1870s is governed partly by aesthetic considerations. What he felt about the conditions of the Dorset labourer is another matter. Michael Millgate's summary of Hardy's assessment of the real situation is particularly apposite:

> But although he profoundly regrets the isolated, static, inte-grated rural life that he once knew, he is by no means the im-passioned advocate of a return to a Golden Age.[10]

Despite Hardy's great affection for the old ways of the country-side he understood also the serious hardship that the work folk too often had to endure. In his article, *The Dorsetshire Labourer*, he flatly condemns anyone who, from a sense of misguided sentimen-tality, would wish to preserve the picturesque:

> That seclusion and immutability, which was so bad for their pockets, was an unrivalled fosterer of their personal charm in the eyes of those whose experiences had been less limited. But the artistic merit of their old condition is scarcely a reason why they should have continued in it when other communities were marching on so vigorously towards uniformity and mental equality. It is only the old story that progress and picturesque-ness do not harmonise. They are losing their individuality, but they are widening the range of their ideas, and gaining in free-

dom. It is too much to expect them to remain stagnant and old-fashioned for the pleasure of romantic spectators.[11]

The changes taking place in Wessex are part of the background against which the stories are set. The tragedies are those of individuals, but informed and supported by the background. Tess's story might have been told of a factory girl, but the advantages of the rural setting are very important. In the local Cerealia of the club-walking, the legend of the white hart, the old d'Urberville family and its stories, the hills spread out like the breasts of Cybele, the legendary material strengthens and dignifies the figure of the woman; it transforms her from simply a dairymaid and farm labourer to a woman of universal significance.

Tess wanders across Wessex as a migrant farm worker, and as personal disasters strike her, she comes at last to her days of drudgery at Flintcombe Ash. The role of the woman agricultural worker in such circumstances has been described by other observers than Hardy, and some of their accounts have been collected in E. Royston Pike's admirable volume, *Human Documents of the Victorian Golden Age*. The Children's Employment Commission (6th Report, 1867, p. 91) provides this anecdote, reminiscent of Tess set to work hacking swedes:

> A girl whom I took in to live, because she has no home to go to, came back today from the gang all dripping wet from the turnips. If you don't feel any hurt from the wet when you are young, you do afterwards, when you are old and the rheumatism comes on . . .[12]

From the Rev. J. Fraser's report, Employment of Women in Agriculture (1st Report, 1867, pp. 16–17), comes the following:

> Some of the work in which women are frequently employed, such as serving the threshing machine, weeding the wet corn, drawing turnips or mangolds, is work to which, on physical grounds, they never ought to be put at all. Exposure to wet or cold, from which no farm labour can claim exemption, is likely, owing to the greater susceptibility of the female constitution, to be specially injurious to them.[13]

Nowadays we take a more optimistic view of a woman's strength and powers of endurance, but the two writers quoted above were appalled not only by the back-breaking toil, but also by a moral question. With the best intentions in the world, the writers of these reports held the same notions concerning the importance of woman's purity that Hardy condemns in *Tess*. For them, there were debased women and pure women, and no circumstances could mitigate that distinction.

The Rev. J. Fraser comments that farm 'employment almost unsex[es] a woman, in dress, gait, manners, character, making her rough, coarse, clumsy, masculine;' and that 'it generates a further very pregnant social mischief, by unfitting or indisposing her for a woman's proper duties at home.'[14] He continues:

> The farmers, almost to a man . . . express the opinion that the proper place for a young single girl is in the household, and not upon the land. It is admitted that the intermixture of the sexes is one great cause for demoralization; yet such is the nature of farm work that it would be difficult even by the best contrived arrangements—it would be almost impossible by legislation—to secure effective separation . . . even more corrupting than the intermixture of any number of men and women in their work is said to be the influence of two or three debased members of their own sex . . .[15]

Another writer, J. E. White, in his report on the Agricultural Gangs (Children's Employment Commission, 6th Report, pp. 83–4), enlarges on the problems of immorality inherent in this class of agricultural work:

> With so many evil influences at work upon the character it is not to be supposed that persons thus employed will be religious. The clergyman, however anxious to discharge his duties, has few, if any, opportunities of seeing them or conversing with them. They go out so early and return so late that he can seldom find them at home, and if he does so they are not disposed to listen to any remarks he may make about their conduct or religious duties . . . Even if night schools for females were common in our country villages, it is doubtful whether they could or would attend them. Their impatience of restraint, their bodily weariness, and their want of application, would all be causes to prevent their attendance . . . With views of this kind they are not likely to attend places of worship, and they often spend the Lord's day in either utter idleness or in vicious pursuits.[16]

Hardy was determined to present Tess as a pure woman and he set out to accomplish this in the teeth of priggishness and prudery, by two means: first, by the character of Tess herself, and secondly by associating her with a body of legendary and traditional material some of which celebrates essentially female strengths and virtues.

As Michael Millgate says, 'Nothing is more remarkable in the novel than the extraordinary passion with which Tess is described and justified, and the "pure woman" formulation only serves to make explicit what is everywhere implicit—that Tess's personality makes it impossible to accommodate her within any of the conventional categories suggested by the crude facts of her situation and story . . .'.[17] We must listen to Hardy himself on the matter of Tess's purity and his conviction that the dual standard of morality should be brought into the open and discussed. In conversation with Raymond Blathwayt he said:

> I still maintain that her innate purity remained intact to the very last; though I frankly own that a certain outward purity left her on her last fall. I regarded her then as being in the hands of circumstances, not morally responsible, a mere corpse drifting with the current to her end.[18] I do feel very strongly that the position of man and woman in nature, things which everyone is thinking and nobody saying, may be taken up and treated frankly. Until lately novelists have been obliged to arrange situations and *dénouements* which they knew to be indescribably unreal, but dear to the hearts of the amiable library subscriber. See how this ties the hands of a writer who is forced to make his characters act unnaturally, in order that he may produce the spurious effect of their being in harmony with social forms and ordinances.[19]

Hardy liked women and he understood them very well indeed. In the world of his novels, his sympathies lie with the women who must struggle with the dual morality imposed on them by society. It is a fact of their lives, which they accept in one sense, but the circumstances of their lives inspire them to fight against it for their personal survival. In their individual ways they try to deal with it—some are overwhelmed by it, some compromise and gain a shallow and unsatisfactory solution, and some fight and triumph in defeat.

Because of this social censure, Tess in her wanderings is an extremely lonely figure. Her vitality and her sexuality attract her to Alec, her intelligence and sympathies attract her to Angel, but neither is a whole man and a fit companion for Tess. Tess has been associated with a series of great female figures: Ceres, Cybele the many-breasted who in mythology was served by a priest who took a vow of chastity and then broke it, Artemis, Demeter, Eve, and the Magdalen. All of these are life-enhancing figures. Those of Graeco-Roman origin serve and impose natural laws which Hardy seems to feel are superior to the narrow lip-service Christianity of the Clare brothers, for example. The Christian figures, Eve and the Magdalen, recapitulate in themselves the whole Christian story from the innocence of Eve, mother of us all, to the Magdalen, forgiven and loved by Christ.

NOTES

1 Unpublished letter (c. 1894) inserted in a presentation copy of Life's Little Ironies. Quoted in part in the Catalogue of the Ashley Library, collected by T. J. Wise (1930), X, 123.

2 F. E. Hardy, The Early Life of Thomas Hardy, 1928, pp. 147–8.

3 'Forty Years in an Author's Life: A Dozen Letters (1876–1915) from Thomas Hardy', annotated by Carl J. Weber, Colby Library Quarterly, Series IV, No. 6, May 1956, pp. 116–17.

4 F. E. Hardy, The Later Years of Thomas Hardy, pp. 32 and 228.

5 Letter to Dr. Caleb Saleeby, 2 February 1915, in F. E. Hardy, The Later Years of Thomas Hardy, 1930, p. 271.

6 William Archer, Real Conversations, 1904, p. 37.

7 Letter to Rider Haggard, March 1902, in F. E. Hardy, Later Years, p. 94.

8 Evelyn Hardy, Thomas Hardy's Notebooks, 1955, p. 51.

9 All references to Hardy's novels are to the Macmillan Library Edition (London, 1949–1952), pp. 10–11.

10 Michael Millgate, Thomas Hardy: His Career as a Novelist (New York, 1971), p. 220.

11 Harold Orel, ed., Thomas Hardy's Personal Writings (1967), p. 181.

12 E. Royston Pike, ed., Human Documents of the Victorian Golden Age (1967), p. 220.

13 Pike, pp. 222–23.

14 Pike, p. 222.

15 Pike, p. 223.

16 Pike, pp. 219–20.

17 Millgate, pp. 268–69.

18 Laurence Lerner and John Holmstrom, eds., *Thomas Hardy and His Readers: A Selection of Contemporary Reviews* (New York, 1968), p. 95.
19 Lerner and Holmstrom, p. 97.

7

Science and Art in
Jude the Obscure

by PATRICIA GALLIVAN

> Since Art is science with an addition, since some science under-
> lies all Art, there is seemingly no paradox in the use of such a
> phrase as 'the Science of Fiction'. One concludes it to mean that
> comprehensive and accurate knowledge of realities which must
> be sought for, or intuitively possessed, to some extent, before
> anything deserving the name of an artistic performance in narra-
> tive can be produced.[1]

Hardy published those lines in 1891, when *Jude the Obscure* was
advancing from conception to achievement, from a 'series of
seemings' to 'shape and coherence'.[2] The essay in which they
appear, 'The Science of Fiction', develops a careful ambivalence
towards its subject. The 'science' of fiction, Hardy wrote, is essential; it must come 'before' the addition of art. But the 'science'
in art is not to be confused with mere 'science', and while the
phrase, 'the science of fiction', may be 'seemingly no paradox',
Hardy does not release it from contradictions. The dual means of
attaining it, Hardy says, is 'a power of observation' when that
is 'informed by a living heart'; it is the product of 'the mental
tactility that comes from a sympathetic appreciativeness of life
in all of its manifestations'. Hardy holds this 'science', or 'knowledge', or 'observation' in tense balance with what is 'living',
'intuitive', 'sympathetic'. The language really does edge towards
paradox: 'To see in half and quarter views the whole picture, to
catch from a few bars the whole tune, is the intuitive power that
supplies the would-be story writer with the scientific bases for
his pursuit.' In another essay, Hardy put his position more con-

ventionally: what we look for in art, he said, is 'representation of life, construed, though not distorted, by the light of the imagination'.[3]

Hardy's essay on 'The Science of Fiction' comes from the period in his career which produced *Tess of the d'Urbervilles*, most of the stories in *Life's Little Ironies*, some of the 'dreams, and not records' of *Wessex Tales*,[4] and the serial version of *The Well-Beloved*. When he wrote the essay, Hardy had had *Jude* in his mind for some time: the novel began, he says, in notes he made 'from 1887 onwards'; it becomes a 'scheme' in 1890, an 'outline' in 1892, and a finished book in 1895.[5] In all of his works of this period, Hardy addresses the subject of his 1891 essay. All of those works touch upon the ways in which reality can be construed or distorted in the light cast by the imagination. No work presents the theme more directly than 'An Imaginative Woman', a story he revised while *Jude* was in his mind. In that story, the relation of the mind to the world it inhabits and creates is dramatised with shocking, if erroneous, clarity: the imaginative woman shapes the child she is carrying to the likeness not of the child's father but of the man she is in love with. Hardy appealed to 'science' to justify the tale: it presented, he claimed, 'a physical possibility that may attach to a wife of vivid imaginings, as is well known to medical practitioners and other observers of such manifestations.'[6] *Jude the Obscure* is a far more complex representation of the ways in which the soft light of imagination can produce flinty realities, and it is also a complex representation of 'the science of fiction' as Hardy described it in the opening lines of his essay on the subject. In *Jude*, his last 'artistic performance in narrative', Hardy derives basically shaping material from his reading in contemporary scientific literature.

While *Jude* moved through the stages of its long preparation, Hardy continued to copy passages from his reading into the commonplace books he had begun to keep in 1876. What he copied he intended to use: it was, as Robert Gittings says, 'raw material'.[7] During these years, Hardy made notes on, among other things, two subjects which comprise important context for his work on *Jude*. One of these subjects is a familiar interest in the notebooks; the other is not. The familiar subject, to which Hardy gave a good deal of his attention in these years, is literary, the explicit subject of 'The Science of Fiction', the opposing claims of realism and naturalism on the one hand and of symbolism and romanticism on the other. The new subject, which can be seen as a development of Hardy's broad interest in science and philosophy, is what one of the writers he quotes calls 'la nouvelle science', the science of psychology. In *Jude*, those two interests converge.

Hardy's notebook entries are reflected in more than one way in his work. Sometimes the reflection is mere glitter, only an item in the colour, as when, for instance, in 'An Imaginative Woman', Hardy describes the poet, Trewe, as 'little attracted by excellences of form and rhythm apart from content', as 'neither *symboliste* nor *décadent*'.[8] Before revising the story, Hardy had copied into his notebook long passages from an article in the *Revue des Deux Mondes* called 'Symbolistes et Décadens'. In his story, the article's title becomes simply raw material relocated, a merely transferred detail.

Sometimes the notebook entries surface more importantly in the work, as significantly developed ideas or events. Hardy copied the following passage, for instance, from Havelock Ellis's *The New Spirit* (1890):

> A woman, married: former lover returns: she wants to fly with him. Husband at length consents to allow her to choose as she will. Then at once she feels able to decide against the lover. The moral is that without freedom of choice there can be no real emancipation or development.[9]

Hardy subscribed to the moral, though it is unlikely that he borrowed it. What he did borrow was the instance: it becomes part of the second Avice's reaction to Pierston's decision to take her home, after bringing her to London, and in *Jude* it becomes a piece of Sue's tortured inconsistency. 'It is a curious thing,' she says to Phillotson the morning she leaves him, 'that directly I have begun to regard you as not my husband, but as my old teacher, I like you.' 'According to the rule of women's whims,' she says to Jude, 'I suppose I ought to suddenly love him, because he has let me go so generously and unexpectedly' (286). But Sue goes on, perversely, to blame herself—'I am so cold, or devoid of gratitude, or so something'—for failing to obey the rule of whim. And later, when she does go back to Phillotson, that is not because his generosity has given her freedom, but because she has abandoned choosing and rejected entirely any idea of emancipation. In the pressure of Hardy's ironic contexts, Ellis's merely moral instance gains in significance, becomes complexly expressive of Sue's character and circumstances.

Some of the material in Hardy's notebooks, however, acquires a much greater importance in the works than that. Some of it is reflected as the very bones of the work, as ideas transmuted to form or as characterising elements of Hardy's own attitude towards his creation. His reading in psychology is this last sort of raw material: it is relevant to his preoccupation, during the years of *Jude's* evolution, with perception, and it partly shapes the intention of the novel.

While *Jude* was in his mind, Hardy made notes from an article in the *Revue des Deux Mondes* for 1 April 1888, in which Paul Janet aimed to justify the recent establishment, at the Collège de France, of a chair of experimental and comparative psychology.[10] The 'new science' he described was 'la psychologie physiologique', the science of the brain. It was now, Janet said, a 'science naissante', even though its history reached back to Descartes, because it had now acquired a wholly new importance. It was being advanced, he said, in several countries—in France by Charcot and Broca, in Germany by 'le savant Wund', and in England by Huxley, Maudsley and Carpenter. Hardy transcribed Janet's description of its subject-matter:

> Les localisations cérébrales, et en particulier l'aphasie, le sens musculaire, l'hérédité, la suggestion, le dédoublement de conscience, etc., tels sont . . . les faits les plus intéressans parmi ceux que l'on a récemment étudiés.

Elsewhere in his notebooks, Hardy pursued some of these subjects (the location in the brain of specific functions, for instance), but what he took from Janet's article was information of obvious interest in a study of *Jude*. He made entries on *la folie à deux*, or contagious rather than hereditary madness, on *le dédoublement du moi*, on hypnotic suggestion, and on *la folie suicide*.

At about the same time as he made notes on those psychological phenomena, Hardy was reading a book which was to give him a great deal more material, for *Jude* and for other works, on the operations of the human mind. The book was *Natural Causes and Supernatural Seemings* by Henry Maudsley (1835–1916), who left his name, and a founding grant, to the psychiatric teaching hospital in the University of London. He published the book in 1886 (the year in which Freud returned to Vienna after spending a year in Paris with Charcot—who is mentioned in Janet's article —at work on hypnosis and gathering information which was to be important in the evolution of psychoanalytic theory). By the time Hardy seems to have made his notes from Maudsley's book, it was in its second edition.

Maudsley examines 'causes of belief in the supernatural' or, as he puts it elsewhere, sources of error in seeing and believing. His purpose, his 'scientific obligation', was to argue against supernatural explanations for phenomena: 'That many theories concerning the supernatural have had their origin and sustenance in the operations of disordered mind cannot be disputed' he says (162). For him, Mohammed and St. Paul were epileptics, St. Theresa the victim of hallucination. The appearance of supernatural effects from natural causes appealed to Hardy during the years in which *Jude* took shape. 'The Withered Arm', for instance, leaves it open to the superstitious reader to believe in a supernatural cause of the young wife's withering and of her death, and Hardy's reading of Maudsley on the supernatural's relation to 'disordered mind' is directly relevant to the religious crisis to which he submits Sue Bridehead at the end of *Jude*. Maudsley's book supplied, however, more than that to *Jude the Obscure*. To his interest in 'supernatural seemings', Hardy added another, amply reflected in his notebook, in the mental operations Maudsley details. Maudsley devotes two-thirds of his book to what he calls the 'Fallacies Incident to the Natural Operations of Sound Mind' and to 'Unsound Mental Actions'. He sees the healthy human mind as in development, carrying with it still remainders from its earlier stages and so subject, naturally, to errors from 'causes which are habitually working in human thought now, and which were more largely operative in its more primitive stages of development.' (2) The healthy human mind, he says, makes mistakes in observation—that is, in perception—and in reasoning, and it is propelled into error by the irrepressible activity of the imagination, which is, he says, 'a prolific faculty or function always eager and pleased to exercise itself'. The imagination, says Maudsley, always 'hastens to fill the voids of knowledge with fictions' (116). The activities of unsound mind to which Maudsley gives his attention are hallucinations and illusions, which he sees as distortions of sense, and mania and delusions, which he sees as overpowerings of reason. Although he has strong views about what constitutes unsound mental action, Maudsley allows that 'to run a distinct line of division between sound and unsound mental functions, however desirable in theory, is impossible in fact' (149).

Like Hardy in *Jude*, Maudsley writes with an eye to future generations. That is a natural consequence of his evolutionary views: 'wiser descendants shall wonder', he writes, 'to think that rational beings could ever have been so very irrational as their forefathers' (8). ('When people of a later age look back upon the barbarous customs and superstitions of the times that we have the unhappiness to live in,' says Sue, 'what *will* they say!' 258–59) Maudsley's view of irrationality and madness is linked to his developmental view of the brain: these phenomena are a droppingback on the ladder, a 'reversion to the old belief of savages' (161). Maudsley could not have believed in a family curse, but he *did* believe in 'in-born structure', in the inherited tendency to diseased mental function.

Hardy copied passages from *Natural Causes* . . . into eight pages of his notebook. He made entries on the near-impossibility of advancing human thought or action beyond the social norm; on the causes of error in normal perception; on the inheritance of neurotic tendencies; on the constitution of the brain; on the closeness of imagination to delusion; and, at length, on hallucination. The relevance to *Jude the Obscure* of Hardy's reading in Maudsley is immediately apparent. In *Jude*, Hardy represents every one of those subjects, and though the novel does not offer passages of conventional analysis of motives, it does provide dramatisations of its characters' states of mind which amount to psychological analysis and which use as their theoretical base the psychology Hardy found in Maudsley. 'Every one knows how many tricks the mind plays in sleep,' says Maudsley, 'but few persons realize, until they observe themselves closely and reflect on what they observe, how many like tricks it plays habitually in waking life' (31). In *Jude*, his novel of 'dreams' and 'visions', Hardy shows some of the tricks of the waking mind.

Hardy's very conception of Jude and Sue is deeply affected by his reading in psychology. *Natural Causes and Supernatural Seemings* describes the psychology of the kind of brain which is the 'fit instrument which nature provides . . . to prevent stagnation' (209) and shows how that psychology can produce a 'tragedy of unfulfilled aims':

> So great is the weight of tradition, custom, habit, conformity, enveloping and penetrating the mental being, and pressing like an atmosphere on every thought and feeling, that the vast multitude of persons are unable even to conceive the notion of deviation; and the majority of the small minority who can be other-minded dare not . . . what courage [an innovator] must display in facing the questioning surprise, the silent disapproval, or the open ridicule and remonstrance, of all those who, because of his difference from them, regard him as eccentric or lunatic!
> (208)

The mind which will dare to be different, says Maudsley, is not the 'well-balanced brain, adjusted aptly to its surroundings' (209). It is an 'inspired rashness' or a 'certain divine impetuosity' (208) which may bring about change in human history, though the change, Maudsley says in a passage Hardy transcribed, may be 'at a ruinous cost to the individual.' (196) Hardy copied the following passage into his notebook:

> . . . A narrow intensity of temperament, whereby a notion of a particular kind is cherished with exclusive fervour, without regard to limitations [in the actual] & pushed with eager energy without regard to occasions & hindrances, is sometimes a very useful practical force in the world . . .
>
> (cf. Maudsley, 152)

He also transcribed this sentence: 'For evolutional [originality], a brain is required wh. is not in well-balanced equipoise of faculties & circumstances.' The idea of imbalance in the faculties derives from Maudsley's conception of the constitution of the brain. It is a confederation of faculties, he says in a passage Hardy took down, 'inseparably connected with their nervous substrata . . . these are disposed & united in the brain in the most orderly fashion . . . forming in the sum a complex aggregate or confederation of nerve-junctions & nerve-tracts, each of wh. is capable of more or less independ.^{t} action . . .' In the well-adjusted, healthy, and unoriginal brain, the faculties move together in a well-oiled action; in a brain fit for 'evolutional originality', as in a brain in a state of disintegration, the balance is disturbed.

132

Those ideas went into the making of Jude and Sue. On each of them, Hardy confers the imbalance requisite to social reform. Each is tormented by inconsistency: Sue shows a 'colossal inconsistency' (210), Jude himself is 'dazzingly inconsistent', each displays a 'curious double nature' (251). Hardy combines Jude's imagination with what Jude describes, when he puts his case on 'Judgment Day', as 'impulses—affections—vices perhaps they should be called [which] were too strong not to hamper a man without advantages' (393). He gives Sue an 'intellect [which] sparkles like diamonds' (276) and a nervous frailty which is partly the weakness of her sex and partly the outcome of the family curse, the 'in-born structure' of heredity. Jude and Sue are conceived as nature's instruments, shaped to strive against what Maudsley calls, with the wonderful detachment of science, 'the medium': the brain of the evolutional original, according to Maudsley, is 'possessed with a sort of inspired or instinctive unrest, and is prone to discharge itself in the disruption of the old medium.' (209) To this 'supersensitive couple' (367), Hardy gives the fate of 'pioneers' (425) in a world in which the medium is obdurate. 'It takes two or three generations to do what I tried to do in one', Jude says in his self-justifying, self-judging speech on 'Humiliation Day' (393). 'Why was I half wiser than my fellow-women?' Sue asks, 'and not entirely wiser!' (408) The symbolism of Jude's and Sue's first meeting—at the Martyrs' Memorial—is not obscure.

The major contrast of the novel Hardy said was 'all contrasts' is that between the opposing intellectual developments of Jude and Sue. The two halves of the 'one person split in two' (276) describe, in their developments, the antithetical possibilities of their 'instinctive unrest'. Jude moves through what Maudsley calls a 'process of progressive disillusioning' (243), a correction of error in 'seeing and believing'. Sue moves back into guilt and fear and orthodoxy, suffers a 'reversion to the old belief of savages' (Maudsley, 161). Jude enacts his freedom from dogma when he burns his theology books; Sue enacts her retreat to orthodoxy when she burns her embroidered nightgown.

In Jude, Hardy traces a familiar though paradoxical path, the 'coming to know' of the novel form. He moves from stage to stage of disillusion, shedding 'husks of prejudice', primitive remainders, so that his loss, theoretically at least, is gain. At the end of the book, Jude sends his early deceiver, Vilbert, packing down the stairs, and he looks into a light which makes darkness plain. The bitter light is both his triumph and his defeat. Hardy's repeated imagery of ascent—the boy's toiling up the 'long and tedious ascent to the downs' (16), the ladders, the lantern of the Sheldonian—suggests Jude's aspiration and his climbing to intellectual clarity. His helpless proneness at the end of the book, when his disillusioning is complete, is the image of his destructive triumph. Jude's intellectual clarity makes him the victim of what Maudsley calls 'the transcendent irony of fate—that the complete accomplishment of disillusion shall be the close of development and the beginning of degeneration.' (367) In that sentence, Maudsley has in mind the development of mankind, but he quotes Amiel on the similar development in the individual: ' "La désillusion complète serait l'immobilité absolue. Celui qui a déchiffré le secret de la vie finie, qui en a lu le mot, est sorti du monde des vivants, il est mort de fait." ' (367n.) Jude's disillusioning is an intellectual triumph, but he dies of fact.

In Sue, Hardy gives the reverse of Jude's intellectual development: 'she was once a woman', Jude says to the Widow Edlin,

> whose intellect was to mine like a star to a benzoline lamp: who saw all *my* superstitions as cobwebs that she could brush away with a word. Then bitter affliction came to us, and her intellect broke, and she veered round to darkness.
>
> (484)

'Where is your reason?' Jude asks Sue. 'You seem to have suffered the loss of your faculties!' (470) And when he says that he cannot understand her 'blindness' to her 'old logic', she replies:

> Ah, dear Jude, that's because you are like a totally deaf man observing people listening to music. You say 'What are they regarding? Nothing is there.' But something is . . . I am convinced I am right—that I see the light at last.
>
> (424)

Jude sees perfectly well what has happened to Sue: 'Our ideas were fifty years too soon to be any good to us. And so the resistance they met with brought reaction in her' (484). The imagery of treacherous light has shifted: Sue's final deceiving light is the counterbalance to Jude's early deceived vision.

Seen in Maudsley's terms, Jude's imagination is an ambiguous benefit. On the positive side, Maudsley saw the imagination as 'forward-reaching', the 'incentive and initiative of progress'. 'What but imagination', he asks, 'has enticed and stirred men to enter upon the unknown, the vague, vast and mysterious, by presenting to them images of distinct paths and rich territories there'? (122–23) On the negative side, he thought that the imagination produced 'multitudinous errors' (122) in belief. The man in the grip of an intense notion was, he said, and Hardy noted the passage, 'constitutionally incapable of weighing evidence . . . commits all the faults of bad observation and reasoning' (cf. Maudsley, 152). 'Venturing in search of those paths and domains' suggested by the imagination, a man is likely to find himself 'beguiled and deceived' (123), faced with 'hard and dreary realities' (124) of a world uncoloured by his own vision. He may, in the process of proving his own deception, have 'made new paths . . . , laid out definite districts, and appropriated the country for use and profit' (123). He will have achieved that, of course, at the cost of his vision.

Hardy gives Jude that ambiguous power. It is Jude's imagination which moves him, stirring him by the image of Christminster as rich and mysterious territory, and which is the basic condition of his tragically unfulfilled aims. Jude's imagination leads him into beguilements and deceptions, and his blindness is therefore a condition of his vision. His steady escape from blindness, his accumulation of proof of his own deceptions, implies the steady impairment of his 'vision'.

As Maudsley conceives it, the 'blindness' of a man of vision is not merely metaphorical. What Maudsley means, when he says that a man of vision cannot see, is that the organs of perception are over-ruled by an idea. *Natural Causes* . . . like Maudsley's earlier *Common Source of Error in Seeing and Believing*, and his 'Hallucinations of the Senses', which appeared in the *Fortnightly*, treat the issue of disturbed perception. It is very likely that Hardy would have read Maudsley's *Fortnightly* article (since he read that journal regularly) and so have learned, before reading Maudsley's book, of the psychiatrist's view of the 'process by which we perceive'.[11] Under the heading, 'Hallucination', Hardy copied several passages from *Natural Causes*. In one of the passages he transcribed, Maudsley describes the operation of normal perception:

> A person for the most part sees only a very small part of that
> wh. he thinks he sees, the mind contributing, by virtue of its
> former experience, what is necessary to fill up the image . . .
> Of ordinary perception it may truly be said, then, that it is in
> great part illusion . . .
>
> (cf. Maudsley, 188–89)

Maudsley goes on: 'no one . . . actually has nearly so much of
the objective experience as he seems to have . . . he sees a part
only, which, being sufficient to suggest the whole, is the symbol
of much that he does not see, but takes for granted.' (189) What
Maudsley says in *Natural Causes* he had put more directly before: a person 'sees what he believes he sees, not necessarily that
which really is'.[12] 'This dominion of the idea over the sense, which
has its consummate effect in the production of hallucination,'
according to Maudsley, 'is really the most fruitful source of error
and defect in common observation, an ever active, and never to
be neglected, cause of fallacy.'[13] Hallucination, Maudsley says, is
closely linked to the normal activity of the imagination, and error
creeps into human thought through the 'easy opening' (189) that
is provided by the fact that the ordinary perception consists very
largely of filling in the blanks between sensations with ready-
made information. Powerful suggestion or false experience can
over-rule the truth.

To Hardy, whose interest in visual perception is, as Norman
Page shows, a distinguishing feature of his work, those passages
from Maudsley must have exercised a particular appeal. Perhaps
they account for the fact that it is in *Jude* that Hardy makes
most evident the 'metaphorical function of vision and blindness,
modes of seeing and failing to see, interpretation and misinter-
pretation of the visible'.[14]

What Maudsley wrote on perception and hallucination, and
what Hardy read in *Natural Causes* and elsewhere on suggestion,
constitute background to Jude's power of 'vision' in general, and
to his first, confirming 'ecstasy or vision' (19, 30), the birth of
his 'ruling passion' (401), in particular. Jude approaches his vision
of Christminster with intense desire: 'he prayed', we are told,
'that the mist might rise.' (19) When the mist does dissolve, and
the city shows itself, it shows itself in motion: the vision seems
to drift across the sky, the veil lifting, the veil descending, the
'vague city' resembling, as Sue might have put it, 'a stanza or

melody composed in a dream' (19–20, 413). It is not for a moment static, and its motion disturbs our sense, so that when Hardy offers, at the end of the visionary paragraph, the possibility that what Jude saw was 'miraged', he settles on a word for the instability of reality we have already seen. The ambiguity of the visionary passage comes from its unceasing movement. It is as though what we had seen was perception enacted, as though we had watched Jude's mind filling in the blanks between sensations. That Jude fills the blanks with poetic information, with a description of the New Jerusalem, confirms the impression that 'the spectator' who 'gazed on and on' has made his own vision. 'A proved efficient cause of hallucination,' Hardy read in Maudsley,

> is a vividly conceived idea which is so intense, and so isolated thereby from transmission of its energy along the tracks of other ideas in reflection, that it is projected outwards into what seems an actual perception—in the case of sight, for example, a mental image so vivid as to become a visual image; in the case of hearing, an idea so intense as to become a voice.
> (191)

Jude's vision leaves him disturbed: like a 'supernatural seeming', it has troubled his deepest, most primitive imagination. He 'started homewards at a run,' Hardy writes, 'trying not to think of giants', since he 'knew that he had grown out of belief in these horrors' (20).

By the time Jude actually arrives in Christminster, he is firmly committed to his transmuting vision, actively engaged in the suppression of information that does not suit the ideal: when the bell sounds a hundred and one strokes, Jude revises the number to the perfect hundred; when an object does not fit the harmony of the whole, Jude allows himself not to see it (91). That is because the vision is more real than the real city. 'That the hallucination should be seen more vividly, and seem more real sometimes than the actual object,' Maudsley wrote, as a footnote to the above passage on hallucination, 'is not surprising when we reflect that perception is always an internal experience' (191n.). What Jude is engaged in when he actually reaches the City of Light is the 'voluntary intensification of ideas unto the pitch of hallucination' ('Literary Notebook'; cf. Maudsley, 196). Hardy copied this further passage from Maudsley under his heading, 'Hallucination':

Mental represent[n] so intense as to become mental presentation is a faculty of mind apt especially to be met with among certain artists . . . 'You have only to work up imagination to the state of vision & the thing is done' (Blake). Dr. Wigan (*Duality of the Brain.* Alf[d] Wigan, M.D.) relates . . . skilful painter . . . required only one sitting . . . 'When a sitter came I looked at him attentively for ½ an hour, sketching' . . . Afterw[ds] placed the chair, imagined man in it, referred to the imaginary figure, & worked as if he had been there. 'When I looked at the chair I saw the man.' . . . After a time he lost the power of disting[g] between imagin[y] & real . . . became insane.

(cf. Maudsley, 194)

At Christminster, Jude consciously summons his vision. The real people disappear, and he composes himself—puts himself into a trance, almost—for his act of imagination:

> Knowing not a human being there, Jude began to be impressed with the isolation of his own personality, as with a self-spectre, the sensation being that of one who walked but could not make himself seen or heard. He drew his breath pensively, and, seeming thus almost his own ghost, gave his thoughts to other ghostly presences with which the nooks were haunted.
>
> (92)

This time, we are certain that the spectator has made the vision: Jude has prepared himself for years for just this venture. Summoning his ghosts, 'Jude found himself speaking out loud, holding conversations with them as it were, like an actor in a melodrama who apostrophizes the audience on the other side of the footlights' (94). Like the artist, Jude is capable of 'mental representation so intense as to become mental presentation'. His abandonment to illusion is by now complete, and it is voluntary. The night he learned that he must marry Arabella, he learned that he believed his 'idea of her' to be 'of most consequence, not Arabella herself' (65). By the time he arrives in Christminster, Jude prefers to occupy the city when the real people are in bed, to watch Sue without being seen. Jude's story is composed of linked moments of vision or hallucination and of his painful correction, from the information derived from experience, of their distortions of the truth. Like the visionary of Maudsley's psychology, he is 'constitutionally incapable of weighing evidence . . . commits all the faults of bad observation and reasoning'.

138

Hardy deals with the distortion of reality in Sue's story no less than in Jude's, but Jude's distortion of sense, his imaginative revision of its data, is altogether more appealing than Sue's distortion of reason in her bleak progress from clarity and courage to breakdown and fear. She is, as she says, 'driven out of [her] mind by things' (409). Her defeat deprives her of Jude's tragic status. Jude's tragedy depends upon his growth in consciousness. It is given to him to correct his vision and to look with direct eyes into his mistakes:

> He fell asleep for a short while, and when he awoke it was as if he had awakened in hell. It *was* hell—'the hell of conscious failure,' both in ambition and in love. He thought of that previous abyss into which he had fallen before leaving this part of the country; the deepest deep he had supposed it then; but it was not so deep as this. That had been the breaking in of the outer bulwarks of his hope; this was of his second line.
>
> (147)

Sue is denied that kind of awareness. Her fate depends upon the development of her primitive unawareness. It is the victory of her nerves.

The 'nerves' which seemed to an early reviewer of Jude to qualify Sue Bridehead as the 'first delineation in fiction of . . . the woman of the feminist movement' prepare her from the beginning for her final abandonment of independent choice.[15] She is seen as a 'pert little thing . . . with her tight-strained nerves' (131), as 'all . . . nervous motion' (105), as an 'ethereal, fine-nerved, sensitive girl' (263). Like Jude's, Sue's personal strength is an ambiguous benefit. The 'fine nerves' which make her sensitive constitute her exceptional vulnerability, and just as he shows the stages in Jude's disillusioning, Hardy shows the steps in Sue's weakening for the 'mental volte-face' (429) which is her defeat. Hardy shows these stages in language which gives slightly more weight to their psychological than to their personal emotional character. After Sue and Phillotson agree to live separately in the same house, for instance, 'the irksomeness of their position worked on her temperament, and the fibres of her nature seemed strained like harp-strings' (271). When she actually leaves Phillotson and joins Jude, her behaviour is marked by 'discontinuity' (287), the cause of which, as will shortly appear, is nervous. When the disaster of the children's deaths occurs, 'Sue's nerves utterly gave way . . . throwing her into a convulsive agony which knew no abatement.' (405) Finally, when she sacrifices herself on 'the altar of what she was pleased to call her principles', her nerves, we are told, have made their outrage visible on her body: 'the strain on her nerves had preyed upon her flesh and bones, and she appeared smaller in outline than she had formerly done' (445). Sue's shrunken outline is not merely physical, for by the time she had decided to go back to Phillotson, to allow the triumph of orthodoxy, she had already become 'such a mere cluster of nerves that all initiatory power seemed to have left her' (434).

Sue's nervous frailty is perhaps partly a consequence of her sex ('If he had been a woman', Jude thinks, 'he must have screamed under the nervous tension which he was now undergoing' 148), but it is derived chiefly from her inheritance. Jude shares the family curse, of course: he becomes the hanged man. But it is in Sue that Hardy works out the theme of hereditary frailty, and it is a theme for which he found support in Dr. Maudsley's book.

Hardy's transcriptions from Maudsley make two points in explanation of Sue's final delusion. The first accounts for the 'discontinuity' of her behaviour under stress: 'The mind is not a single function or faculty,' Maudsley wrote, 'but a confederation . . . In hallucination & illusion a certain tract of the brain has taken on a morbid function. In brains with a predisposition to insanity the confederate centres are loosely bound together, more apt to act separately . . .' ('Literary Notebook'; cf. Maudsley, 156, 168). The second point in explanation of Sue's behaviour is Maudsley's account of the relation to inheritance of an imbalance in the mental faculties:

> It is probable that the extraordinary states of apparent mental disintegration are owing to the separate or irregular function of certain mental nerve-tracts & to the coincidental suspension of the functions of all the rest . . .
> [This irregularity is often] the individual's evil heritage from a line of ancestral development . . .
> ('Literary Notebook'; cf. Maudsley, 314, 315)

Everybody, Hardy transcribed, 'in the main lines of his thoughts, feelings & conduct, really recalls the experiences of his forefathers.' (cf. Maudsley, 318). Sue's inheritance is that of the mad wife of the hanged man.

Sue's flight to religion is, in both Maudsley's terms and her own, when she has a flash of truth, a step backwards, a 'reversion to the old belief of savages'. 'I am getting as superstitious as a savage!' she says in a moment of recoil from her idea that 'the ancient wrath of the Power above us has been vented on us' (413, 414). 'You threw off old husks of prejudices', Jude says to her 'and taught me to do it; and now you go back upon yourself!' (424). Hardy gives Sue the kind of delusion in which, Maudsley says,

> the afflicted person is in a state of abject fear and misery, full of vague apprehensions of evil to come, incapable of heart in his affairs or of hope of them, apathetic, inert, and despairing, and sure that he is, or is about to be, overwhelmed by some unspeakable calamity—perhaps it is that he is forsaken by God and given over to eternal damnation.
>
> (231)

Sue's calamity, of course, is not imagined, but her self-punishing fantasy of a 'persecutor' (413) is as much an exercise of her primitive imagination as Jude's boyish fears of Herne the Hunter or of giants. She does not share in his 'process of progressive disillusioning' (Maudsley, 243).

Hardy's use of that psychological material in *Jude* suggests several points. The first is that he cared a great deal that the 'fable' of this novel should be 'realistic', its 'tragedy' inevitable. That he gathered information for his portraits from contemporary medical authority should have ensured the first, and the character of the psychological theory which gave Jude and Sue their mental gifts and limitations did ensure the latter. It was very possibly Hardy's reading in psychology, furthermore, which enabled him in *Jude* so successfully to combine, as Barbara Hardy says, 'animated and realistic psychology' and 'ideological pattern',[16] not only because it provided matter for the characters but also because it took a specific attitude towards its matter. In what he read, Hardy found not only information, but also the attitude of experiment; and to a certain extent Jude and Sue are shaped for experiment, as Jude's Remembrance Day speech makes clear: 'It is a difficult question, my friends, for any young man—the question I had to grapple with, and which thousands are weighing at the present moment in these uprising times' (392–3).

At the same time as it served the realism of *Jude the Obscure*,

141

Hardy's reading in psychology was very much at the service of the poetry. In Maudsley, and possibly in others, Hardy found scientific fact, or at least scientific theory, to support the particularly ambiguous dominant metaphor of his novel. Like the symbols of 'An Imaginative Woman', the far more complex symbols of *Jude* are supported by information from 'medical practitioners and other observers'. What Maudsley says about hallucination (as the overwhelming of the data of observation by a powerfully held conception) provides a reason for seeing the most vividly imaged passages of *Jude* as passages of pure psychological realism.

It seems likely that such a possibility would have pleased Hardy in the years in which he worked on *Jude*—and produced *The Well-Beloved* and the stories in which the real and the spectral are often confused. What Maudsley said about perception and hallucination, furthermore, seems likely to have had particular interest to Hardy as a writer who declined to accept an easy distinction between realistic and non-realistic writing. At about the time he was reading Janet and Maudsley, Hardy was making entries, sometimes extended, on the debate in France about the opposing claims of realism or naturalism and symbolism. The debate as he recorded it (usually in his own translations, often in the original French) reveals itself as purely a literary version of the same question of perception. Hardy copied the following, for instance, about naturalism:

> All the processes of naturalism have only for their object, in the novel as in the painting, the putting the artist on his guard against the thousand means he has of deforming the reality . . .[17]

On the other hand, the following on symbolism:

> [The symbolists hold that] between external nature & ourselves there are 'correspondences', latent 'affinities', mysterious 'identities', & that it is only so far as we seize them that, penetrating to the interior of things, we can truly approach the soul of them.[18]

One of the powerful themes of *Jude*, and the central issue in other things Hardy wrote while *Jude* was in preparation, is the power of the mind to make its own reality. Jude persists in his 'gigantic error', Jocelyn Pierston in his 'gigantic fantasy', Joshua Halborough in his 'forward visions', and all of them, like Mrs.

Marchmill, the 'imaginative woman', make their lives take a shape which is determined by their dreams. Maudsley's book on the operations of the sound and unsound mind may well have appealed to Hardy for the freshness of its inquiry into the relation of the perceiving, imagining subject to the world. Hardy's first notebook entry from *Natural Causes* is the following:

> To every one a *thing* is neither more nor less than what he *thinks* it—in effect, a *think*; & to think a new thing he must first use the old thought. How can he do otherwise before new experience has enabled him to organize a new *think*? The old *thing* or *think* represents object *plus* subject; a new thing, therefore, is no thing to him until it is asselfed in a think, for until then it is object *minus* subject.
>
> (cf. Maudsley, 33)

That passage, in spite of its cumbersome expression, makes it clear that Hardy's interest in Maudsley's psychology is by no means remote from his aesthetic thought.

NOTES

1 Hardy, *Personal Writings*, ed. Harold Orel (1967), pp. 134–38.
2 Hardy, 'Preface to the First Edition', *Jude the Obscure* (1912; repr. 1920), p. viii.
3 'The Profitable Reading of Fiction', *Personal Writings*, p. 114.
4 'Preface', *Wessex Tales*, introduction and notes by F. B. Pinion (1976), p. 11.
5 'Preface to the First Edition', *Jude the Obscure* (1912; repr. 1920), p. vii. Further references to the novel, given parenthetically in the text, are to this edition.
6 Hardy, *Life's Little Ironies* and *A Changed Man*, ed. F. B. Pinion (1977) [p. 10].
7 *The Older Hardy* (1978), p. 2.
8 *Life's Little Ironies*, p. 15. Cf. *Revue des Deux Mondes* 90 (1 Nov. 1888), 213–26.
9 The passage is transcribed here as it appears in the notebook. This quotation is from 'Literary Notebook—II'; all other notebook passages quoted below are from 'Literary Notebook—I'.
10 'Une Chaire de Psychologie', *Revue des Deux Mondes*, 86 (1 Apr. 1888), 518–49.
11 'Hallucinations of the Senses', *Fortnightly Review*, 24 (1 Sept. 1878), 374.
12 *Common Source of Error in Seeing and Believing* (1881), p. 6.

13 *Ibid.*, p. 12.
14 Norman Page, *Thomas Hardy* (1977), p. 82. This book gives a full analysis of visual perception in Hardy's works.
15 Hardy, 'Postscript', *Jude*, pp. xi–xii.
16 Barbara Hardy, *The Appropriate Form* (1964), p. 70.
17 The quotation is from F. Brunetière, 'Les *Nouvelles* de M. de Maupassant', *Revue des Deux Mondes*, 89 (1 Oct. 1888), 693–704.
18 F. Brunetière, 'Symbolistes et Décadens', *op. cit.* (note 5).

8

Stories in Stones

by PHILIPPA TRISTRAM

Much of life is passed within four walls, whose presence, with the objects they enclose and the prospects upon which they open, can assume a variety of meanings for those who inhabit them. But the degree of their importance to the individual novelist is unpredictable, and their significance, being partly dependent upon theme, even more so. Interiors are given little attention by Defoe, though isolated objects may be emphasised. Through much of Richardson rooms are interchangeable prisons, and furniture places of concealment for crow quills or designing suitors. Houses in Jane Austen indicate qualities of life, though rooms may matter less than position in them, signifying the proximity or distance of their occupants. In Dickens domestic contexts so upstage their owners that subsequent novelists can no longer afford to ignore them; thus Kingsley's hero, Alton Locke, admits 'I have as yet given no description of the old eccentric's abode—an unpardonable omission, I suppose, in these days of Dutch painting and Boz'.[1]

Hardy is by no means immune to Dickens's influence, especially in his early writing,[2] but it is significant that his second novel, *Under the Greenwood Tree*, should be subtitled 'A Rural Painting of the Dutch School' rather than 'A Dutch Interior'. It is natural for a reader of the Wessex novels, those of 'character and environment' in Hardy's definition,[3] to envisage figures in landscape rather than withindoors; whilst in earlier tales buildings themselves tend to merge with their natural settings. The church at Endelstow, 'cutting up into the sky from the very tip of the hill . . . seemed a monolithic termination, of one substance with the ridge, rather than a structure raised thereon' (*PBE* 22). To restore such a building appeared to be 'a not less incongruous act

than to set about renovating the adjoining crags themselves'
(Pref.). At times it seems that Hardy's landscapes subsume both
men and their less frail constructions: 'But compare the age of
the building with that of the marble hills from which it was
drawn!' he writes of Tintern Abbey in 1873 (*LTH* 93). Yet in
1876 he notes in his diary:

> An object or mark raised or made by man on a scene is worth
> ten times any such formed by unconscious Nature. Hence clouds,
> mists, and mountains are unimportant beside the wear of a
> threshold, or the print of a hand.
>
> (*LTH* 116)

The habitations of men move him more than 'unconscious
Nature',[4] as much, at times, as the fortunes of men themselves:
a ruined house is 'a hideous carcase . . . in a green landscape, like
a skull on a table of dessert' (*LTH* 114). 'Dust thou art and to
dust thou shalt return' is a truth as relevant to buildings as to
men. Like Dickens's, Hardy's houses have a being of their own,
but their life is quieter and more separate from their occupants,
as though they recall their origin in earth and anticipate their
return to it.

That strongly responsive sense of stone is developed largely
in the Wessex novels; in the earlier works of 'ingenuity' or
'romance' Hardy's attitude to buildings is objectively professional, predictably so since he was a practising architect at the
outset of his career as a writer, and undecided between the two
professions. The writer moreover never lost the architect's enthusiasm; visits to Cathedrals, even in his final years, regularly
punctuate the *Life*, whilst within weeks of his death his second
wife records: 'He said that if he had his life over again he would
prefer to be a small architect in a country town, like Mr. Hicks at
Dorchester, to whom he was articled' (*LTH* 443). The architect's
vocabulary is at times obtrusive in his prose: the Duke of Hamp-
tonshire owns 'a castellated mansion . . . ornamented with make-
believe bastions and machicolations' (*GND* 218); Athelhall derives
its name from the central room 'covered with a fine open-timbered
roof, whose braces, purlins, and rafters made a brown thicket of
oak overhead' (*CM* 40); Enckworth Court presents a contrast
in styles, 'the hooded windows, simple string-courses, and random masonry of the Gothic workman, stood elbow to elbow with
the equal-spaced ashlar, architraves, and fasciae of the Classic

addition' (*HE* 345). An architect's prejudice may also intrude: 'the mullioned and transomed Elizabethan' is regarded as 'that never-to-be-surpassed style for the English country residence' (*CM* 28); Salisbury Cathedral is 'the most homogeneous pile of mediaeval architecture in England';[5] the 'gurgoyle' of Weatherbury Church, whose 'doings' desecrate the grave of Fanny Robins, prompts the comment that 'there is not truer criterion of the vitality of any given art-period than the power of the master-spirits of that time in grotesque' (*FMC* 369). Hardy's sketchbook, with its punctiliously accurate drawings, is never far away; Giles Winterbourne's view of Sherton Abbas is not his own description:

> The churches, the abbey, and other mediaeval buildings on this clear bright morning having the linear distinctness of architectural drawings, as if the original dream and vision of the conceiving master-mason were for a brief hour flashed down through the centuries to an unappreciative age. Giles saw their eloquent look on this day of transparency, but could not construe it.
>
> (*W* 41)

Hardy's experience as an architect has however left its mark in ways more intrinsic on his novels of 'ingenuity' or 'romance and fantasy', which were written largely in the decade following his first publication. A number of his characters are architects, whilst the circumstances of an architect's life—uncertain social status, training, professional ethics and attitudes to restoration—are all employed in the interests of factual substance.[6] In these novels professional engagements pave the way to romance, but the architect's perception may also prompt a short story, as the dating of two houses does in 'The Duke's Reappearance'. In Hardy's later writing life as a poet, this early experience becomes a lyric theme; in 'The Heiress and the Architect', for example, the patron's expansive plans are reduced by the professional to smaller and smaller size, until she finally pleads for ' "Some narrow winding turret, quite mine own, / To reach a loft where I may grieve alone!" ' but even this quaint staircase is refused by 'the man of measuring eye' who requires space ' "To hale a coffined corpse adown the stairs" ' (*WP* 68). All houses reduce themselves to that final house.

Appropriately enough, architecture is more often the frame to events than their occasion. In his preface to *A Pair of Blue Eyes*,

Hardy explains 'that an imaginary history of three human hearts
. . . found in the ordinary incidents of such church renovations a
fitting frame for its presentation.' Such frames may however contrast with what they enclose, as the substantial securities of a
Georgian watering place do with 'A Committee Man of "The
Terror" ', a tale of the French Revolution. Contrasts such as these
are an invitation to symbolism. Enckworth Court presents a
fictitious façade where brick is veneered with freestone, and a hall
in which paint and plaster masquerade as marble: 'What was
honest in Enckworth Court was that portion of the original edifice
which still remained, now degraded to subservient uses' (HE 347).
Marriage to Lord Mountclere is, in many senses, a deceptive pretence at genuine materials, and Ethelberta's honest, though
humble, stock is put to menial use.[7] In Two on a Tower the social
difference, signified by Lady Constantine's mansion and Swithin's
thatched cottage, is literally transcended by the tower with its
telescope, where the two see their 'infinitesimal lives against the
stupendous background of the stellar universe' (Pref.). It is no
wonder that Hardy discerned in Gothic building certain principles of
literary structure, as the Life explains in a sustained analogy between architecture and poetry.[8] But the contrast between the solid-
ity of those structures and the frailty of the human lives which produce, and are then contained by them, later becomes a potent
lyric theme, verbally presented in 'Her Dilemma' and visually
illustrated in the early editions of Wessex Poems.[9] The two lovers,
one 'soon to die', are sketched like vertical effigies, dominated
above by a cross-section of pointed arches, emphasised below by
horizontal corpses beneath the floor of the church. From the first
such vivid images are not infrequent in the novels.[10] When Cyth-
erea marries Manston in Desperate Remedies, they leave the vestry
only to see, amongst the effigies 'damp and green with age . . .
sculptured in cadaverous marble' of the Aldclyffe chantry, the
living cadavre of the rejected lover Springrove 'almost hanging
to the monument' (DR 288).

The architect's experience proved a fruitful resource for Hardy
throughout his writing-life; yet one may at times feel, particularly in the novels of 'ingenuity' and 'romance', that the trained
analytic eye can be counter-productive. Whether focused on factual substance, or on structure, theme and symbol, the professional view seems unduly deliberate, distancing the reader from

the narrative. The studied detail of Springrove's figure in the chantry is melodramatic; the contrivedly symbolic structure of *Two on a Tower* forms a factitious bridge between two worlds; the division between a real professional and an unreal personal, life is felt in all those stories where architects figure. It is a paradox that the Wessex novels, from which autobiography in a direct sense is absent, should be characterised by that unmistakable intensity of personal feeling which is conspicuously absent in stories that bear a closer relation to events in Hardy's own life.[11] One may wonder then whether Hardy does not assume the architect's persona as a means of keeping intensities of feeling at a deliberate distance, and recall the invalid burgher at the oriel window with its 'raking view' who tells the story of 'A Changed Man' as it passes before him. This dispassionate spectator strongly contrasts with the emotional intensities of Lucetta and Elizabeth-Jane as they gaze through the windows of High Place Hall onto the market below. Hardy, so carefully private when writing the *Life* in his anonymity and his omission of painful incident, is private too in his suppression of genuine emotion in the autobiographical novels.

In 'A Dream or No', written after the death of his first wife, Emma, he wonders at his fascination with the Cornish village where he first encountered her:

> Why go to Saint-Juliot? What's Juliot to me?
> > Some strange necromancy
> > But charmed me to fancy
> That much of my life claims the spot as its key.
> > (*SC* 327)

The assistant whom Crickmay dispatched from Dorchester to rebuild the tower of that church must have been as unconcerned at the restoration as he was ignorant of the waiting Emma. He cannot at the time, any more than the fictitious Stephen at Endelstow, have regarded the workmen as 'six iconoclasts in white fustian';[12] but he was later to deplore such projects as the *Life* relates:

> Much beautiful ancient Gothic, as well as Jacobean and Georgian work, he was passively instrumental in destroying or altering beyond identification; a matter for his deep regret in later years.
> > (*LTH* 31)

But the loss of the tower of St. Juliot, along with the north aisle and transept, was a personal one: 'Hardy much regretted the obliteration in this manner of the church's history . . . the building as he had first set eyes on it having been so associated with what was romantic in his life', is his deceptively dry comment (*LTH* 79). When Hardy remarked that he was 'an awful imposter' as an architect (*LTH* 345), he may have been thinking less of his professional competence than of his emotional inhibitions, at least as a restorer. Buildings came to have too *much* meaning for him; to destroy them, in part or in whole, was like tampering with a living body.[18] Where their associations were personal, that repulsion was doubly intense: in the sequence of poems which follow Emma's death, place and person have a lacerating connection. 'We two kept house, the Past and I' Hardy writes of that period (*SC* 290), but, in relation to his early life, he was careful to avoid this 'strange, still housekeeping'; he can bring himself to visit his childhood home, or, in another mood, to 'haunt' it, but not to live in it (*WW* 820):

> . . . the rapt silence of an empty house
>> Where oneself was born,
>> Dwelt, held carouse
> With friends, is all of silences most forlorn!
>> (*WW* 826)

It was however *A Laodicean*, not *A Pair of Blue Eyes*, that Hardy described as the most autobiographical of all his novels;[14] it might have been truer to say that it was the most architectural. Like Hardy himself and Springrove in *Desperate Remedies*, George Somerset is divided between that profession and poetry (it is interesting that the fictional characters remain architects). A commission, in this case the restoration of Castle de Stancy, again proves the path to romance; but the profession is pivotal in this novel where it merely provides local colour in *Desperate Remedies* and the frame for *A Pair of Blue Eyes*. Somerset describes the proposed restoration of her castle to Paula 'much as a comparative anatomist reconstructs an antediluvian from fragmentary bones and teeth' (91), and that dispassionate professional eye informs the entire novel, from its detail to its structure. In demonstration of a lecture on dating, the hands of the two explore the undercutting of a capital—and join (102). The novel is structured around the old and the new. Paula, 'a personification of the modern spirit', is symbolised by the utilitarian Baptist chapel at which Pugin would shudder, and the tunnel her father constructed, 'a triumph of science' (whilst exploring *that* she betrays her feelings when she assumes that Somerset has been hit by a train). The old is the de Stancy family who provide Paula with a companion and an alternative suitor; these are represented by the castle, though both are brought up in the 'genuine roadside respectability' of Myrtle Villa, where kitchen activities are audible in the parlours. Paula's romantic nostalgia for the past is eventually overcome, the castle is burnt down, and the spiritual descendant of Archimedes espouses him of Pheidias —though not without regrets: ' "I wish my castle wasn't burnt, and I wish you were a de Stancy!" ' (500).

If the characters carry no conviction, neither does the castle.[15] It is never, like a street in Lisieux, a place 'for a mediaevalist to revel in, toss up his hat and shout hurrah in, send for his luggage, come and live in, die and be buried in' (460). It is as improbable as the Greek court that Paula wants to introduce within it; it has to be destroyed: ' "We'll build a new house beside the ruin, and show the modern spirit for evermore" ' (499–500). One may recall that in Hardy's last 'autobiographical' novel,[16] Jocelyn Pierston, in the revised ending, acquires 'some old moss-grown, mullioned Elizabethan cottages, for the purpose of pulling them down because they were damp; which he afterwards did, and built new ones with hollow walls, and full of ventilators' (205–6). The Well-Beloved, in all her manifestations, once inhabited cottages such as these; not only do crucial scenes occur within them, but they are part of that formative sense of place, for buildings on the Isle of Slingers are constructed from 'the huge lump of freestone which forms the peninsula' with 'slabs of stone as the common material for walls, roof, floor, pig-sty, stable-manger, door-scraper, and garden-style' (*TM* 314). Not content with the death of his obsession, Pierston levels the monuments of past passion.

Hardy was not averse to modernity: in 1863 he won a silver medal from the R.I.B.A. for an essay 'On the Application of Coloured Bricks and Terra Cotta to Modern Architecture', and the small Tite prize for his design of a country mansion.[17] Some twenty years later, an established writer, he moved to Max Gate, the new house near Dorchester which he designed himself. At a similar stage in her career Ethelberta exchanged a 'sailor's pretty cottage' for a 'porticoed and balconied dwelling', in order that the 'dash and pretentiousness' of this new development of villas for the professional classes, 'far beyond the mark of the old cottages', should impress Lord Mountclere (338). It is possible that an attempt at enfranchisement from his past prompted Hardy too; certainly Max Gate was not only new, but also unlike any other house in Dorchester at the time.[18] Yet a stronger motive has already been mentioned—Hardy's peculiar sensitivity to the presence in old houses, not only of his personal family history, but of other lives quite separate from his. Where Yeats treasured the company of ghosts in his Tower, Hardy retreated from them; just as Somerset wishes to build a new house 'unencumbered with the ghosts of an unfortunate line' preserving the ruined castle as a prospect only (L 499), so Hardy, in building Max Gate, used its windows to frame the bleak countryside south and west of Dorchester, with its intensity of personal and historic associations.[19] Ghosts, however, are resilient. Whilst sinking the well for the new house, Romano-British urns and skeletons were uncovered: 'Hardy and his wife found the spot was steeped in antiquity, and thought the omens gloomy; but they did not prove so, the extreme age of the relics dissipating any sense of gruesomeness.'[20] Their intrusion was only postponed, for not only did Emma come to haunt the silent rooms in Max Gate after her death in 1912,[21] but imagination pictured a future in the year 2,000 where another couple pretends to the same impunity:

'Some folk can not abide here
    But we—we do not care
Who loved, laughed, wept, or died here,
    Knew joy, or despair.'

(*LLE* 550)

But if Hardy felt the past was intolerable, he also found it essential. He tried at Max Gate to keep his distance from Wessex, but he chose to live in it. Writing on his refusal of an invitation to the United States, he describes his paradoxical aversion to a land which claims to be free 'From that long drip of human tears / Which peoples old in tragedy / Have left upon the centuried

years.' Though his 'own Being bear no bloom', as a writer he needs
that context 'scored with prints of perished hands' in order to
'trace the lives such scenes enshrine, / Give past exemplars
present room, / And their experience count as mine' (*PPP* 99–
100).

The essential reason why Hardy was a writer, not an architect,
surely lies here. In 1887 he noted:

> In a work of art it is the accident which *charms,* not the in-
> tention; *that* we only like and admire. Instance the amber tones
> that pervade the folds of drapery in ancient marbles, the dead-
> ened polish of the surfaces, the cracks and the scratches.
>
> (*LTH* 191)

This love of the accidental interfers with the professional view;
thus Somerset is distracted from measuring a church by the
warmth of its stone, from observing the castle by the mosses on
its walls, or its chapel by the markings on the pews.[22] Once these
incidentals became essential to him, Hardy would have had no
future as a restorer. His address in 1906 to the Society for the
Protection of Ancient Buildings, with its stress on their human
associations so often sacrificed to an 'artistic and architectural'
emphasis, must have caused some bewilderment.[23] The architect's weakness is, however, the artist's strength. When Hardy
praised Crabbe for his 'microscopic touch', 'giving surface without
outline, describing his church by telling *the colour of the lichens*'
(*LTH* 284), he indicated one of his own most memorable qualities, although his detail more usually has a human mark—'the
wear of a threshold or the print of a hand.' Worn steps, for
example, tell a multitude of tales. 'The sycamore tree . . . / With
its roots forming steps for the passers who care to call' makes
poetry of Stephen's story (*HS* 701); it also prompts a prose tale,
'Interlopers at the Knap', where its 'bared roots' form 'a convenient staircase from the road below to the front door of the
dwelling' (*WT* 181). Steps can inscribe for the lover a more immediate history: 'Christopher . . . imagined what a trifle of the depression worn in each step her feet had tended to produce'
(*HE* 94). Whether those associations are personal, or historic as
in paving worn to a gutter 'by the ebb and flow of feet . . . since
Tudor times' (*TM* 28), they haunt Hardy with the sense of un-
told stories:

Here is the ancient floor,
Footworn and hollowed and thin,
Here was the former door
Where the dead feet walked in.
(PPP 152)

These, not the constructs fabricated from them, are the true stories in stones. The most suggestive buildings are not necessarily the great ones; like Melbury's house in Little Hintock, 'of no marked antiquity, yet of a well-advanced age', quite modest dwellings may awake 'instincts of reminiscence more decidedly than ... remoter, and far grander, memorials':

> It was a house in whose reverberations queer old personal tales were yet audible if properly listened for; and not, as with those of the castle and cloister, silent beyond the possibility of echo.
> (W 26)

These places shelter a more ordinary life: despite its past consequence, Melbury's house is devoted to the business of a timber-merchant; an ancient inn gives a 'healthful stretch to the eyes' of an hostler, and Hardy is glad to see a mill at Wimbourne escape demolition 'having as great a repugnance to pulling down a mill where . . . they ground food for the body, as to pulling down a church where they ground food for the soul.'[24] His descriptions are convincing in their actuality, like that of Overcombe Mill which expresses at one end the practical humanity of the Love-days, 'a hard-worked house slipping into the river', at the other the relative cultivation of the Garlands whom they sustain, 'an idle, genteel place, half-cloaked with creepers . . . having no visible connection with flour' (TM 12). As Hardy notes in his preface of 1895 to Tess, his description of 'old English architecture . . . in this and its companion novels has been done from the real'; in that year he conducted the etcher, Macbeth Raeburn, around Wessex so that he could make sketches on the spot for frontispieces to the Wessex novels (LTH 267).

Tess herself, latterly so real to Hardy, was physically suggested only by a briefly glimpsed figure;[25] her true origin lies in the sense of place which permeates her, for 'beauty to her, as to all who have felt, lay not in the thing, but in what the thing symbolised.'[26] The house of her childhood seems 'part of her body and life . . . the slope of its dormers, the finish of its gables, the broken courses of brick which topped the chimney, all had something in common with her personal character' (446). Like their owners, houses may fall on evil days—with the illness of Joan 'stupefaction' comes over the 'features' of the Durbeyfield cottage—but they also have their own tragedies of circumstance. High Place Hall, though declaring ' "Blood built it, and Wealth enjoys it" ', has difficulty in claiming a tenant because it overlooks the market-place; Bathsheba's farm was once a manorial hall whose 'vital principle . . . had turned round inside its body to face the other way'; a thatched cottage on the new estate of the Stoke d'Urbervilles 'was indifferently turned into a fowl house', outraging the sensibilities of the descendants of bygone owners.[27] Aggregates of such modest houses form a composite sense of place, like the open doorways of Casterbridge which afford a view 'as through tunnels' of the 'mossy gardens at the back' with their 'floral blaze . . . backed by the crusted grey stone-work remaining from a yet remoter Casterbridge' (MC 71); or the 'tall stems of smoke' ascending from Little Hintock 'which the eye of imagination could trace downward to their root on quiet hearthstones,' the smoke itself becoming an image of the surrounding woodland (W 5).

Hardy's interiors often concentrate on those quiet hearthstones; with few exceptions, his houses do not gaze out through their windows, but turn in on themselves, away from the world of work.[28] The glazing of Geoffrey Day's cottage distorts that external life, 'scattering the spokes of cartwheels, and bending the straight fir-trunks into semicircles', and his firm separation from labour is marked by a large nail in the central beam 'used solely and constantly as a peg for Geoffrey's hat, the nail was arched by a rainbow-shaped stain, imprinted by the brim of the said hat when it was hung there dripping wet' (UGT 123). The genteel Mrs. Garland whitens over a related 'brown circle' in Miller Loveday's house, and eradicates records of past conviviality—the 'shining dirt imprinted along the back of the settle by the heads of countless jolly sitters' and 'the tawny smudges of bygone shoulders in the passage . . . without regard to a certain genial and historical value which they had acquired' (TM 138). The ear may attend without to the summons to work or sleep, as Marty South listens to the sparrows making their dawn way down the long holes in the thatch, and dusk is marked by the 'tread' of their return (*HS* 730). Leisure, however, deliberately insulates itself from diurnal tasks, making a room within a room around the fire. The chimney corner in Geoffrey Day's cottage, in common with 'most chimney corners in the neighbourhood', is large enough to accommodate himself, his wife, her chair and table 'without danger or even inconvenience from the heat of the fire'.[29] The settle gives definition to this room within a room, 'the necessary supplement to a fire so open that nothing less than a strong breeze will carry up the smoke':

> It is, to the hearths of old-fashioned cavernous fireplaces, what the east belt of trees is to the exposed country estate, or the north wall to the garden. Outside the settle candles gutter, locks of hair wave, young women shiver, and old men sneeze. Inside is Paradise. Not a symptom of a draught disturbs the air; the sitters' backs are as warm as their faces, and songs and old tales are drawn from the occupants by the comfortable heat, like fruit from melon-plants in a frame.
>
> (*RN* 166–7)

Such chimney corners as this one at Bloom's End are convivial centres of life; the house is a different place when Clym sits lonely there, listening to the wind, the rain, and the clicking of the garden gate 'as if invisible shapes of the dead were passing in on their way to visit him' (447). Those firelit occasions, often connected with Christmas, seem islanded images of a long-past childhood, whilst the older Hardy sits alone, like Clym attentive to the ghosts of the past. The creaking of a little table speaks 'Of one who gave you to me' (*LLE* 613), and he sees on the furniture

> . . . the hands of generations
>   That owned each shiny familiar thing
> In play on its knobs and indentations
>   And with its ancient fashioning
>   Still dallying.
>
> (*MV* 456)

When the awaited ghost returns she is is discouraged by the change in her 'once own quarters', and rejects him along with her former home, preferring the 'roomy silence' of her grave and the 'mute and manifold' company of the dead.[30] Not only the personal past but that of others can be haunting: 'The worst of taking a furnished house is that the articles in the rooms are saturated with the thoughts and glances of others', Hardy once complained (*LTH* 254). That presence is so vivid that it can destroy a later relationship:

> As if the intenser drama
>   Shown me there
> Of what the walls had witnessed
>   Filled the air,
> And left no room for later passion anywhere.
>
> (*SC* 342)

Sometimes Hardy turns upon these intrusive presences, accusing the universe itself of indifference; the tenant-for-life who remarks on his care for the house is told by the sun:

> 'Oh friend, it matters not, I say;
>   Bethink ye, I have shined
> On nobler ones than you, and they
>   Are dead men out of mind!'
>
> (*PPP* 148)

At others the indifference lies in the successors from which the house itself suffers: 'Their raw equipments, scenes, and says / Afflicted its memoried face' (*LLE* 609). But interlopers, like those who succeed the Durbeyfields, may be merely 'precious innocents', fortunate in their indifference to 'the histories of others, beside which the histories of these were but as a tale told by an idiot' (483). The indifference here lies in nature, in the Spring birds who sing 'as if they thought there was nobody missing in particular.' The birds at least should have remembered Tess, but even that Hardy can, on occasion, forgive:

> 'Life laughed and moved on unsubdued,
>   I saw that Old succumbed to Young:
> 'Twas well. My too regretful mood
>   Died on my tongue.'
>
> (*MV* 435)

Such places as the Durbeyfield cottage are expressive of unrecorded history, of inconspicuous lives like Anne Garland's, who reflects as she watches George III reviewing his troops that she is 'looking into the stream of recorded history, within whose banks the littlest things are great, and outside which she and the general bulk of the human race were content to live on as an un-reckoned, unheeded superfluity' (*TM* 114). But Hardy is moved by the record too; his native Bockhampton's 'bare list of owners' conjures 'a series of scenes!' These concern the immortals of history, like Mr. Pitt 'notorious for his shabby clothes', but the buildings themselves commemorate those 'superfluous' lives, whose aggregate is the subject of the social historian, for 'the nation of every country dwells in the cottage'.[31] The climate of the Poor-houses, which preceded the institution of workhouses, and once stood 'just at the corner turning down to the dairy', is recaptured by the tale their recollection prompts of an old pauper found there prostrate on the floor amongst scattered pennies and halfpennies, endeavouring to discover 'for once in his life' how it felt to roll in money (*LTH* 395). The ancient buildings of Casterbridge are 'a record of 500 years in stone', and their demolition violates the writing of history: 'Milton's well-known observation in his *Areopagitica*—"Almost as well kill a man as kill a good book"—applies not a little to a good old building; which is not only a book, but a unique manuscript that has to follow.'[32] In *The Laodicean* Havill accuses Paula of doing as much damage to the castle's 'history in stone' as all the battery of civil wars (122); even 'artifices of blending or restoration' are deplored, because they will hoodwink 'the seeker for history in stones . . . in time to come' (*HE* 345). When a child in the theatre at Fiesole gave Hardy 'an ancient coin / That bore the image of a Con-stantine', she raised for him 'better than all books' the 'swift perspective' of Europe's history under the Caesars.[33] For Hardy, true history is written in the three dimensions of that coin, or of the vast kitchen of Chene Manor where 'breakfasts had been cooked for John of Gaunt' (*GND* 65). Christopher Swetman's house, on the outskirts of King's Hintock, can still, though greatly altered, revive the Monmouth Rebellion; casual relics, like an 'outhouse door riddled with bullet-holes,' can renew the ten-sion of Napoleon's anticipated invasion.[34] County records, 'at first sight . . . as barren of any touch of nature as a table of logarithms', are transformed into 'palpitating drama' by 'the faintest tradition of what went on behind the scenes',[35] and their language may be preserved in describing their location: ' "a faire yellow freestone building, partly two and partly three storeys; a faire halle and parlour, both waynscotted; a faire dyning roome and withdrawing roome, and many good lodgings" '—too 'faire' altogether to house a bastard child (*CM* 243).

More remotely still, levelled ruins and earthworks may speak of times too distant for record in books or manuscripts, although the voices of their 'superfluous' occupants have long been 'silent beyond the possibility of echo.' Henchard's Casterbridge, already itself a memory when Hardy wrote the novel, is ghosted by 'old Rome in every street': 'It was impossible to dig more than a foot or two deep about the town fields and gardens without coming upon some tall soldier or other of the Empire, who had lain there in his silent unobtrusive rest for the space of fifteen hundred years' (83). Inhabitants who might have objected to skeletons more recent were undisturbed by a past so remote as that; but to the established antiquary such evidence is so valuable that he will even dig illegally to prove where the King's house stood, and whether the stronghold was Celtic as well as Roman (*CM* 182–3). Though the natives of Casterbridge consider those times 'so un-like the present' as to be irrelevant, the writer is sadly sensitive to their similarity:

> Then grinned the Ancient Briton
> > From the tumulus treed with pine:
> 'So, hearts are thwartly smitten
> > In these days as in mine!'
> > > (*SC* 370)

Of the antiquarian, however, he enquires 'What if it is Roman?' (*CM* 183). 'Quasi-scientific' history is 'mere charlatanism' to Hardy, 'because events and tendencies are not reasoned or vol-untary', but 'the outcome of *passivity*—acted upon by unconscious propensity' (*LTH* 168). It is a stream, not a tree, having no systematic development or organic growth: 'It flows on like a thunderstorm-rill by the road side; now a straw turns it this way, now a tiny barrier of sand that' (*LTH* 172).

Whatever its accidental course, that stream is itself unchang-ing. A professional may rightly claim that Hardy is no historian, because history is concerned with change where the writer's sub-ject is the immutable.[36] In that imaginative certainty, barriers between the present and the past or future are apt to slip away, and if Hardy is not a historian as such he knows more of its immediate meaning. The archaeologist 'is living two thousand

years ago, and despises the things of the moment as dreams'
(CM 184); the ageing woman dwells in past events 'not as one
who remembers, / But rather as one who sees' (TL 258); under
the sway of his own obsession, a place may have for the poet
'a savour that scenes in being lack, / And a presence more than
the actual brings' (SC 332). As Hardy once reminded the Wessex
Society of Manchester, if dreams of the Wessex past are vain,
so are present Manchester lives (LTH 336). Whether the eye
travels upstream, 'looking at the grain of a floorboard, and medi-
tating where it grew', or downstream 'picturing under what
circumstances the last fire would be kindled in the . . . chimneys',
it alights alike on the unchanging (WT 145). That sensation of
suspended time is often connected with the contemplation of
objects, and Mother Cuxom's *requiescat* for Susan Henchard
is not the less moving because it derives from domestic trivia—
the future life of her keys, her cupboards, and little secret things
(MC 144). In the silent sickroom, just before her mother's death,
Elizabeth-Jane is dislocated in 'that chaos called consciousness' by
the objects that surround her—why they should be as they are
and helpless to be otherwise. To her the tick of the clock is
hurrying onward, where Captain Hardy in the lull of battle
imagines it marking time in his childhood home:

> The placid look of the grey dial there,
> Marking unconsciously this bloody hour,
> And the red apples on my father's trees,
> Just now full ripe.

> (DI 97)

For Grace Melbury time has moved on, but her old bedroom with
its face estranged declares that it has stood still: 'The world of
little things therein gazed at her in hopeless stationariness, as
though they had tried and been unable to make any progress
without her presence' (W 55). Tess, in the silence that follows her
confession, is aware of the altered, ironic expression of objects
around her; nothing in the substance of things has changed, but
their essence has (293). Time may race, keep pace, stand still,
anticipate or run back; to Knight, hanging on the Cliff without
a Name, it does all these things, just as, in his position, the world
is upside-down and rain descends from below. At first he can
think neither for future nor past, but, under the stress of death's

approach, he lies 'hand in hand with the world in its infancy. Not a blade, not an insect, which spoke of the present was between him and the past' (*PBE* 251). An embedded fossil expresses 'immense lapses of time' which 'closed up like a fan before him' until the lifetime of the trilobite is 'a present and modern condition of things' (253). In half a minute awareness returns to the actual present, then instantly races forward to anticipate a world without him and his unknown future.

These moments of dislocation are normally the product of crisis, but they represent nonetheless an enduring truth. Though no stories connect themselves with the ancient Aldclyffe Manor House 'now', the past predicts them and the future realises them. At the beginning of *Desperate Remedies*, the coachman remarks:

> ' 'Tis jest the house for a nice ghastly hair-on-end story, that would make the parish religious. Perhaps it will have one some day to make it complete.'
>
> (69)

It has, by the novel's end, one horrid enough, with its murder, disinterment and subsequent execution. The insight into necessity, externalised here, is later internalised to those who are sensitive to their environment, who feel that they have no volition, that the stream has swept them up like so much flotsam as it obeys the law of its nature and pursues its random course. This sensation is subtly and extensively present in *The Mayor of Casterbridge* and *Tess of the d'Urbervilles*. A night in the Norman portion of Wenlock Abbey made Hardy feel 'quite mouldy' (*LTH* 268), and the years in ancient Casterbridge engrave their mark on the Henchards, although all three are strangers to the place. The cottage in which Susan awaits her remarriage has a view of tumuli and earthforts; a pleasant spot in itself, it thus acquires 'the usual touch of melancholy that a past-marked prospect lends' (97). A hopeful Elizabeth-Jane, on her first visit to her future home, High Place Hall, is distressed by a decaying mask made 'ghastly by the weakly lamp glimmer' which forms the keystone of the arch by which she leaves (168). In his defeat, Henchard retreats to the 'sad purlieu' of Jopp's cottage, built from the stones of the dismantled priory (226). Susan's prospect of married life, Elizabeth-Jane's of companionship, or Henchard's hope of a renewed existence with his step-daughter, are not frustrated by these contexts; they merely dispose the responsive mind to anticipate disappointment. To Tess, who by disposition and descent is part of her context, fatalism is unavoidable. Even her brief summertime at Talbothays is passed in adjacency to the former estates and the vaults of the d'Urberville family, whilst the first fatal night of her marriage is spent in the mutilated farmhouse which was once their mansion.

Only when Tess is an outcast from all human habitations does she achieve liberation from the past, and a momentary happiness beneath an unfamiliar roof. Branshurst Court, a 'desirable Mansion to be Let', its furniture under dustsheets, provides a sanctuary where no memories intrude on her (503). For the space of that brief idyll, time is suspended:

'Don't think of what's past! . . . I am not going to think outside of now . . . All is trouble outside there; inside here content.'
(506–7)

With their discovery by the caretaker, time resumes its march: ' "Ah, happy house—good-bye! . . . My life can only be a question of a few weeks" ' (509).

'. . . every hearth has a ghost, alack,
And can be but the scene of a bivouac
Till they move their last, nor care to pack!'
(SC 367)

In freedom her final resting place is the prehistoric altar at Stonehenge with its roof of stars.

In his last novel, Hardy's Jude and Sue have no home; they are always on the move from lodging to lodging, increasingly so as events gain catastrophic momentum, from years at Aldbrickham, through months or weeks 'elsewhere', to that final day in the 'old intramural cottage' at Christminster where the children die. Sue is, and Jude becomes, amongst the rootless, although their travels are the circumference of a circle whose centre is Marygreen, not Jude's adopted Christminster or Sue's London. In this they reflect the changing countenance of the time, whose mobility is not only social and spiritual but has a geographical aspect. In his first novel Hardy described a 'characteristic and handsome specimen of the genuine roadside inn of bygone times' with its long line of derelict outhouses and its grass-grown stable-yard: 'The railway had absorbed the whole stream of traffic which formerly flowed through the village, and along by the ancient door of the inn' (*DR* 144). In his last, that altered map is insistently traced: the great western highway is deserted, a place for the wind to play with straws and haystems (169); railways have become the arteries which connect the country towns, and stations alter their former orientation (363). Scenes no longer occur beneath ancestral roofs, but within the doors of lodgings, pubs and railway carriages. A return to more permanent dwellings is always ominous: in the ancient schoolhouse at Shaston Sue feels ' "crushed into the earth by the weight of so many previous lives there spent" ' and foreshadows her return to the circle's ancestral centre, her living burial at Marygreen (254).

In another way too, though with a difference, *Jude* resumes a theme common to the architectural novels. He considers the externals of buildings and his eye is professional, but his relation with stone is responsive, not analytic:

> The numberless architectural pages around him he read, naturally, less as an artist-critic of their forms than as an artisan and comrade of the dead handicraftsmen whose muscles had actually executed those forms. He examined the mouldings, stroked them as one who knew their beginning, said they were difficult or easy in the working, had taken little or much time, were trying to the arm, or convenient to the tool. (99)

Buildings for Jude are neither hieroglyphics nor symbols; when in disrepair they move him 'as he would have been moved by maimed sentient beings' (99). As to Hardy, the accidental is not distraction to him, but the essence of their charm: 'They had done nothing but wait, and had become poetical' (100), and the renovator's precision cannot match itself adequately with that broken line. Jude himself has antecedants in the earlier novels: Ethelberta's brothers, Sol and Dan, are country joiners, unspecialised in their trade as Jude is in his;[37] Stephen Smith's father is a master mason, who has left an enduring mark on the buildings amongst which he was born (*PBE* 85). He too is an unspecialised country craftsman, 'despised by Adam Smith on that account and respected by Macaulay, much more the artist nevertheless' (101). These figures are incidental in the early novels, but after *Jude* they acquire a poetic status. It is a labouring man who discerns, in a 'time touched stone' in the British Museum, no 'ashen blankness' but the echoed voice of St. Paul (*SC* 358); another who loses his livelihood with his refusal to demolish an Elizabethan house in Dorchester, a protest which lives 'where deathless things abide!' (*PPP* 140). It is a mason who perceives in the crystallisation of ice a key to the secret of Perpendicular style, to Hardy the only true English architecture (*LTH* 357); its inventor is persuaded that the discovery is not his but 'Heaven's outshaping', and dies disappointed and anonymous (*SC* 379). The architect's dispassionate view and the poet's felt one find their meeting place in the mason's responsive craft.

Hardy's response to stone, both in natural forms and as a presence in buildings, is closely related to his understanding of the history of societies and the fate of individuals. His determinism is less an intellectual doctrine, than a recognition that finer sensibilities are vulnerable, as he was, to the formation of circumstance and setting. Only those of coarser grain, like Arabella, can direct themselves along the stream of history more or less where they will. As a state of intense contextual awareness, fatalism is inescapable for those more sensitive, whilst the presence of stone is an enduring part of that context. Hardy does not sentimentalise the past; like Angel he is ' "politically . . . sceptical as to the virtue of [the] old" ', but ' "lyrically, dramatically, and even historically" ' he is as ' "tenderly attached" ' to it (*TU* 215). He never discounts the harshness of former times, and 'politically' welcomes the development of itinerant labour reflected in *Tess*:

> The seclusion and immutability, which was so bad for their pockets, was an unrivalled fosterer of their personal charm in the eyes of those whose experiences had been less limited. But the artistic merit of their old condition is scarcely a reason why they should have continued in it when other communities were marching on so vigorously towards uniformity and mental equality . . . They are losing their individuality, but they are widening the range of their ideas, and gaining in freedom.[38]

Nonetheless, the poet regrets the results of this development, from the destruction of local traditions to that of cottage gardens (*LTH* 205).

Hardy's dilemma is captured in a letter he wrote to *The Times* in 1906, where he describes his witness in 1865 of a public address given by one of the pioneers of modern thought, John Stuart Mill. Hardy recalls him as 'a man out of place', for 'the religious sincerity of his speech was jarred on' by the uncomprehending crowd below him, whilst his head was etched 'in relief against the blue shadow of a church which, on its transcendental side, his doctrines antagonised.' Such a 'perilous exposure' of conviction was emphasised by 'his vast pale brow . . . sloped back like a stretching upland'.[39] In the final weeks of his own life, Hardy paused for the last of many times to watch 'a goods train carrying away huge blocks of Portland stone'. The ancient rock of Portland had supported human habitations for centuries, and its stone had long been exported to make others; St. Paul's itself had set sail from that shore:

> He seems never tired of watching these stone-laden trucks. He said he thought that the shape of Portland would be changed in the course of years by the continual cutting away of its sur-**face.**
>
> *(LTH 443)*

To turn to hillside, take the shape of stone, is for Hardy no retreat from that conflict between past sanctities and future change, for stone itself is expressive of such things.

NOTES

1 *Alton Locke*, Everyman edition, p. 73. *Sketches by Boz*, 1st complete edition, 1837–9; *Alton Locke* 1850; Hardy's first novel, *Desperate Remedies*, 1871. Hardy's novels and *The Dynasts* will be indicated by initials with page references to the Macmillan Pocket Hardy, with the exception of *The Well-Beloved*, where the New Wessex Edition is cited. Poems are indicated by the initials of the original volumes, but page references are given to the *Collected Poems*, 4th edition, 1930. LTH denotes *The Life of Thomas Hardy* by Florence Emily Hardy (though largely Hardy's own writing), 1962.

2 Gittings notes a Dickensian interior in *DR*, *Young Thomas Hardy*, Penguin edition, p. 202. See also Farmer Springrove's house, *UGT* 37–8; the Inns of Court, *PBE* 149–50; Overcombe Mill, *TM* 12–14. Possibly because the last novel is historical, the influence of Dickens is detectable throughout.

3 In his general preface to the Wessex Edition of 1912. Hardy's second group includes 'Romances and Fantasies'; his third 'Novels of Ingenuity'.

4   Cf. *LTH* 261 where he comments on a painting of Grindelwald and the Wetterhorn: 'There is no real interest or beauty in this mountain, . . . The little houses at the foot are the real interest of the scene.'

5   *LLI* 89; cf. *LTH* 295: 'the most marked instance in England of an architectural intention carried out to the full.'

6   In *DR*, Ambrose and Owen Graye, Springrove and Manston; in *PBE*, Smith; in *L*, Somerset, Havill and Dare. The circumstances mentioned are touched on, together with others, in all three novels, and are central to *L*.

7   Cf. *GND*, 'The First Countess of Wessex', where the modesty of Falls Park and the ambition of King's Hintock Court dramatise the heroine's alternatives.

8   *LTH* 381. The relation is explored by D. Drew Cox in 'The Poet and Architect', *Agenda*, Vol. X, Nos. 2–3, Spring-Summer 1972.

9   *WP* 10. The poem is dated 1866; the sketches are 'recently made' according to the preface of 1898.

10 Cf. *PBE* 453–4; *HE* 229; *CM* 122–3.

11 Particularly *PBE*, which is based upon Hardy's courtship of his first wife Emma at St. Juliot in Cornwall. *DR* and *L* draw heavily on his early experience as an architect, and *HE* obliquely on his struggles as a writer of humble origin.

12 *PBE* 191; cf. 372–3 where Knight regrets the old tower as 'a local record of local art' and Swancourt celebrates the replacement 'designed by a first-rate London man—in the newest style of Gothic art, and full of Christian feeling.'

13 Cf. the debate between Troy and Oak, *FMC* 278, where the steady Oak is for preserving Bathsheba's house, whilst the fickle Troy is for changing it. See also 'A Man', *PPP* 140–4, who refuses 'to help lay low a house so fair!'

14 Cf. Gittings, *The Older Hardy*, 1978, p. 23.

15 Gittings attributes the novel's imperfections to Hardy's illness, but these weaknesses are perceptible from its beginning; *ibid.*, 22–4.

16 *Ibid.*, pp. 70–1; the three Avices relate to Hardy's three Sparks cousins, Rebecca, Martha and Tryphena, all widely separated in age, all attractive at different times to Hardy.

17 See Gittings, *Young Thomas Hardy*, pp. 100, 103, 104.

18 See Betjeman, 'Hardy as Architect', *The Genius of Thomas Hardy*, ed. Margaret Drabble, 1976, p. 152. Gittings, in *The Older Hardy*, attributes the building of Max Gate to Hardy's failure to find a suitable house for sale in Dorchester, pp. 37–8. This is Hardy's own explanation, *LTH* 163, and may be disingenuous. It does not account for his doubts about the wisdom of building in the year of the move, Gittings *ibid.*, p. 43. See also 'The Two Houses', *LLE* 563, where the old and the new are contrasted, 'Architectural Masks', *PPP* 147 where the new house harbours the cultured and the old does not, and *TU* 43–4, where the new estate of The Slopes bears some resemblance to Max Gate.

19 Betjeman, *ibid.*, p. 152.

20 *LTH* 163; the preceding sentence paradoxically claims that 'the only drawback to the site seemed to him to be its newness.'

21 Cf. Gittings, *Older Hardy*, p. 170, who adds to the number of ghosts.

22 *L*, 3, 25, 125. Cf. 'Copying Architecture in an Old Minster', *MV* 411, where ghosts gather at the stroke of the old clock, and the sketcher drops his drawing.

23 *LTH* 331. The preference of the Victorians was for 'middle-pointed' and restorations on the scale of St. Juliot, intended to establish architectural uniformity, were frequent. See also *LTH* 188, where Hardy as an architect supports the stripping of parasitic growths from the ancient buildings, but wishes personally that he had paid his visit to Rome before it occurred.

24 *HE* 3, *LTH* 151. See also the house, barely 100 years old, of Jacob Paddock, a market gardener, *CM* 147–8, which prompts the story 'Enter a Dragoon'.

25 See Gittings, *Older Hardy*, pp. 67–8.

26 *TU* 381. This feeling is conspicuously absent in the displaced Fitzpiers, *W* 155.

27 *MC* 167; *FMC* 80–1; *TU* 69. See also the old Aldclyffe Manor House, *DR* 118–20; Oxwell Hall, *TM* 45–6; Fitzpiers' familys' former castle, *W* 203–4; the former seat of the Drenghards, *GND* 201.

28 *The Mayor of Casterbridge* is a clear exception, accounted for by the origin of Elizabeth-Jane in a passage Hardy copied out from Short-house's *John Inglesant*: 'From those high windows . . . young girls have looked out upon life, which their instincts told them was made for pleasure but which year after year convinced them was . . . given over to pain.' Gittings, *Older Hardy*, pp. 41–2. See also the idle Fitzpiers, *W* 161.

29 *UGT* 124. See also the chimney corners in *DR* 340, and *TU* 155, 270.

30 *SC* 326. Hardy's refusal to permit change at Max Gate irritated his second wife, cf. Gittings, *ibid.*, p. 173; she did, however, alter some things, cf. pp. 160, 185.

31 Quoted by Mrs. Pine-Avon from John Bright, *W-B* 79.

32 *LTH* 352. See also preface to *FMC* which describes the destruction of 'the thatched and dormered cottages that were once lifeholds'; the existence of lifeholds is crucial in *W*, and is a chapter in social history. Hardy can regard demolition ironically, as in 'The levelled Churchyard' *PPP* 144 and 'The Obliterate Tomb' *SC* 361.

33 *PPP* 92; see also 'Rome: Building a New Street in the Ancient Quarter', *PPP* 93, where the broken masonry is 'an open tome / Top-lined' with the inscription: 'Dunces, Learn here to spell Humanity!' Cf. R. J. White, *Thomas Hardy and History*, 1974, p. 60: 'a peculiarly Hardyan type of history, history derived from "living documents".'

34 *CM* 255, *TM* Pref. See also Hardy's poem on Keats' Hampstead house, *LLE* 544, and his fascination with the two houses in Rome where Keats wrote and died, *LTH* 188.

35 *GND* Pref. The entire collection of stories supposedly stems from such records and traditions concerning them.
36 White, *op. cit.*, p. 11.
37 *HE* 116–7 cf. JO 91–2, 117.
38 Quoted by White, *op. cit.*, p. 6, from Hardy's essay of 1883 on 'The Dorchester Labourer.'
39 *LTH* 330. Hardy admired Mill, and had read widely in him as a young man; cf. Gittings, *Young Thomas Hardy*, p. 152.

9

Hardy, House-Style, and the Aesthetics of Punctuation

by SIMON GATRELL

From his earliest years Hardy was responsive to music; he related how as a child he was moved to tears by a tune, and danced to hide his emotion. Later he learned the violin and played at dances with his father, and he was himself fond of dancing until his late middle-age; only a poet with an ear for melody and rhythm could have written the 'Lines to a Movement in Mozart's E Flat Symphony', and indeed the search through his novels for moments of heightened or exalted emotion will often discover them associated with music and dancing; it is no coincidence that *The Fiddler of the Reels* is one of Hardy's most powerful stories.

If it is accepted that Hardy was sensitive to the patterns of music, that he felt vividly their power and their intoxication, and that he often transmitted this feeling to us through his words, it should hardly be novel to suggest that he was also concerned with the nature of the pauses which dictate the rhythm of his words, that his punctuation responds carefully to the cadences of speaking and narrative voices. Yet such a suggestion has never been made. This is partly, I imagine, because punctuation is a matter which, when compared with the words an author wrote, seems hardly worth considering except by an editor debating the choice of copy-text; but it is also, with Hardy at least, partly because what we see when we take up one of the Macmillan texts or its derivatives is not Hardy's own punctuation.

Many writers of fiction in the nineteenth century accepted that the publisher or printer would alter their MS punctuation in accordance with the house's accepted practice, regularising it and thereby, it was assumed, making better sense of their words; there was always the safeguard of author's proof against ghastly compositorial error.[1] This concept of house-style is a familiar one, but difficult to show in operation without extensive quotation, and thus not often considered in detail. Its chief virtues are generally held to be accuracy and uniformity, the establishment of a correct system of punctuation over an often sketchily pointed manuscript in a consistent manner. Of these two qualities, accuracy or correctness is very much a matter of fashion, which a comparison of the punctuation of the extract from a nineteenth-century manual on p. 183 below with any similar contemporary passage, or with one from the mid-eighteenth century, will amply show; moreover it is possible for two authorities to hold opposite views on the utility of a mark during the same period, as is seen by comparing the extract already referred to with that on p. 184 below. Since in the end punctuation is a subjective matter which will never be regulated by all the rules in grammar books, it is only through comparison of individual examples that we can evaluate the relative value of two systems of punctuation imposed on the same text; the second part of this essay will attempt such an analysis. The matter of uniformity, on the other hand can more easily be tested statistically, and it is with the accepted assumption that in a given printing house at a given time in the last third of the nineteenth century there was a version of punctuation which was in general use by the compositors, and that they imposed what has been called the tyranny of house-style on the manuscripts they composed, that I should like to begin this essay. At the same time I will show some of the ways in which Hardy's manuscript punctuation was lost.

In order to achieve a spread across Hardy's novel-writing career, I have chosen *Under the Greenwood Tree* (1872) and *Tess of the D'Urbervilles* (1891)[2] to provide the illustrations in this first part of the essay; the manuscripts of both novels were used as printer's copy and bear a complete system of compositorial stints (though it occasionally breaks down in *Tess* where pages are missing from the MS).[3] In *UGT* there are five compositors who do 95% of the work, in *Tess* there are seven who do 98%, and I have confined my analysis to these men, though taking the rest into account in the total figures.[4] In the tables that follow there are three sets of figures that follow the name of each compositor; the first is simply the number of times that he makes the specified alteration; the second is the number of times he makes it per hundred lines of the Wessex Edition text,[5] permitting direct comparison between compositors; the third is the percentage of his total changes this particular change represents, making it possible to see whether any compositor has a bias within his own work.[6] I begin with some details from a comparison of the manuscript and the first edition of *UGT*, Table I showing the number of times each compositor adds a comma where the manuscript was blank.

TABLE I

JONES	296	20·2	43%
NORTH	257	20·2	46%
GILES	308	18·8	46%
STEWART	204	16·8	44%
DODD	119	14·7	39%
TOTAL	1281	18·8	45%

The most striking feature of this Table is the sheer volume of commas that were added to Hardy's text, on average more than seven per page of the Wessex text, accounting for 45% of all the differences between the first edition and the manuscript; and though I will look at the effect of this more closely in the second part of the essay it must be said here that such a large importation of a single mark into any text is bound to have a decisive effect upon the rhythmical structure of the language, for good or ill.

On the question of uniformity the table is inconclusive; it is true that each compositor adds a large number of commas, and this might be seen as evidence that a house-style is working; on the other hand the difference between Jones and North, who add nearly eight commas to a page and Dodd who adds considerably less than six, is not negligible. There is a certain amount of individuality of treatment; we might say that Dodd has a slightly greater tolerance than Jones for Hardy's unpunctuated prose.

Hardy's dash (a mark of which he is fond) does not fare much better, as Table II shows—it details the number of times his dash was either altered to some other mark, or else removed altogether.

171

TABLE II

GILES	140	8·5	21%
NORTH	89	7·0	16%
JONES	93	6·4	14%
DODD	39	4·8	13%
STEWART	55	4·5	12%
TOTAL	440	6·5	15%

Rather more than two of Hardy's dashes have vanished from each page of Wessex text and this too alters the balance of his prose. Here we have evidence of a significant divergence in compositorial behaviour, since Giles removes a dash almost twice as often as Stewart, and the alteration forms a much higher proportion of all Giles' changes than of Stewart's. The figures suggest that Stewart had some sympathy with Hardy's use of the dash, and it is possible to confirm this by looking at specific examples in the text.[7]

There is a further vivid example of compositorial inconsistency connected with the dash that may be noted here: there are thirty places in the text where one of Hardy's manuscript dashes is altered to either ,— or ;— in the first edition, and of these, 25 were changed by North, and 5 by Dodd—in the work of the others this kind of compromise is never seen.

If it is felt that the case for Stewart's independence of house-style in the matter of the dash admits of some doubt, then a more clear-cut case can be made with regard to Dodd's attitude to the semicolon. Table III shows the number of times a semicolon is either added to the text or substituted for another mark.

TABLE III

JONES	114	7·8	16%
STEWART	79	6·5	17%
NORTH	81	6·4	14%
GILES	85	5·2	12%
DODD	21	2·6	7%
TOTAL	408	6·0	14%

Dodd makes this kind of change half as often as the compositor immediately above him in the table, and Jones at the top makes it three times as often; this must be considered significant evidence of compositorial independence, and it is possible to support such a conclusion if the number of times one of Hardy's relatively infrequent semicolons is replaced by another mark is considered. Then the order in Table III is completely reversed, Dodd removing three times as many semicolons per hundred lines as any other compositor, six times as many as Jones. It seems safe to say that Dodd disliked (relatively speaking) the semicolon as a mark of punctuation, and that this dislike has found its way into Hardy's text in the passages that he composed. In fact it is possible to go a little further, and say that Dodd favoured an altogether lighter system of punctuation when compared with his colleagues. It is his marked reluctance to use the semicolon in place of a comma or a dash that puts him at the foot of Table III—he would not be at the foot of separate tables showing the substitution of a semicolon for a stronger mark. The same trend is noticeable when the substitution of a comma for other marks is considered: in this case Dodd does not only have the largest number per hundred lines of comma for semicolon alterations as would be expected, but he also has the largest number of comma for colon, for point and for exclamation mark changes. He is without doubt more eager than the other compositors to add weaker marks to Hardy's already light punctuation. Thus in assessing the amount of independence from house-style that compositors show, not only the volume, but also the nature of their changes should be taken into account; to underline this, while Table IV shows that Dodd was the compositor who interfered least with Hardy's system, it does not show that he favoured a lighter system. This table (in which the third column naturally has no place), shows the sum of the punctuation differences between the manuscript and the first edition.

TABLE IV

JONES	683	46·7
NORTH	558	43·9
GILES	672	41·0
STEWART	463	38·2
DODD	305	37·6
TOTAL	2856	42·0

This total represents over sixteen differences per page of Wessex Edition text, the effect of which may easily be imagined. Dodd alters about three and a half fewer marks per page than Jones, a difference which might be considered striking, until the comparable table for *Tess* is examined. (There are only abbreviated forms of the compositors' names on the *Tess* manuscript; I give the variety which appears most frequently.)

TABLE V

KEV	558	31·5
ROB	432	28·9
AND	765	26·3
R. LAN	653	25·5
DUN	499	22·8
LAWR	443	19·1
FRED	152	11·4
TOTAL	3610	24·1

It is apparent that passages composed by Fred, containing twenty less differences per hundred lines, will be very much closer to Hardy's punctuation than those composed by Kev; or indeed than those composed by any of his colleagues. Compared with the range of interference indicated here, the compositors of *UGT* would seem to have operated a most coherent house-style, though in fact their individuality has already been established.

A second point to notice is that the average number of changes per hundred lines in *Tess* is only just over half that in *UGT*. There are perhaps two main reasons for this; one is that *Tess* was composed for serial publication, *UGT* for the two-volume first edition. The compositors, presented with monthly or weekly copy, are likely to have operated under greater pressure than that normally experienced in book-work, and there is some evidence to support this assumption. Three of the *UGT* compositors also worked two years later on *A Pair of Blue Eyes*, Hardy's third published novel which first appeared in *Tinsley's Magazine*, and Table VI shows the changes made in their stints on that occasion (the numbers are small because only a portion of the MS survives).

TABLE VI

STEWART	216	30·4
NORTH	133	30·2
GILES	48	28·1
TOTAL (whole MS)	1034	34·2

As will be seen by comparison with Table IV, the number of changes per hundred lines is considerably reduced for each compositor, probably because the speed required to meet serial deadlines meant a somewhat closer adherence to the author's punctuation; it is also interesting to note that all three were considerably more conservative than the average, and in this context one other compositor may be mentioned as showing an eccentricity in *A Pair of Blue Eyes* as marked as that of Fred in *Tess*: Hall makes a total of 210 changes in only 378 lines of Wessex text, which is an astonishing amount of 55·6 alterations per hundred lines.

The second contributory factor to the difference between *Tess* and *UGT* is the effect of the passing of time. By 1891 Hardy was an author with a reputation, and as such may have commanded a degree of respect from his printers; he may also (and this seems borne out by an examination of the manuscript), have moved rather closer to an accepted mode of punctuation. The general features of *Tess* are surprisingly similar to those of *UGT*: there are still long unpunctuated stretches; still few commas; still an idiosyncratic use of the dash; still, above all, the sense of rhythm that is so often destroyed by the activity of the compositors. But at the same time there are more semicolons and colons, and fewer dashes, leading to a more orthodox appearance of his text. Nevertheless there remains in the MS a system of punctuation that is recognisably Hardyan, despite the intervention of twenty years and nine novels. The compositors of *Tess* still feel it right to alter well over nine per page of Hardy's marks.

A comparison of the next Table (which shows the commas added to the manuscript text of *Tess* by *The Graphic*), with Table I will show that though the average occurrence of the change diminishes considerably in the later novel, the proportion of all the alterations that this one change represents remains very similar, 43% compared with 45%.

Two compositors here are considerably more at home with Hardy's lack of commas than any in *UGT* or any of their colleagues, but it is interesting to see that while Lawr is genuinely responsive to Hardy's punctuation in this area, since it represents only 30% of all his changes, Fred's special receptivity in this situation is more apparent than real, since he is reluctant to make any kind of change, and this one represents half of all that he

TABLE VII

R. LAN	334	13·1	51%
AND	336	11·5	44%
KEV	203	11·5	37%
DUN	257	11·5	50%
ROB	169	11·3	39%
FRED	79	5·9	50%
LAWR	131	5·7	30%
TOTAL	1528	10·4	43%

made. It should also be noted that though four compositors make the addition an almost identical number of times, suggesting perhaps that some form of uniformity of style is present, the proportion of all their marks that it represents shows a very wide range, indicating that there will be considerable differences when other varieties of alteration are considered; and Table VIII, showing the number of times a comma was removed from the text, bears this out:

TABLE VIII

KEV	79	4·5	14%
R. LAN	87	3·4	13%
ROB	35	2·3	8%
DUN	39	1·8	8%
AND	44	1·5	6%
LAWR	29	1·3	6%
FRED	11	0·8	7%
TOTAL	330	2·2	9%

Here it seems that each compositor has a different view; there is clearly no sense of uniformity, and the column showing the changes per hundred lines moves in a nicely graded descent from 4·5 to 0·8, one five-and-a-half times as many as the other. It might be expected that Fred and Lawr, who let much of *The Graphic* text remain free of new commas, might be tempted to remove more than their colleagues; but this is not the case, and R. Lan who adds more commas than anyone else, also removes more than anyone except Kev. This would seem to suggest that R. Lan had a special interest in the comma, for reference to

Table V will show that he is by no means the most determined reviser of Hardy's punctuation overall; and this is confirmed when we find him the most conservative of the compositors when some other types of alteration are considered.

Much more statistical information could be brought to bear on the subject, but I believe that enough material has been presented to support some general conclusions: firstly that individual compositors have preferences or antipathies towards a particular mark of punctuation; and secondly that some compositors are markedly more conservative than others in their handling of the text. These lead to a third conclusion: that in the face of this diversity in both *Tess* and *UGT* the notion of a consistently viewed and imposed house-style begins to melt—that the punctuation provided by the printer is not a homogeneous thing, it depends in great measure upon the whim of the individual compositor. Sample collations from other of Hardy's novels show patterns similar to those outlined here,[8] and there is no reason to doubt that other writers suffered in the same way.

Hardy's own punctuation system, then, has disappeared beneath a weight of printing-house changes; it is now plain that the compositors themselves have no agreement as to what should be considered normal punctuation. The task in the second part of this essay is to discover whether what was lost has any particular value, using material from *UGT* alone.[9] To do this I shall consider some of the major marks of punctuation in turn, confining myself for the most part to examples that show alteration in the first edition.

Comma

I have already drawn attention to the punctuation of the extract from Wilson's Treatise on p. 183 below; it seems safe to say that by modern standards it is heavily punctuated, especially with regard to the number of commas. It is also probable that this was the kind of model followed by all the compositors of *UGT*, there being no fundamental difference between them in the matter of the addition of commas (as there is between the *Tess* compositors): nevertheless, I have shown statistically that there is no uniformity of application of such guidelines as might constitute a house-style, and it is possible to reinforce this conclusion

by an examination of examples from the text. In nearly every
frequently recurrent situation neither the manuscript nor the first
edition achieve anything like consistency of punctuation. For instance, after an introductory 'Now', the most frequently occur-
ring situation is

Now$<$,$>$ what I want to know is . . .

(II, 19.17)[10]

but is easy enough to find

Now to my mind . . .

(I, 156.15)

where both agree, or

Now Mr Dewy

(II, 30.4)

where they similarly agree, and even occasionally

Now, $<$ $>$ you ought not to . . .

(II, 43.11)

A similar pattern of inconsistency is found before vocatives, before the exclamatory 'why', and before participial clauses and
phrases; the only constant element is that where the two witnesses differ, on the large majority of occasions it will be found
that the manuscript had no comma and the first edition added
one. Often the only apparent effect of this addition is cumulative, but there are many places where Hardy's sparer punctuation
does have significant and individual value.

Frequently some point of emphasis or of intonation which Hardy
made clear through his own punctuation, was obscured or altered
by the standardising impulse of Robson's compositors, sometimes
leading to a shift in the meaning of the passage. Take Fancy's
simple exclamation 'O how vexing!' This is how it appears in the
manuscript, the exclamation mark placing such emphasis as there
is on the last word; and this is presumably what Hardy intended
us to hear when he wrote the passage. In the first edition (II,
7.18–19) it has a conventional comma: 'O, how vexing!' which
alters the rhythm, separating 'O' from the rest of the sentence
and thus stressing it, as if Fancy were really surprised to discover that there was no water left for Dick to wash his hands in;

it is fair to say that neither version is wrong, but even in such a short sentence, they are different, with different implications.

A second, slightly more complex example shows the same kind of thing; again Fancy is speaking, this time in response to an almost innocent statement of Dick's. In the first edition it appears as

> Now, Mr. Dewy, no flirtation, because it's wrong, and I don't wish it.
>
> (II, 37.4–5)

The multiplicity of commas, separating every available fragment of the sentence with apparently equal pause, offer no assistance with the intonation of the speech; indeed it hardly seems like a speaking voice at all, the only guide the reader has towards working out how Fancy said these words is his own active imagination. On the other hand the manuscript version

> Now Mr Dewy—no flirtation, because it's wrong and I don't wish it.

gives precise indications of how Hardy heard Fancy speak in his creating imagination—the dramatic reality is revealed through the punctuation. There is, for instance, the suggestion at the dash of some small movement of flirtatious aversion by Fancy before she ironically prohibits it in Dick; the lack of a comma after 'Now' allows more emphasis whether of real or simulated concern to fall on 'Mr Dewy', where it is most appropriate; the rather rushed end of the sentence has now an air of self-justification about it.

In a third example from Fancy's dialogue there is again a similar situation; here she is appealing to Dick, in a moment of real passion, not to abandon her for another sweetheart. In the first edition it runs thus:

> O, you won't, will you, Dick, for I do love you so.
>
> (II, 92.1–2)

where the most charitable reading will find two of the commas redundant, and even destructive; what Hardy wrote is 'O you won't will you Dick, for I do love you so'. The lack of commas in the first half of the sentence catches exactly the rapid, anxious, almost desperate tone which Fancy in the circumstances must have used. There is hardly any tone at all in the first edition reading, beyond what the words themselves supply.

In narrative too, Hardy's rhythmical structure can be broken by the addition of conventional and inessential commas

> About the room were sitting and standing<,> in various gnarled attitudes<,> our old acquaintance<,> Grandfathers James and William, the tranter . . .
>
> (II, 176.17–20)

The pace is slowed right down by the first edition commas, and if any attention is paid to punctuation while reading, the jerky quality is obtrusive.

Whether or not you agree with these subjective interpretations, the important point still holds, that with Hardy's live pointing there is a stimulus to make such active suggestions; in the flat first edition versions there is no sense of drama, though they may be strictly correct by someone's grammatical rules. And in fact the difference between the two witnesses may be explained quite simply by saying that Hardy composed his manuscript for the ear, that he represented on paper so far as was possible through punctuation the cadences that his imagination created, while the compositors set up their version of the text for the eye alone, so that the contemporary reader should find his grammatical expectations fulfilled, and presumably so that the reading process should be facilitated, though as has already been seen this does not always happen.

Potentially more destructive than the flattening out of Hardy's expressive rhetorical punctuation is the subtle alteration in the sense of his words that can be caused by compositorial interference; naturally this does not happen frequently, but it can be seen in

> Dick Dewy faced about, < > and continued his tune in an under-whistle<,> implying that the business of his mouth could not be checked . . .
>
> (I, 6.10–14)

where Hardy separates the first action from the second by a comma, and the lack of one after 'under-whistle' indicates that it was only the second action which implied anything: the first edition, carefully moving the comma, combines the two actions

into one, and suggests that both actions now imply that which
follows. In itself this may be a trivial enough distinction, but it
does represent a tampering with the author's intention. In the
next example, Hardy's version is clearly more sensible:

> But, < > I don't care who hears me say it, nothing will speak
> to your heart ...
>
> (I, 50.13–15)

His first comma, in a place where he rarely uses one, represents
the pause the speaker makes in place of a word such as 'and';
its omission links 'But' to 'I', instead of to 'nothing' as the manuscript intended, and which is clearly demanded in the context of
the whole of William Dewy's speech. A final example may be
thought even more important,

> ... discovered that the chimney-crook, < > and chain from
> which the hams were suspended, < > should have possessed more
> merits and general interest as playthings than any other article
> in the house ...
>
> (I, 90.19–91.2)

for here modern readers, unfamiliar with rural cottages of the
nineteenth century, most probably would not realise that the
chimney-crook and the chain were two separate objects rather
than components of one unit, unless the distinction were made
clear by Hardy's commas. The matter was further clarified by the
alteration in the 1896 revision of 'article' to 'articles'.

Another marked feature of Hardy's style in which the comma
(or lack of it) plays the largest part, may most appropriately be
mentioned here, though as with the aural/visual distinction it is
a general difference between the manuscript and the first edition.
It will appear from even a cursory examination of the manuscript
that Hardy wrote, and presumably thought, in longer stretches
of unpunctuated prose than the compositors of the first edition
seem to have been prepared to accept. Examples of this abound
throughout the novel, but I have chosen three examples from only
one chapter:

> For several minutes Dick drove along homeward <,> with the
> inward eye of reflection so consciously set on his passages at
> arms with Fancy<,> that the road and scenery were as thin
> mist over the real pictures of his mind.
>
> (II, 14.3–8)

. . . the tranter gave vent to a grim admiration$<,>$ with the mien of a man who was too magnanimous not to appreciate a slight rap on the knuckles$<,>$ even if they were his own.

(II, 18.24–19.4)

Having taken this precaution against vacillation$<,>$ Dick watched his messenger down the road$<,>$ and turned again into the house whistling an air in such ghastly jerks and starts$<,>$, that whistling seemed to be the act the very farthest removed from that which was instictive in such a youth.

(II, 27.19–28.5)

Each passage without commas achieves a more fluent expression, which may stretch the reader's powers of retention, but is in no way unreadable. The first edition on the other hand, especially in the first two examples, is rather awkward, the continuity of the passages destroyed by too many pauses; the effect of this difference between the two approaches to punctuation is again a cumulative one, which can really only be felt over a long stretch of the text.

To end this section on the comma, here is a further example of the damage that can be done by the thoughtless conformity of the compositors; it concerns the preparations for Fancy's bridal, and Mrs. Penny's incantation ' 'Tis to be, and here goes!' Fancy is nervous, and Mrs. Penny relates how the sentence carried her through her wedding, suggesting Fancy should try it. Each character says the charm twice, and Hardy in the manuscript differentiates between the calm matron and the excited bride-to-be by allowing Mrs. Penny both times to pause in the middle, but making Fancy rush right through it, omitting the medial comma each time. The first edition compositor added Mrs. Penny's comma to Fancy's speeches in the name, one imagines, of uniformity; in fact he has obscured what seems to be a deliberate and sensitive distinction of mood that could only be expressed through the difference in punctuation.

As a coda to this discussion, it should perhaps be noted that in Hardy's two major revisions of the text, in 1896 and 1912, for both of which he read and amended proof, a total of 480 commas were removed from the first edition text, 378 of these in 1912. It is certain that Hardy himself was responsible for the removal of almost all of them; by 1912 he had the confidence of an established author to deal with his text in proof as he wished.

Dash

From Table II on p. 172 it is clear that, when the relative incidence of comma and dash in any system of punctuation is taken into account, the compositors of the first edition were at least as anxious to remove the latter from the manuscript as they were to add the former. Yet the mark is most important within Hardy's style of punctuation, being both flexible and precise.

That printing-houses avoided the use of the dash as much as possible, is suggested by the following eloquent passage taken from a contemporary American work, which had some circulation in Britain, *A Treatise on English Punctuation*,[11] written specifically for the instruction of compositors and students:

> Notwithstanding the advantages resulting from the proper use of the dash, the most indistinct conceptions have been formed as to its nature and applications. Many authors, some of them of high standing in the literary world, as well as a majority of letter-writers, are wont to employ this mark so indiscriminately as to prove that they are acquainted neither with its uses, nor with those of the other points whose places it is made to supply. Some use it instead of a comma; others, instead of a semicolon; not a few where a colon is required; and a host, between every sentence and after every paragraph. Others go even further; by introducing it between the most commonplace words and phrases, apparently to apprise the reader, through the medium of his eye, what perhaps he could not discover by his judgement, that the composition before him is distinguished for brilliance of diction, tenderness of sentiment, or force of thought. But surely the unnecessary profusion of straight lines, particularly on a printed page, is offensive to good taste, is an index of the *dasher's* profound ignorance of the art of punctuation, and, so far from helping to bring out the sense of an author, is better adapted for turning into nonsense some of his finest passages.
>
> From these abuses in the application of the dash, some writers have strongly questioned its utility in any way as a sentential mark. So long, however, as modes of thought are different, and the style of composition corresponds with the peculiarities of an author's mind, so long will it be necessary occasionally to use the dash.

This would seem to express succinctly the apparent reluctance of Robson's compositors to transmit Hardy's dashes, although many of them have a useful function. And though Wilson's view was the prevailing one, there were others in circulation at the time, as is shown by a brief quotation from a long and witty vindication of the dash in Justin Brennan's *Composition and Punctuation Familiarly Explained.*[12]

> The introduction of this stop is a most important accession. It completes the system of punctuation, removes all its doubts and difficulties, and leaves its study unembarrassed by subtleties. It puts simplicity in the place of mystery, gives decision in lieu of hesitation, divests ignorance of its imposing mask, and strips artifice of its deceptious solemnities.

Though Hardy would probably not have agreed with Brennan that the dash and the comma might, in all but a few situations, replace with propriety the colon and the semicolon, he did have several distinctive uses for the dash. The most frequent of these may be described as summatory or defining, as in:

> It was a morning of the latter summer time —$<;>$ a morning of lingering dews, when the grass is never dry in the shade.
> (II, 58.3–5)

or also in '. . . to soothe her —$<,>$the captive' (II, 36.7). In the first example the dash indicates that the reader should expect a further definition of an already announced subject; while the semicolon is too heavy in a short sentence, obscuring the close connection between the two parts. In the second there is particularly triumphant or despairing note (depending on the point of view) about the pause represented by the dash that is lost with the conventional comma—a definition of her situation.

That one compositor, it may be added, recognised this as an acceptable role for the dash, is indicated by the few occasions that one was retained by the first edition in such a position:

> Never such a man as father for two things—cleaving up old dead apple-tree wood, $<\ >$ and playing the bass-viol.
> (I, 26.5–8)

—so also at three other places, all of which were composed by Stewart.

One other example of the first edition's alteration of this sort of dash is combined with the second group to be considered:

. . . the lost man —<,> his arms folded, his head thrown
back—<,> his eyes fixed upon the illuminated lattice.

(I, 65.9–12)

The first manuscript dash here is one of the kind discussed
above, introducing an extended definition of the lost man—a
technical use of the dash; the second is different, being dramatic
rather than technical. It separates the final element of the description from the first two with a rather longer pause, as a
speaker of this narrative might pause fractionally longer for effect
before telling us at last that Fancy is the reason for Dick's
absence from the rest of the party. And indeed the comedy of
the next few lines is dependent upon the misunderstanding of
this reason, assumed or otherwise, on the part of the searchers.

This second group is perhaps the heart of Hardy's handling
of the dash; he used it to give the reader, particularly in dialogue, the most delicate indication of both meaning and emphasis.

She'd never have had to work in her old age if he had continued
strong —<,> poor Jim!

(I, 156.1–3)

The dash is most eloquent here, expressing at least a slight re-
flective pause, perhaps more—a shake of the head and a change
in the tone of voice to a new sorrow. Such suggestions are possible when the dash is present, whereas the comma weakens a
potentially varied and dramatic rhythm; it also joins the last two
words more firmly to the rest of the sentence, which is something Hardy certainly did not intend, especially when it is considered that the dialogue continues with news of Jim's death; a
touch of the comedy of Leaf's apparent sorrow over such an
apparently insignificant death is lost in the loss of the dash.

'What was his age when 'a died?'
'Four hours and twenty minutes—<,> poor Jim.'

(I, 156.4–6)

Similarly, the dash has an essential function in the following

Why<,> Shiner is for putting forward that young woman that
only last night I was saying was our Dick's sweetheart, but I
suppose can't be —<,>and making much of her in the sight
of the congregation, and thinking he'll win her by showing her
off.

(I, 186.20–187.4)

The sentence changes direction slightly at 'but I suppose can't be', which is a kind of aside, and the dash represents accurately the slight breath and pause that the tranter must take before returning to the main point of his sentence; the comma in the first edition gives no account of this carefully observed detail. The speech loses tension and contrast, since the punctuation is uniform throughout, and each element in the sentence has apparently the same emphasis; Hardy's punctuation is clearly that of a speaker, the first edition punctuation is designed for a reader —the aural/visual distinction already suggested in the section on the comma.

The two examples so far have involved speech, and the substitution of a comma in the first edition for a dash in the manuscript; the final one shows both that Hardy's fine perception was extended to narrative, and that the first edition could interpret the dash, on occasions, as representing a heavier pause:

> 'But 'tis like all your family were —<,> so easy to be deceived.'
> 'That's as true as gospel of this member,' said Reuben.
> Mrs Dewy began a smile at the answer, then altering her lips and refolding them so that it was not a smile, commenced smoothing Bessy's hair —<;> the tranter having meanwhile suddenly become oblivious to conversation, occupying himself in a deliberate cutting . . .
>
> (I, 21.5–15)

The first dash here is important for the reason that those discussed earlier are, in that a comma cannot represent the pause required by the meaning of the speech. It is the second, however, that is the main interest, for it demonstrates how a dash can indicate a new direction in a sentence without breaking its sequence in the reader's mind. The dash encourages the reader to see a relationship between Mrs. Dewy's smile and the tranter's sudden obliviousness, while the semicolon discourages such a connection; it breaks the sentence into two less strongly connected parts, thus helping the reader to feel that the tranter's interest in cider is unrelated to any consciousness of possible deception on Mrs. Dewy's part. With the dash present, it may be imagined that the 'critical state of affairs' mentioned in the following paragraph refers to both deception and the cider-broaching, a coincidence of crises; it would seem from Hardy's use of the word 'suddenly', that the tranter felt some kind of confusion or embarrassment that needed to be hidden in physical activity. A comma in this place would have been wrong, as it would have taken inadequate account of the shift of direction in the sentence.

There are a few places where the first edition omitted a dash altogether, not replacing it with any mark, often to the detriment of the text

No, no: <,> I mean —< > with a young man;

(II, 52.3)

Here the combination of the colon and the dash convey the kind of delicate consideration that Fancy on occasion feels for Dick. This hesitation constitutes a trait in her character that we can admire; she is thoughtful for his position as well as her own. When the dash is omitted and a comma substituted for the colon the speech appears swift and decided, less alive, and considerably less sympathetic to Fancy. In another case

Very trying —< > it must be.

(I, 204.8)

the omission is almost substantive, the emphasis in one version being so different from that in the other. The manuscript version is to be preferred, since the speech rhythm it represents is clearly more appropriate as a response to the previous statement of the keeper, and also to Dick as a somewhat nervous visitor to his house.

The two great virtues of the dash in Hardy's hands are that it had no fixed place in the sequence of pause value—that it could be weaker than a comma or stronger than a semicolon according to need, and that it could perform special functions none of the other marks fulfilled precisely. The interference of the compositors successfully ensured that this variety was lost in the printed versions of the novel.

Semicolon

In *UGT* Hardy used the semicolon less frequently than other major marks of punctuation, and the compositors rarely altered it when it was present, as may be gathered from Table IV on p. 173; but three examples show that even in the treatment of this mark one compositor at least took an independent line. Take for instance

> This was duly gone through;<,> and no notice whatever seemed to be taken of the performance.
>
> (I, 53.23–25)

where the manuscript semicolon represents much more accurately the pause that the players make at the end of their hymn while waiting for some notice to be taken of it; or compare Hardy's: 'Right William; and so they be!' where the varied, expressive intonation of the speaking voice is vividly conveyed, with the first edition's regular, monotonous, technically accurate version: 'Right, William, and so they be!' (I, 51.12) In a third case,

> 'But for all that 'tisn't in me to call the man a bad man;<,> because I truly and sincerely believe en to be a good young feller.'
>
> (I, 147.10–13)

Hardy's meaning is distorted momentarily for a reader by the removal of the importantly heavy pause; he might take the second clause to be dependent upon 'bad man' rather than on ' 'tisn't in me'; with the semicolon there such an error could not be made—moreover, as he was writing, Hardy probably heard William Dewy make a significant pause at that point.

It should be no surprise to learn that all three of these examples were composed by Dodd, and here we see the effect of the independence he shows from the orthodoxy of a possible house-style.

Colon

Hardy's relatively frequent use of the colon suffered harshly in the compositorial repunctuating, some 190 of them being removed; as might be expected they were mostly replaced by full-points or semicolons, and for the most part the effect of these changes is only felt cumulatively; but on a few occasions the difference between the two versions is felt dramatically. Here, for instance, is the distraught Fancy telling Dick how she followed him:

> 'I ran after you—and I saw you go up the hill and not look back once—and then you plunged in, and I after you: but I was too far behind.'

this is the manuscript version; the first edition reads

> 'I ran after you, and I saw you go up the hill and not look back once, and then you plunged in, and I after you; but I was too far behind.'
>
> (II, 91.3–7)

How much more expressive of Fancy's out-of-breath, sobbing narrative is Hardy's version, the dashes contrasting in pausal value with the single comma to orchestrate the pace of the speech, which is brought to an abrupt halt with the crucially heavy pause of the colon, suggesting the crestfallen, penitent, almost despairing stop and fall in her voice.

One other example will show this same ability Hardy's punctuation has to encourage the reader to see the dramatic energy in a speech; Dick is talking to his rival the vicar, neither knowing the other has been accepted by Fancy:

> Why, she's my sweetheart: <,> and we are going to be married next Midsummer.
>
> (I, 163.21–164.1)

Here the heavy pause of the colon emphasises the incredulity that Dick feels at Mr. Maybold's ignorance, and permits a change of tone in his voice from (say) astonishment to conspiratorial pride, since they are keeping news of the wedding 'rather close just at present'; it also allows us time to imagine the first part of Dick's revelation sinking into the vicar's mind before the second and more violent thunderbolt arrives. The comma, running the clauses swiftly together, allows the reader none of this imaginative richness.

Occasionally Hardy seems to run wild with colons, as he sometimes does with the dash; but however odd it looks there is usually a reason for it:

> 'Tis all right: <;> Dick's coming on like a wild feller: <;> he'll be here in a minute: <. T> the hive o'bees ...
>
> (II, 185.17–19)

This appears at first glance quite eccentric in Hardy's version, yet it is reasonable to suppose that it is intended as a dramatic representation of Nat Callcome the best man calling through the floor at Fancy, pausing heavily to allow the sound to percolate the floorboards, and it is monotonous in rhythm because there have to be pauses for breath when one has to shout out a long-ish piece of information.

Full point

It seems astonishing that even with the full point examples are easy to find where the compositors obstruct Hardy's intentions, but such is the case. I choose four brief examples:

Ay.$<$; a$>$And I see what the pa'son don't see.

(I, 186.19–20)

Here Hardy sins against the rule which doesn't permit a sentence to begin with a conjunction. But that is the way that people speak; of course such a consideration would not be a concern of the compositors. Hardy does the same in the second example

I don't like him indeed.$<$, a$>$And I never heard of his . . .

(II, 49. 5–6)

where the separation of sentences is important, since it emphasises Fancy's denial of affection for Shiner; when the two statements are run together with only a comma between them, that considerable force is lost, as she goes on to change the subject from love to the quire's dismissal. In the third extract

Then she has done as much to he.$<$— r$>$Rot 'em!

(II, 24.11–12)

there is a dramatic difference between the two versions, two quite different ways of saying 'Rot 'em'; Hardy's comes as a further thought, the result of a conscious reflection, while the first edition's is merely an appendage to the previous thought.

The last speech, though the shortest is perhaps the most important:

'Yes.$<$,$>$ I will,' she said.

(II, 157.17)

at this crucial moment in the story, when Mr. Maybold has asked Fancy to marry him, Hardy's point represents her 'faint and broken' hesitancy in replying to him much better than the comma which the compositors see fit to put in its place.

I hope that these examples from *UGT* speak for themselves; the exigencies of space alone have limited their number, and many more may be found by the interested reader that are equally eloquent of the value of Hardy's own system of punctuation. It is inconsistent, but so is the first edition; and there are times, a handful only, where it is frankly inadequate, usually because of the omission of a comma; but it is alive, it is sensitive to tone and the dynamics of speech and narrative, above all it positively helps the reader to take the fullest imaginative charge from the words that it surrounds.

Hardy wrote in *The Early Life* (p. 136), probably in 1875

> The whole secret of a living style and the difference between it and a dead style, lies in not having too much style—being, in fact, a little careless, or rather seeming to be, here and there. It brings a wonderful life into the writing:
>
> 'A sweet disorder in the dress . . .
> A careless shoe-string, in whose tie
> I see a wild civility,
> Do more bewitch me than when art
> Is too precise in every part.'
>
> Otherwise your style is like worn half-pence—all the fresh images rounded off by rubbing, and no crispness or movement at all.

I believe that Hardy would have included punctuation style in this prescription, and it has been the aim of the latter part of this essay to show how the manuscript of UGT actively and effectively employs the theory it contains.

We now read Hardy in texts that surround his words with mechanical and alien punctuation; there is a desperate need for editions of his novels and stories that pay proper attention to *everything* that he wrote. His work comes out of copyright on 1 January 1979, and it is most devoutly to be hoped that the plans of Oxford University Press to publish two of Hardy's novels in scholarly editions will have matured by then, and that they will add others in the due course of time.

NOTES

1   Charlotte Brontë's is a well-documented case; she praised and admired the transformation of the (as she saw it) ill-pointed manuscript of *Jane Eyre* into a novel with a visually acceptable system of punctuation.

2 *Under the Greenwood Tree* hereafter referred to as *UGT*; *Tess of the D'Urbervilles* hereafter referred to as *Tess*.

3 Further information on this and many other matters connected with either novel may be found in two unpublished Doctoral dissertations presented at the University of Oxford: *A Critical Edition of Thomas Hardy's Novel 'Under the Greenwood Tree'* (1973) by S. J. Gatrell, and *A Critical Edition of 'Tess of the D'Urbervilles'* (1974) by J. M. Grindle. I am very grateful to Dr. Juliet Grindle for providing me with the raw collational material upon which this study has been based as far as *Tess* is concerned.

4 There is not space here to present the argument which follows upon analysis of the surviving proof-copy of Hardy's fiction, and which leads to the conclusion that only between five and ten per cent of all the differences in punctuation between the manuscript and the first printing of any of Hardy's texts is likely to derive from authorial proof-correction. This argument may be found in full in my doctoral thesis mentioned in Note 3, pp. 482–85. For the sake of convenience in this essay I have assumed *all* changes to be the work of the printing house in default of proof for either novel; I have also assumed that such proof-correction as there was would have been equally spread over each compositor's work, and would therefore have no decisive effect upon the statistics I present.

5 This is calculated in terms of the Wessex Edition of 1912 so that *UGT*, *A Pair of Blue Eyes*, and *Tess* may be directly compared.

6 Possible differences caused by serial publication are examined below p. 174.

7 See p. 184 below.

8 Some selected details are presented in my thesis mentioned in Note 3, pp. 480–81.

9 For similar examples from *Tess* the reader must consult the introduction to J. M. Grindle's thesis mentioned in Note 3.

10 The pointed brackets in this and subsequent examples enclose the punctuation substituted in the first edition for the manuscript version; the references are to volume, page and line of the first edition.

11 John Wilson (New York, 1873).

12 12th revised edition (London, 1863).

Notes on Contributors

ROSEMARY EAKINS is a graduate of McGill University and of St. Anne's College, Oxford. She has taught English in McGill University and in Oxford, and is now partner and research manager in Research Reports, New York. She is currently working on a book on Browning.

ANDREW ENSTICE is a graduate of the University of Exeter and of Emmanuel College, Cambridge. His first major publication, *Thomas Hardy and the Landscapes of the Mind*, was published in 1978, and he is currently working on a book of poetry.

PATRICIA GALLIVAN is an Associate Professor of English at the University of Alberta. She has published essays on T. S. Eliot and modern poetry, is preparing a critical study of Walter Pater, and is co-editing a book of essays on Hardy's poetry for the Vision Critical Studies series, with Juliet Grindle.

SIMON GATRELL is a graduate of St. Edmund College, Oxford. He has compiled, with T. Bareham, a *Bibliography of the Writings of George Crabbe* (1976), is the author of a number of essays on Hardy, and currently lectures in English in the New University of Ulster.

JULIET GRINDLE is a graduate of Oxford University. She has lectured in English at University College, Cardiff, and now works for an Oxford-based publisher. She has done a critical edition of *Tess of the D'Urbervilles* (O.U.P., 1979), and is currently editing a book of essays on Hardy's poetry with Patricia Gallivan, for the Vision Critical Studies series.

BARBARA HARDY is Chairman of the Department of English at Birbeck College, University of London, and present occupant of its Chair of Literature. She is the author of: *The Novels of George Eliot*; *The Appropriate Form: An Essay on the Novel*; *The Moral Art of Dickens*; *The Exposure of Luxury: Radical Themes in Thackeray*; *Tellers and*

Listeners: The Narrative Imagination; and *A Reading of Jane Austen.* She is also the editor of *Middlemarch: Critical Approaches to the Novel, Critical Essays on George Eliot,* and *The Advantage of Lyric: Essays on Feeling in Poetry.*

ROBERT HEILMAN is Professor of English at the University of Washington, and the author of a wide range of books on literature, from *This Great Stage: Image and Structure in King Lear* (1948) to *The Ghost on the Ramparts and Other Essays on the Humanities* (1974). His work on Hardy includes editions of *The Mayor of Casterbridge, Jude the Obscure,* and *Tess,* and essays on "Hardy's *Mayor* and the Problem of Intention" (*Criticism,* 1963), "Hardy's *Mayor*: Notes on Style" (*Nineteenth Century Fiction,* 1964), "Hardy's Sue Bridehead" (*Nineteenth Century Fiction,* 1966), and "Gulliver and Hardy's *Tess*: Houyhnhnms, Yahoos, and Ambiguities" (*Southern Review,* 1970).

ROSALIND MILES is a graduate of St. Hilda's, Oxford, and of the Shakespeare Institute of Birmingham University, and lectures in English at Lanchester Polytechnic. Her publications include an eighteenth-century acting edition of *Measure for Measure* (1971), *The Fiction of Sex* (1974), and *The Problem of Measure for Measure* (1976). She is currently working on a critical biography of Ben Jonson.

PHILIPPA TRISTRAM is a graduate of Lady Margaret Hall, Oxford, and lectures in medieval English literature in the University of York. She is the author of *Figures of Life and Death in Medieval Literature* (1976), and is currently writing a book on architecture in the English novel.

Index